THE WAR AT SEA

IN PHOTOGRAPHS

1939–1945

CONWAY'S
THE WAR AT SEA
IN PHOTOGRAPHS
1939–1945

Stuart Robertson
Stephen Dent

CONWAY

Frontispiece
The French battleship *Richelieu*, on passage to the Far East
in March 1944.

Page 6
Manning the guns on USS *Arkansas*, 1944.

In memory of J. E. Horwood and D. G. Robertson OBE

A Conway Maritime book

Copyright © Stuart Robertson and Stephen Dent 2007

First published in Great Britain in 2007 by
Conway
an imprint of Anova Books, The Old Magistrates Court,
10 Southcombe Street, London W14 0RA
www.anovabooks.com

Reprinted 2007

British Library Cataloguing in Publication Data
A record of this title is available on request from the British Library.

ISBN 13: 9 781844 860456

Edited by: Alison Moss and John Jordan
Designed by: Nichola Smith, Stephen Dent and Georgina Hewitt

Printed and bound by CT Printing Ltd, China

CONTENTS

Acknowledgements

The authors wish to express their grateful thanks to the following people and institutions for their assistance: Ian Proctor, Matt Lee, Thom Eaton, Yvonne Oliver, and the rest of the staff at the Imperial War Museum photographic and film archives; Laura Waayers, Ed Finney, Charles E. Brodine Jr and William Dildo of the US Naval Historical Center; Debbie Corner, Keeper of Photographs at the Royal Navy Submarine Museum; Jo Lawler, Director of Explosion! Museum of Naval Firepower; Brian Williams, Mark Frost and John Iverson of Dover Museum; Kevin McLaren, Kristina Watson and Lydia Fisher at the Royal Commission on the Ancient and Historical Monuments of Scotland; Leon M. A. Homburg, curator, Marinemuseum, den Helder; Gerry Rendle and Paul Burkhalter of Devonport Dockyard and Museum; Commander Erminio Bagnasco, director, *Storia Militare*; Volkmar König; Terry McGovern; Dave Bassett; Jean Hood; Bert Purches; DK Brown; Stephen Johnson; Geoffrey Hudson; William J. Crawford; Dee Dent; Al Fox; Leo van Ginderen; Hans Lengerer; Waldemar Trojca; Charles Blackwood; David Evans; Martin Le Poidevin of *Flyer* magazine; Andy Field; Katy Goodwin; Geoff Dennison; Ian Hancock; Tony at ColorWorks, Bath; Steve Mclaughlin, Bill Schleihauf; the staff of Bath Central Library; and John Lee and Alison Moss at Conway. The authors would like to thank their families, friends and publisher for their forbearance.

In particular, this book could not have been compiled without the aid of a number of people who generously provided images and caption information from their own collections, as well as their time and knowledge. Principal among these are several contributors to Conway's naval annual *Warship*. First and foremost our thanks go to John Jordan. John Jordan is the editor of *Warship* and also the author of two books on the Soviet Navy, and is at present working on a book on the navies of the inter-war period. Enrico Cernuschi is the author of *Ecero Tutti il Loro Dovere* (Rome: Rivista Marittima, 2006), now a standard text on the history of the Italian Navy commissioned by the Italian Naval Academy. Vince O'Hara is the author of *German Fleet at War 1939-1945* (Annapolis: Naval Institute Press, 2004) and *The U.S. Navy Against the Axis: Surface Combat 1941-1945* (Annapolis: Naval Institute Press, 2007). Henk Visser is a retired officer of the Royal Netherlands Navy, and works at the Marinemuseum, den Helder. He is the author of *De Koninklijke Marine, 1922-1964*. Conrad Waters is a member of the group working to return the World War Two frigate HMS *Whimbrel* to the UK as a permanent memorial to the Battle of the Atlantic. Chris Savill is an aviation and social historian who works at The National Archives (formerly the Public Record Office) in Kew, London, and has written a number of books on aviation history. Richard Worth and Vladimir Yakubov are the authors of *Raising the Red Banner: The Pictorial History of Stalin's Fleet 1920-1945* (Spellmount, 2007). This book has benefited greatly from all their input; any errors of fact or interpretation remain the sole responsibility of the authors.

The Camera at Sea

As that generation of men and women who experienced World War Two at first hand recedes into history, to gain an impression of what life was like for them we must rely on the sources left behind by the participants. The photograph, perhaps better than any other means of communication, can bring us face to face with the scenes that once confronted the people there and then.

Some photographs of that global conflict are so famous as to have acquired a meaning of their own as enduring symbols, even works of art: the Nazi leadership strolling arrogantly in front of the Eiffel Tower in subdued Paris; the raising of the US flag on bloody Iwo Jima; the Soviet emblem flying stiffly over the Reichstag in devastated Berlin. But many other pictures, never destined to achieve such iconic status, also have powerful immediacy and speak perhaps more accurately of what it was like to be in a time and place affected by war.

The vast majority of photographs created between 1939 and 1945 remain unpublished and little known and yet collectively they represent the biggest source of tangible evidence for what, nearly seven decades ago, the experience of war was really like. Not all the photographs have dramatic impact or military significance. Yet each photograph represents a composite of not only the facts of a scene – as far as they may be evident – but also the photographer's choices which led him to select and record that scene. Each image thus reflects the world beyond the lens but also the human processes behind it. Like all wars, World War Two created an environment punctuated with action and drama but, as ever, most combatants and civilians spent the majority of their time waiting for something to happen. The photographic record reflects this variable state of affairs, though most pictorial histories of war prefer to ignore it.

Early photography involved cumbersome yet frail technology; the length of exposure did not make it easy to capture sharply focused action images, not least in fluid environments. It was not until dry plate technology arrived at the end of the 1870s that it became possible properly to photograph the motion of the sea and objects upon it. And as soon as photographic technology matured enough it was put to military application. World War One witnessed total war on land, an environment often ripe for sympathetic visual treatment using new photographic equipment, including the Speed Graphic camera, which became the dominant portable professional camera. World War One also saw the first widespread use of photographic reconnaissance on land and over it. At sea, aerial reconnaissance was conducted from airships and primitive aircraft, originally for the spotting of enemy vessels and for the corrective direction of shellfire in an engagement.

By the early 1930s, technology – and official interest in photography – had grown such that the art had become an integral aspect of war, scientifically and doctrinally woven into forces' modus operandi. Photographs were also a powerful medium for recording successes and failures of operations, and could be used by navies and governments to promote certain selected ideas.

During that troubled decade – of Depression in America and elsewhere, the rise of fascism and Nazism in Europe, of totalitarian communism in Eurasia and militant nationalism in Japan – photography cemented its position alongside the printed word as a valuable commodity and a tool. European newspapers and periodicals such as *Paris Match* and the *Berliner Illustrierte Zeitung* employed photographers in greater numbers than any armed forces ever did, though the burgeoning Nazi state cleverly blurred the lines between reportage and propaganda in print and on moving film. The techniques of photojournalism matured as an increasingly globalizing world sought information on events such as the Italian conquest of Abyssinia, the Spanish Civil War and the Japanese invasion of China.

By World War Two, large numbers of photographers were occupied in recording the enormities and intimacies of war, either for immediate military application or for propaganda and even deliberate posterity. All German and Soviet official photographers were part of the armed forces, and almost every photograph they took was subject to official sanction based on its usefulness in 'winning the war'. Censorship and official control was rife. The same held true for Allied photographers. Photographs had to undergo a long chain of official vetting before they could be released for publication. The true realities of war, as captured on film, were seen by the public only after the war's end.

The 35mm single-shot camera – the Leica and the Contax in particular – and the compact twin-lens reflex Rolleiflex dominate much of the photographic reportage of the war years. Alongside official

Introduction

forces' photographers, other skilled practitioners – often buccaneering freelancers with a keen nose for a story and luck for being in the right place at the right time – shaped the way the war was seen both at the time and in retrospect. Billeted with specific combat units or on officially-sanctioned roving commissions, freelance photographers could document what they saw and sell the vetted fruits of their labours to magazines feeding the news-hungry populaces at home. They made much use of the versatility and durability of these new compact and robust cameras, which could operate in changing light and unpredictable stability – the sort of conditions encountered while standing on the bridge of a destroyer manoeuvring at speed under air attack, or while wading ashore under fire on a Pacific beach – such that a distinctive gritty, realistic black-and-white style emerged as the signature motif of their war photography. It remains the archetype of war photography to this day.

Yet colour photography was employed to great effect for the first time between 1939 and 1945. Colour film had first appeared in America in 1925, and became popular in Germany by 1931. Almost all colour film shot during World War Two was shot either on German Agfa Gasparcolor, or American Eastman Kodak Kodachrome colour negative film. Nazi Germany, with its Goebbels-run *Propaganda Kompanien*, was in the vanguard of developing novel and effective means of creating and employing propaganda, and in the colour photograph they found a perfect medium to showcase their ideology. *Signal* was the most famous of a breed of publications designed to bring vividly to life the Nazi war through painstakingly selected or prepared images. Published in several languages, by 1943 *Signal* was being read by a total of 2.5 million people; one third of the images were in colour, despite the shortages that had begun to affect Germany as the tide of war turned against it.

German war photography was superior to virtually all others due to its insistence on technical discipline and an editorial policy founded on an organized propaganda basis. The German Navy in particular had been a popular subject of photography and cinematography since the turn of the century, when the German Navy League nationalist pressure group, using a touring exhibition, began to promote naval expansion as the chief means of attaining Germany's 'place in the sun'. In essence, the medium, if not the message, was not very different in 1939–45.

Rivalling Germany's dedication to the visual documentation of the war, the United States married significant material advantage with a broad base of talented camera-operators. Unlike the British, whose photographers were usually accorded an NCO rank, most American war photographers were given commissioned officer status. This gave them even greater mobility and access in the field. Likewise, freelance or staff photographers of civilian publications such as *Life* magazine (later *Time Life*) enjoyed a particularly good relationship with American commanders. Lieutenant Commander Edward Steichen was in charge of the US Navy's photographic unit. He and his team – many of them advertising and fashion photographers before the war, including Wayne Miller, Fenner Jacobs and Victor Jorgensen – were charged with recording all the operations of the US Navy, particularly in the Pacific. Attached to aviation, surface and amphibious combat units, Steichen's department produced some of the finest images of what was fundamentally a far-flung naval war in the East. David Douglas Duncan pioneered the method of taking shots through the Perspex nosecones of bombers and even designed his own manned photographic pod slung under the aircraft's wing.

However, the unpredictable nature of war meant that events could unfold outside the attention of official or assigned freelance photographers – such as the Japanese surprise attack on Pearl Harbor – and our record for these is provided usually by amateur photographers and sometimes civilians. Similarly, official photographers, while on the 'front line' inside operational ships and aircraft, could not always obtain good coverage of what were often widely-dispersed battles. Reflecting the realities 'on the ground', good photographs were more easily attainable during amphibious landings – as Robert Capa's much-lauded shots of D-Day show – or in the ravaged aftermath, as W. Eugene Smith's portfolio from the Pacific testified to great effect. Photographs involving humans in close-up – their faces contorted with fright or determination, often with dead or injured comrades in the vicinity – generated a different kind of emotional reaction to the more aloof macro-scale shots of comparatively impersonal warship or aerial combats. Action photographs taken aboard ship also tended to be more blurry, especially if the subject being photographed was an aircraft whose speed relative to the point of photography was great.

The saying goes that 'the first casualty of war is truth'. A proportion of all wartime photographs – particularly colour shots – were staged, either to give false impressions for propaganda purposes or in an effort to capture the visual essence of situations for which genuine images did not exist. And many photographs in today's private collections were 'illegally' shot for sailors as souvenirs by official photographers while aboard ship – known to the British photographers as 'rabbit work' – to supplement their wages.

The British attitude to official photography was less comprehensive than that of the Germans and Americans. Generally the three British service film and photographic units used colour far less than their opposite numbers. The Royal Naval Photographic Unit had been set up in 1919 and was designed to support the fleet's reconnaissance and publicity activities; by 1939 it had expanded to provide coverage to all the theatres where British naval forces found themselves. By 1945 it employed 200 women.

As the war progressed, initially small photographic units grew into complex bodies within each armed service, employing men equipped and trained by them. This also included cine film. By the invasion of Normandy in June 1944, the Allies were highly organized; pre-battle preparations were clear and efficient, and the priority – the rapid dispatch of photographs back from the landing beaches – was aided by the setting up of mobile vetting centres through which film could be channelled to the rear before being released to the public. Having already covered the Salerno and Anzio landings for *Life*, Robert Capa's surviving 'slightly out of focus' shots of the American landings at Omaha beach are world-famous; notable British photographers include George Rodger and Sergeant Jimmy Mapham, operating further east on Gold and Sword beaches. As with many areas of the war, it is the enduring work of these eyewitness photographers – operating despite great personal danger – which has heavily influenced our emotional fascination with the events of 6 June 1944, subsequently expanded upon in cinema.

Nevertheless, photography of the war has its limits. Having won a battle, the victors naturally found it fundamentally easier to record the progress of their victory than the defeated their defeat. Consequently, by natural process, many photographs reflect a state of access peculiar to the fortunate eye-witness. The Germans produced the best images of the first two years of the war. The evacuation of British troops from Dunkirk is an exception that proves the rule – Operation Dynamo was recorded not by official photographers (long since departed), but only amateurishly by a few British and German participants.

The transfer of films to be developed was also problematic at sea in a way it was not on land or in the air. Until dark-rooms were established aboard large warships, or unless special contingencies had been put in place, photographs taken at sea (whether for official war-fighting purposes or for reportage) could take days or even weeks to arrive at the developing stage. Thus, up-to-date photography of the war at sea was at a premium for contemporary media and naval authorities, and remains so today. There was, of course, no such thing as an immediately available electronic image file in World War Two. Many private photographic collections only saw the light of day after the war, and continue to do so.

The work of Japanese and Soviet naval photographers is particularly elusive. It is recorded that Robert Diament acted as the official Soviet Navy photographer, working mostly with the Northern Fleet, covering Arctic operations and focussing frequently upon the heroic aspects of the individual sailors involved. In the case of Japan, many of the official records were destroyed at the end of the conflict, both by the devastating Allied bombing campaign and then at the hands of the Japanese themselves. During the war Japanese propaganda photography was exhibited on the home front, even displayed in Tokyo department stores. In December 1943, by law, Japanese photographic manufacturers and photographers were forced to focus on the war effort. Photographs taken by German and Soviet civilians remain the most elusive due to the wartime and post-war conditions of those countries.

Furthermore, while sea war was one of three overlapping and competing areas of fighting, it was usually the least immediate in terms of its effect on populaces and on the services themselves. Steady pressure, patient stalking, and monotonous voyages across wide ocean routes – these were the underlying hallmarks of the sea war. And just as most of the maritime war was fought out of sight of the land, the images of it can feel similarly detached and subject to the same barrier of impersonality. Of all the wars, the one fought at sea was perhaps the least human in scale. Yet paradoxically, to prosecute the sea war, each of its basic units – the ships – gathered more men together cheek-by-jowl in one place to fight this impersonal war than either the land or air war necessitated. Visually, the war at sea reflects this potent and varied mixture of the size, scale and faces of battle.

The photographic record presented here includes stills from many theatres of war – the Pacific, Arctic, Atlantic, Mediterranean, Indian – from shore to ship, beneath, upon and above the sea. Characteristic of photographs of sea war is the open sea-space and the natural frame provided by the lens upon a ship or other object against the ocean. The impersonal nature of a war fought at great distances contrasts with the often claustrophobic human conditions of life aboard ship, aeroplane or submarine. And yet naval war is no less vivid and dynamic on celluloid than other methods of fighting. Few scenes from World War Two can rival the sheer fiery terror of a massed *kamikaze* attack, the panic of an 'abandon ship' or the adrenaline of an amphibious landing on an enemy-held shore.

Each photograph has a different story to tell, and by placing them in a broad narrative context we can go some way to catching a glimpse into remarkably diverse, fascinating, and in many cases largely forgotten areas of the war at sea between 1939 and 1945.

World War Two: The Naval Background

War at sea can be waged in many forms, each with a specific purpose but all with one fundamental aim – the injuring of an opponent's capability to use the same sea to his own ends. For hundreds of years, sea power has been created and deployed to defend and extend interests, and deny the ability of others to use the sea as a highway for trade, communication, influence and military power. As a result, few aspects of the recent past have been unaffected by the ability of nations to use the sea for political ends.

World War Two saw the greatest deployment of sea power in the history of mankind. Huge resources were spent around the globe on creating and maintaining the tools to fight at sea. In many ways the conflict was primarily a maritime war. Without the possession and exercise of sea power in its wide variety of guises, Japan could not have over-run the Pacific and then been driven back, and the United States could never have projected its power across the Atlantic to defeat Nazi Germany. Britain could not have reinforced the home island by way of

Edward Steichen
In command of the US Navy's Photographic Institute, Commander Edward J. Steichen was a leading figure in the photography of the war at sea in an organizational as well as creative capacity. Here he perches on a platform overlooking the flight deck of an American aircraft carrier, studying his surroundings. Photograph by Lieutenant Victor Jorgensen.

continued communication with the nations of the Commonwealth and the USA, nor held its positions around the Mediterranean. Sea power formed the launch pad of many of the great land offensives, or delivered the materiel for others to fight on land and in the air. Allied victory on the high seas enabled the reinforcement of the Soviet Union and the projection of American power into Western Europe, contributing to the ultimate defeat of Germany and Italy, while Japan was almost exclusively defeated by the application of sea power. And the pursuit of a maritime war on essential trade became the sole means by which Germany could bring Britain to defeat. Through the application of sea power, Britain did not succumb. And in sum, sea power was the only way that Allied victory could be brought about through the delivery, application and sustenance of military power on land.

At the close of the 1930s, seven nations possessed large navies and many others maintained some kind of maritime force. Each was a serious investment for the nation in question, perhaps the most complex, resource-heavy organization a state could pursue. Certainly it was one of the hardest national enterprises to get right. And each navy was the result of myriad competing strategic, geo-political, ideological and economic considerations. None of them could make precise and exact predictions about the opportunities and threats they would encounter. Their predictions were shackled not just by their not knowing what the future would bring but also by their familiarity with the present.

Four of the world's biggest navies were European – belonging to Britain, France, Germany and Italy. The Soviet Union's fleet was also based largely in European waters. Outside Europe the two largest maritime powers were Japan and the USA, eyeing each other across the enormous expanses of the Pacific Ocean.

The French Navy

The French Navy – the *Marine Nationale* – was principally designed to contest the Mediterranean against the Italians, using a fleet of modern, fast, and well-armed capital ships, cruisers and destroyers to protect French security but also defend imperial interests in North Africa, the Middle East and further afield in French Indochina. Its principal bases were at Brest and Toulon in France, and ships and squadrons were sometimes deployed to North African ports and anchorages, which included Dakar and Casablanca. In the agreements reached at the 1922 Washington Naval Treaty, the French accepted parity with Italy with a ratio of 1.75 each for capital ships, beneath Japan's 3 and Britain's and America's 5 each. During the 1930s, as tensions grew on the European continent, French naval planners worked to create a fleet to equal Italy plus Germany. In response to German re-armament, the French accepted a *détente* with Italy, but the Italian-Abyssinian crisis of 1935–6 saw France choose to rely on Britain, with an increasingly expansionist Italy turning towards a 'Pact of Steel' with Nazi Germany.

In 1939 the French Navy possessed one slow, converted aircraft carrier (the *Béarn*) with two under construction but never to be completed, two modern and five older battleships, eighteen cruisers, fifty-eight destroyers, thirteen torpedo boats, seventy-six submarines, and over thirty smaller warships. Three battleships, one cruiser, twelve destroyers and thirty escort vessels were also under construction, with one new battleship ready in 1940. Many other vessels were authorized, but construction had not begun and all were cancelled on the outbreak of war. Alone, this fleet, under the leadership of Admiral François Darlan, Chief of the Naval Staff, was just about superior to the Italian Navy in the Mediterranean. In the last year before the outbreak of war, the French had developed an offensive strategy that it hoped would preserve French security in the Mediterranean and Atlantic regions. This strategy was based around the *Bretagne* class battleships and *Duquesne* and *Suffren* class cruisers to counter Italian designs upon North Africa, while releasing the modern 13-inch gunned hybrid battleship/battlecruisers *Strasbourg* and *Dunkerque* for use against the likelihood of German surface raiders in the Atlantic.

Traditional enemies, the French and British navies were increasingly forced to look upon each other as partial guarantors of each others' Mediterranean strategy; with British involvement, Anglo-French naval power could dominate the region and keep the powerful German surface fleet in check elsewhere. While the French Navy had good ships – especially its large *contre-torpilleur* fleet destroyers – it lacked certain elements of an integrated maritime system; it did not enter the war with radar, its naval aviation was weak and its submarines, while technologically sound, suffered problems with operational doctrine. On a fundamental level, the French Navy's strength was divided by having to look south to the Mediterranean and north and west to its northern and Atlantic flanks.

The Italian Navy

The *Regia Marina*, though cultivating a reputation for élan and dash with speedy rather than well-armoured ships (for instance the 'Condottieri' type light cruisers), was essentially a fleet in being which could focus all its power in one theatre, take few unnecessary risks and stay in harbour, venturing out only when the *Supermarina* high command decided the odds favoured direct action. Italy held colonies in Libya and the Red Sea region, which threatened British control of Egypt, the Sudan and Suez. A signatory to the 1922 Washington Naval Treaty (where she accepted the 1.75 ratio equivalent to France), but deciding not to ratify the follow-up 1930 London proceedings, Italy ignored the displacement limits on heavy cruisers when building the *Zara* class cruisers and the *Bolzano* during the 1930s. Though Italy was more successful than her allies and rivals in upgrading older capital ships during the pre- and war years (the four battleships of the *Cavour* and *Duilio* classes were by far the most radical modernizations of older battleships of any of the five treaty navies), many of her warships that at launch had been modern and swift were rather worn out, less potent and consequently more vulnerable by the time of her entry to the war in 1940 – a factor increasingly important as operational demands took their toll.

Nevertheless, Italy alone dominated the central Mediterranean, and it was obvious to many that in the event of war with Britain, Italy would seek to close the route to the east via Suez, and seek to defeat the French battle fleet. The Italian invasion of Abyssinia in 1935–6 had risked a war with Britain in the Mediterranean, but British fears of Italian air power (Mussolini described the Italian peninsula as 'a natural aircraft carrier') made it prudent for them to avoid war and remain at base in Alexandria in Egypt instead of Malta. Meanwhile the Italian Navy, despite awareness of British naval shortages, feared a defeat to a British battle fleet should it force the issue. The result of the crisis, and of the later involvement of the Italian Navy in submarine 'pirate' patrols in the Spanish Civil War in 1936–7, was that more bases were built in the south of Italy, and numbers of destroyers, torpedo-boats and submarines were increased as Italian naval expenditure rose by over 40 per cent in 1938.

A less than fully motivated Italian populace, and opportunistic declarations of war on France and Britain in June 1940, tended to take the shine off Italian naval prestige, and her standing among her Axis partners was never high throughout the war. Italy was not rich in raw materials and supplies (she lacked large reserves of oil in particular), and her naval build-up for war, despite big budgetary increases, was slow as a result. The country was also not blessed with an abundance of skilled crews to man the newer ships, particularly the larger capital ships. Deficiencies in realistic training would be exposed against the British. In January 1939 the Italian Navy had no aircraft carriers, two reconstructed battleships (the *Duilios* were not fully worked up until after June 1940), twenty-one cruisers, forty-eight destroyers, sixty-nine torpedo-boats, 104 submarines and thirty-four smaller escort and patrol vessels. With the first of the excellent new *Littorio* class battleships due to complete in 1940, this would almost constitute a match for the French Navy. Organic naval air power was weak, the sole Italian aircraft carrier *Aquila* remaining uncompleted. Instead, the navy had to rely on the Italian air force. The *Regia Aeronautica*, influenced by General Guilio Douhet's doctrines of an independent (and cheap) strategic bombing arm, was averse to torpedo- and dive-bombing and preferred level bombing where possible. The mainstay of the torpedo-bomber force was the modified tri-motor S.79 Sparrowhawk. Though Italian air-launched torpedo technology was quite advanced, its bombs were not very effective against ships. The *Regia Aeronautica* was found to be an indecisive tool, which never functioned well when used in support of the navy; reconnaissance was poor, and a lack of organic fighter aircraft would also hamstring the navy's ability to exploit opportunities against the British battle fleet during the war.

The Imperial Japanese Navy

In Japan, the doctrines derived from the work of American naval historian Alfred T. Mahan – that the apogee of sea power was the battle fleet – were so prevalent among naval planners that the *Nihon Kaigun* was almost exclusively focused on offensive big ships, the design of which was informed by a technological-determinist approach to war at sea. This impressively narrow focus came at the expense of provision in more defensive areas of maritime operations. Consequently forces for the protection of sea lines of communication – a vital consideration given Japan's island position and reliance on imported resources – were relatively neglected. Meanwhile the symbolically powerful and aggressive battleships, aircraft carriers, cruisers, destroyers, naval aviation and patrol submarines were intended to achieve victory in decisive battle.

From 1902, as an ally of Britain to counter Franco-Russian pretensions, and with a modern navy modelled in many ways on the Royal Navy, Japan had steadily grown in military, economic and trained manpower throughout the first three decades of the century. Undefeated in battle against German forces in Asia in the World War One, the conflict had shown that Japanese tactics and equipment were advanced, largely due to British input. These Anglo-Japanese ties were severed in 1921 under American and Commonwealth pressure. The end of the Anglo-Japanese Alliance and the cooling of relations after 1922 were a real problem for the Japanese. They were thrown back on their own resources, and this led the Japanese military – in particular the navy – to seek new resources in order to introduce new technology, including intensive efforts to acquire German submarine know-how. In some areas this process led to important innovations but in others – notably underwater protection and anti-submarine warfare – the Japanese fell behind.

Meanwhile, Japanese naval policy, fuelled by internal dissension and upheaval over the Washington Treaty, veered between co-operation with the west and endemic xenophobia, partially coloured by the many examples in Japan's history when she had been forced to bow to western pressure on matters of international prestige. The 1922 treaty presented opportunities to Japan as well as curtailment; she was allowed to build unlimited numbers of cruisers, destroyers and submarines, and agreement had been reached that prevented the fortification of US bases in the western Pacific. Yet in 1930, at the London Naval Conference, limitations were called for by Britain and America that targeted the size of Japan's cruiser fleet. Obsessed with their inferior numerical position, the Japanese developed weapons and tactics to give them a qualitative superiority. Expertise in torpedoes produced a 24-inch oxygen-fuelled torpedo, the Type 93 'Long Lance', capable of running for 12 miles at nearly 50 knots, almost twice the range of rival navies' torpedoes.

By 1927 the Imperial Japanese Navy possessed almost four times as many aircraft as the Royal Navy, and by the late 1930s Japanese industry was turning out new carrier-borne aircraft that were at least as good as the best land-based foreign aircraft, while new-build and converted aircraft carriers had begun appearing from 1922. Until 1932 an attitude of uneasy international co-operation predominated, but the economic effects of the Great Depression reversed this, and Japan began to pursue an expansionist policy at the expense of her neighbours in East Asia, beginning with an advance into Chinese Manchuria in 1931, which some historians trace as the true beginning of the World War Two. Internal dissent inside the armed forces created conditions enabling the 'fleet faction' to become the mainstream of the Japanese Navy, attaining further popularity among the younger, radical anti-Western naval officers.

Increasingly, Japan acted antagonistically towards both the United States and the USSR, but it was the 1937 invasion of mainland China (with large-scale naval, air and amphibious support) which really increased the tension. At the same time, naval expenditure was doubled. A desire to achieve economic self-sufficiency, military security and economic leadership of Asia, and a need to act before the United States' naval re-armament programme reached its scheduled maturity in 1944, informed an increasingly militaristic and fatalistic outlook.

Japan was, like Britain, dependent on many imported raw materials and the embargo placed upon these, in particular on oil, by the US began to bring matters to a head in the western Pacific. With France and Holland defeated by Germany by mid-1940, and with the US oil embargo biting hard throughout 1941, Japan's moment seemed to have arrived and the advance into South East Asia began at the end of the year.

Both the Japanese and the Americans had planned on the basis of a Japanese attack and capture of the Philippines at the outset of any war in the region. The Japanese expected an American counter-drive west from its base at Pearl Harbor in Hawaii, as outlined in the longstanding American Plan Orange, which would be met by Japanese submarine and aerial attack in the central Pacific prior to a general fleet action in the Sea of Japan. But Japanese plans changed during 1941. The US oil embargo failed to bring Japan back 'into line' and Japan pre-empted Plan Orange, taking a huge gamble on its fate.

In December 1941 the Japanese Navy had ten battleships, ten aircraft carriers, eighteen heavy and twenty light cruisers, 112 destroyers and sixty-eight long-range submarines, the latter designed to intercept the US battle fleet and soften it up for a meeting with the Japanese battle fleet. Until the 1930s, her naval air power consisted of only around three hundred aircraft, which allowed the British to remain calm about the threat to their battle fleet should it be called to the East. But by the time Japan entered the war, that air power, including shore-based strength, had increased to around a thousand machines. Its carrier aircraft – the Nakajima B5N 'Kate' torpedo-bomber, the Aichi D3 'Val' dive-bomber and its fighter, the Mitsubishi A6 'Zeke' (better known as the 'Zero') – were all potent leading-edge designs at the outbreak of the Pacific war. The remainder of the Japanese naval air arm comprised land-based twin-engine bombers such as the 'Betty', intended for forward deployment to Japanese-held islands, and flying boats such as the 'Mavis', which were used for long-range reconnaissance.

Considering that one of the principal means of achieving an expansion of territory would be amphibiously, Japanese landing craft were relatively unsophisticated until defensive imperatives prompted a need for better amphibious craft later in the war. And perhaps most importantly, despite an emphasis on their own technological superiority, the Japanese Navy failed to appreciate the extent to which it might need to defend itself against similar weapons; it went to war without radar and with only partially effective anti-submarine sensors, part of the cost of the loss of the Anglo-Japanese alliance.

The United States Navy

The United States was blessed with the greatest industrial capacity of all the leading powers, and geographical security. America had no far-flung empire to defend, though this also meant it had a dearth of forward bases. Congress consistently refused to grant enough money to the US Navy such that it did not build up to its 1922 Washington treaty allocation until the late 1930s. Nonetheless, it possessed a burgeoning two-ocean navy that surpassed the Royal Navy in numbers and quality of capital ships if not in 1939 then certainly by 1945. Planning and preparation for a war with Japan dominated thinking in the 1920s and 1930s. Admiral Moffett, Chief of the Navy's Bureau of Aeronautics, argued cogently for aircraft carriers and a greatly expanded aviation corps to form the linchpin of America's strategy against Japan, reasoning that they were essential to any lightning strikes across the Pacific west of Hawaii, and could take on the task of mopping up island-by-island resistance by aerial bombing rather than risking valuable battleships against coastal fortifications and land-based enemy aircraft. American aviation outclassed all except the Japanese, and her submarine force was powerful though rather hidebound by its tactical doctrine. But on balance the US Navy was still a traditional big gun navy. The new battleships of the *South Dakota* and *North Carolina* classes were armed with 16-inch guns mounted in triple turrets, surpassing anything building in Europe. Without worldwide bases, American cruisers had to be large, long-ranged and well armed, with the *Brooklyn* class epitomizing the style.

By the late 1930s, the US Navy enjoyed control of a large and growing organic air power with rugged types of radial-engined fighters, torpedo-bombers and dive-bombers (such as the Grumman Wildcat, Douglas Devastator and Douglas Dauntless), but still did not wholly think that air power had supplanted the place of the battleship.

While President Roosevelt had much sympathy for Britain fighting alone from June 1940 against Germany in Europe, much of his electorate felt differently. There were significant pro-German and anti-British lobbies in the USA. American isolationism had characterized much of the inter-war period and despite American financial aid and a 'Destroyers-for-Bases' agreement in favour of Britain in 1940, this view would not see a wholesale change until early 1941 when German submarine operations increasingly affected American merchant shipping in the Atlantic. The US Naval hierarchy was understandably pre-occupied with the Japanese threat in the Pacific but could also see that German domination of Europe was unacceptable to American interests. By the spring of 1941 the US Navy joined its Canadian neighbours in the western Atlantic convoying of Allied shipping to Britain, and had

agreed to a policy of 'Lend-Lease' to Britain and the Soviet Union. Meanwhile, the oil embargo imposed on Japan pushed the Japanese Navy into final preparations for war in Asia. American strategists were convinced that the margin of fifteen US Navy battleships to nine for Japan, established by the Washington Treaty, was sufficient to defeat the Japanese fleet in a decisive battle.

By December 1941 the US Navy possessed seven fleet carriers and one aviation transport, seventeen battleships, eighteen heavy and nineteen light cruisers, 214 destroyers and 114 submarines. Three 16-inch gunned battleships were operational compared with the Imperial Japanese Navy's two, and two further newly completed ships had already been working up for several months. The US Navy was unequally split between the Pacific and the Atlantic oceans, with the focus of American power having been placed in the Pacific since 1922.

The Royal Navy

For the Royal Navy, World War One had been a disappointment. The battle of Jutland had not broken the deadlock let alone won the war, and the German U-boat had come close to exhausting Britain. In 1922 the Washington Naval Conference reflected the widespread hope and conviction that such a war should never happen again. For the first time, the British accepted parity with another naval power, the USA. The Conference established a ten-year 'building holiday' for capital ships; it also established qualitative limits for 'auxiliary vessels' – all other surface ships – but no quantitative limits were agreed on these.

The London Conference in 1930 focused for the first time on cruisers, destroyers and submarines, and brought forth an extension of the capital ship 'building holiday' to December 1936, at which point the Japanese stated their intention to withdraw from the Treaty system. The British, despite owning a merchant fleet far larger than the Americans', were forced to accept parity in cruiser tonnage; the US Navy wanted a fleet of big 8-inch cruisers to scout for the battle fleet across the Pacific in a future war with Japan. Meanwhile, Germany, Italy and Japan began to produce overweight ships. At the same time, the parsimony of the Treasury deprived British yards and factories of any fresh orders, forcing closures and a failure to keep fully abreast of the latest shipbuilding technologies, which by 1939 translated into a substantial capacity shortage.

A major problem of block obsolescence in British warships and equipment – created by the building boom of 1917 and exacerbated by international agreements and a frugal Exchequer – adversely affected the state of the Royal Navy in 1939, when many of its major warships were rather long in the tooth. The belated rebuilding of the 1930s had modernized only about half of the fleet by 1939; the rest consisted of unmodified 1918 designs. This delay manifested itself in a number of worrying ways, not least the inadequate state of anti-aircraft provision. The Royal Navy had been the first navy to adopt commonality of AA guns across the fleet, but this had been in the 1920s so by 1939 her ships were fitted with eighteen-year-old technology in an arena of war which developed the most quickly. Effectively, in 1939 the British suffered from being first in the field twenty years prior, though most other navies also struggled to produce reliable tachymetric fire control.

Nevertheless, as war broke out in September 1939 the British still possessed the largest and most formidable navy of the combatants, with

Devastator torpedo-bombers on USS *Enterprise*, 1941
Crewmen on the American aircraft carrier *Enterprise* (CV-6) service Douglas TBD-1 Devastator torpedo-bombers on the deck, at sea off the Hawaiian base of Pearl Harbor.

nine aircraft carriers and six building, fifteen capital ships with five building, sixty-four cruisers with nineteen building, 216 destroyers and escort vessels with many more planned, and thirty-eight submarines with eleven building. A large fleet was necessary since her duties were manifold and onerous. The Royal Navy's tasklist still included the local defence of colonies and the protection of the veins of trade on the high seas. Half of Britain's food supplies and two thirds of her raw materials were bought abroad. The Royal Navy had a large presence in the Mediterranean, with Malta the centre of the British naval world there. But the main factor in 1930s war planning was defence of the eastern empire. The British planned to send their main battle fleet to the East and expected that their next major battle was likely to be fought from the incomplete base at Singapore against the Japanese battle fleet, and not in the North Sea against the Germans or in the Mediterranean against the Italians.

The Naval Staff planned on a return to the traditional two-power standard to counter the growing German and Japanese threat, intending to achieve this strength by the mid-1940s, meanwhile ignoring the US Navy as the 'next biggest' fleet. A major building programme was commenced in 1936–7, funded by an increase in the defence budget of £20 million to £81 million (and later to £105 million), consisting of a projected nine new battleships, six aircraft carriers, twenty-four cruisers, twenty-four destroyers (including powerful 'Tribal' class destroyers

mounting eight 4.7-inch guns) and twelve submarines. None of the major warships would be ready for another four years.

By the end of the 1930s Britain faced an acute strategic dilemma should war break out with two or all three of the Axis powers. The British merchant marine was huge and, while a source of strength, required protection around the globe. The need to defend long imperial shipping routes determined the necessary number of trade-protection cruisers. Surface raiders and aircraft were seen as the most serious threat to sea communications, whereas it was believed that the threat of the U-boat, successfully (but only just) defeated in 1917, would be controlled by Asdic/sonar (recent experience of which had been gained by participation in neutrality patrols against Nationalist, Italian and German submarines during the Spanish Civil War) and by Germany not having direct access to the open Atlantic – an incorrect set of assessments, as it turned out, but ones that the *Kriegsmarine* high command also subscribed to. In fact, the U-boat threat was not underestimated by the Admiralty, but realistically seen as only one facet of the expected German campaign against British trade.

While most British cruisers and destroyers were of reasonably modern design and construction, the battle fleet was old and but partially updated (only two new battleships built since the end of World War One, and only one modern aircraft carrier – compared to three Japanese and four American). Aviation, a growing science in which the Royal Naval Air

Service had enjoyed a lead after 1914, had only in 1937 been recovered from the Royal Air Force and most operational and projected types of aircraft were obsolescent compared to their Japanese and American naval counterparts. The Fleet Air Arm used the monoplane Blackburn Skua and Fairey Fulmar as fighter-bombers and the vintage Fairey Swordfish biplane as a torpedo-bomber, the latter remaining so dependable that it outlasted its planned successor, the Fairey Albacore.

But the Royal Navy had plenty of strings to its bow. New fire control gear, based on the Dreyer system in service during World War One, had been installed. Night fighting became the special competency of the British – particularly within the Mediterranean fleet, often the cradle of leading British tactical performance and innovation. In 1939, alliance with France seemed to bring added security to the Mediterranean and, combined, Anglo-French naval strength dwarfed that of Germany, with two battlecruisers, twenty-two battleships and eighty-three cruisers between them as against three 'pocket battleships' and eight cruisers. And the Royal Navy still retained a priceless asset in its fighting skills, confidence and reputation, which counted for much.

The German Navy

Much younger and with a lot to prove, the German *Kriegsmarine* was almost wholly offensive in composition. The surrender of 1918 and the imposition of the Versailles Treaty – when the German Navy, limited to an establishment of only 15,000 men, was forbidden to possess submarines or an air arm, and was confined to a coastal pre-dreadnought capability – was a source of great rancour in post-war Germany. The rebirth of the German Navy under the Nazi party – including the clandestine growth of the U-boat arm under Admiral Karl Dönitz, and a building programme of surface warships once Hitler had openly renounced the Treaty of Versailles in March 1935 – formed the bedrock of the World War Two *Kriegsmarine*.

Adolf Hitler's confident rejection of international opinion while simultaneously expanding Germany's armed forces enabled Nazi forces to look overseas for opportunities to practise and propagandize. As with the *Luftwaffe*'s Condor Legion, the navy took an active role in the Spanish Civil War, in concert with Italian vessels in the western Mediterranean. The 'pocket battleships' *Deutschland* and *Admiral Scheer* were deployed to Spain along with a core of U-boats and mine-laying *Schnellboote*, operating against Republican shipping and bases and, at times, coming into contact with neutral warships including British and French.

In 1935 an Anglo-German Naval Agreement – a formal bilateral agreement – allowed Germany considerable freedom to increase its U-boat strength while pursuing the construction of a surface navy up to 35 per cent of British overall strength (a size which German naval staff calculated could not be achieved until 1942 anyway). With a view to maximizing the number of hulls while staying within the overall tonnage limits agreed with Britain, Dönitz opted for the 650-ton Type VII rather than the 1,000-ton Type IX U-boat as the mainstay design. In the U-boat, Dönitz had a potentially war-winning weapon. But few pre-war *Kriegsmarine* planners relied on the bold prediction that Norwegian, Dutch or French coastlines might come under their control – and in general, few staff officers shared the zealous optimism that Dönitz held in the 1930s about the importance of the U-boat in any future war against Britain.

Not intended to confront the British fleet in any large-scale surface battles, nonetheless Germany's well-designed, over-displaced and powerful capital ships were a threat to British supremacy on an individual basis, and their very existence would divert significant British naval resources.

The *Kriegsmarine* suffered from confusion at a strategic level about the fundamental principles of its existence, and, furthermore, Hitler, despite consistently making the navy his last priority of the three armed forces of the Nazi state, was renowned for his almost schizophrenic and negligently ill-informed personal meddling in military and naval affairs. Labouring under a less aristocratic class structure than the German Army, the political views of its servicemen were quite diverse though not often attracted by the more extreme flavours of Nazism.

By 1939 the German Navy was still small, having not been given the time it needed to prepare properly for the war that Hitler precipitated by annexing the Sudetenland in October 1938. The *Kriegsmarine* high command were deeply disappointed when hostilities commenced only eight months after the establishment of their Z-Plan in January 1939 (planning eight aircraft carriers, ten battleships, fifteen pocket battleships, five heavy cruisers, sixty light cruisers and 249 U-boats). The Z-Plan was formulated on the assumption that general war would not break until 1945 at the earliest, and was also dependent on the unrealistic assumption that Britain would not take competitive remedial action in the meantime.

In the event Germany went to war with two battlecruisers, three 'pocket battleships', eight cruisers, twenty-two destroyers, twenty smaller escorts and fifty-nine U-boats. The Z-Plan was necessarily abandoned and the German Navy, ostensibly committed to surface raiding with its 'pocket battleships' and heavy cruisers, was forced to concentrate on increasing its numbers of submarines and finishing the construction of ships already well advanced.

While small in number, German ships were modern, built since at least the late 1920s, with efficient main and anti-aircraft armament, excellent fire-control, optics, damage control and manned by well-trained crews. While one of the first navies to grasp the potential of radar in fire-control, the *Kriegsmarine* was unable to equip itself with efficient and reliable radar sets. Trade protection was not an issue, and on the eve of war she had only twenty-two destroyers, mainly for offensive fleet work, and thirty torpedo boats. With one aircraft carrier, the *Graf Zeppelin*, never completed, its naval aviation was shore-based and under the control of the *Luftwaffe*. This mainly tactical air force run by Hermann Goering was not well-tuned into the needs of its maritime counterparts, and never developed an effective air-dropped torpedo. Nevertheless, the British expected air power to be used to deliver a knockout blow to British infrastructure – ports, roads and railways – as well as shipping. As a predominantly land-based power, German amphibious needs were primarily defensive, in order to conduct operations on the fringes of its campaigns on the European continent.

The Soviet Navy

The USSR, with ports and fleets in the Baltic, Arctic, Black Sea and Pacific theatres, had no overseas colonies to defend or supply and little ocean-going trade tonnage, and its navy was primarily designed for the offensive application of coastal defence. It remained a relatively minor force despite ambitious building programmes instigated in the 1920s and 1930s unhampered by the Washington and London naval treaties. It was reliant on foreign technical aid, much of which was unsuited to the peculiarities of Soviet design requirements. Soviet shipbuilding was in a backward state during much of the inter-war period. It had retained several large ships of World War One vintage – and even some smaller vessels dating from the Russo-Japanese War of 1904–5. Soviet naval officers were sent to instruct and command Republican forces fighting Nationalists in the Spanish Civil War, and weapons, troops and aircraft were also dispatched. Officer purges between 1935 and 1938 served to diminish the leadership quality, while the core of seamen resident in the Baltic states was not recovered until 1940. A naval programme was undertaken after 1926 but its effect was limited, and folded into the larger Five-Year Plan of 1929–33. The fruits of this were largely confined to unsatisfactory designs of four *Kirov* class cruisers and forty-six 'Gordy' and 'Leningrad' class destroyer leaders and 'Uragan' patrol boats. In 1938, the USSR commenced a major capital ship building programme, the flagships of which were four 60,000-ton *Sovietskiy Soyuz* battleships and two 35,000-ton battlecruisers of the *Kronshtadt* class, mounting nine 16-inch and nine 12-inch guns respectively. Construction progress was good considering the parlous state of Soviet shipbuilding capacity and skills, and with American, Italian and German assistance the ships were well advanced by the time the decision was taken in 1941 to scrap them.

By 1929 a modest submarine building programme had been launched, consisting of small 200-ton 'Maliutka' class coastal boats and 600-ton medium boats of the 'Shchuka' class, developed with German assistance. The Soviet Navy also operated large 'S' and 'K' class oceanic submarines of 900 and 1,500 tons displacement respectively, from the mid-1930s. Various designs of motor torpedo boats were employed in large numbers with all four fleets; the G5 type was reported to make a terrifying 50–60 knots unladen. Naval air power was non-existent in an organic sense, and amphibious capability was neglected despite the importance of the Soviet littoral regions to its communications and security.

The Baltic fleet fought some actions against Finland in 1939–40. Against the Germans from June 1941 onwards, a significant proportion of the Soviet Navy would be occupied not at sea but fighting in marine battalions in defence of Soviet bases and port cities. Meanwhile, Soviet destroyers and submarine-chasers would make brave efforts in Arctic waters assisting Allied convoys. In the Baltic and Black Seas, the Soviet Navy was less able to operate successfully in a true maritime war against the *Kriegsmarine*, mainly due to the dominance of the *Luftwaffe* and the need to act in support of the army.

Other Navies

The British Dominions of Canada, Australia, New Zealand, South Africa and India contributed trained manpower to the Royal Navy in 1939 and when Canada came to organize its own naval force for war it had to build almost from scratch as a result. Starting out with a handful of destroyers and minesweepers, and only 5,000 men, but concentrating on the production of corvettes, the RCN would prove a vital adjunct to the Royal Navy, particularly in the twenty-seven months of fighting and convoying before full American co-belligerency. Right until the end of the war – by which time it had expanded to over 90,000 men – the Canadian Navy would take a disproportionately keen interest in fighting U-boats.

The launch of the *Admiral Graf Spee*, 1934
The launch of the 'pocket battleship' *Admiral Graf Spee* was a strong sign of the re-emergence of German naval power.

Adolf Hitler at Wilhelmshaven, 1936
Hitler attends the launch of the powerful German battlecruiser *Scharnhorst* on 3 October 1936. Also present was Grand Admiral Erich Raeder, Commander-in-Chief of the *Kriegsmarine*.

Grand Harbour, Malta

This photograph shows units of the British Mediterranean and Home Fleets tied up at their buoys in Grand Harbour; in the background are Valletta and Floriana, with their sixteenth- and seventeenth-century ramparts, while to the left is Corradino, site of the naval ordnance depot. The battleship in the centre of the photograph, in the darker grey of the Home Fleet, is the flagship *Nelson*, while beyond her, in the paler grey of the Mediterranean Fleet, are the battleship *Malaya* and two *London* class cruisers. The stripes on the 'B' turrets of the warships (as well as the letters 'NE' on *Nelson*'s 'C' turret) indicate that this photograph was taken during the time of the Spanish Civil War, when ships of the British and French fleets carried these markings in their national colours to facilitate identification from the air.

(opposite) Swordfish dropping a torpedo

The mainstay of the Fleet Air Arm's torpedo-bomber force, the biplane Fairey Swordfish was an outdated design by 1939 but would give sterling service to the British in the Atlantic and Mediterranean. Here a Swordfish Mk I, from the Torpedo Training Unit at Gosport, drops a practice torpedo during training in June 1938.

The Royal Australian Navy, and its neighbour the Royal New Zealand Navy, preferred to buy and man British-built cruisers. Australia ordered two 'County' class cruisers *Australia* and *Canberra* in the mid-1920s and purchased three modified *Leander* class cruisers in the 1930s. They also ordered two Overseas Patrol Submarines – *Otway* and *Oxley* – in the 1920s and built a seaplane carrier, the *Albatross*, at the Cockatoo Naval Dockyard. The submarines were later sold back to Britain, and the *Albatross* was transferred in 1938 as part-payment for the *Leander* cruisers. These ships – to be joined by destroyers and escort craft – were to be used to protect Australian waters and the Royal Navy had no direct jurisdiction over their deployment. Australia and New Zealand also sent pilots to the Fleet Air Arm in Britain. The RAN would expand to nearly 40,000 men operating over three hundred vessels by 1945, including four cruisers, eleven destroyers, eight frigates and sloops and three landing ships. The RNZN expanded to roughly 10,000 men by the war's end. For political and recruitment reasons, South African and Indian contributions remained small for their populace size, but between them they provided over ninety small escort and minesweeping vessels and sent thousands of officers and men to the Royal Navy.

Other considerable navies existed, on the periphery of the naval world yet influential in their own spheres. The Netherlands, historically a very important naval power, still maintained an enviable fleet of modern, well-equipped warships led by forward-thinking commanders. Pioneers in several fields, but particularly in submarines (they invented the *Snort* breathing tube, better known as the *Schnorkel* in German use) and effective anti-aircraft defence, the Dutch also had colonial responsibilities throughout South East Asia and planned on defending them in the event of hostilities in the region, using a force of three cruisers, seven destroyers and fifteen submarines. The exiled Dutch government exercised control over the navy, though individual warships would be integrated into British command. Likewise, Poland possessed a small navy of four destroyers and five submarines in 1939, and would later send men to man Royal Navy cruisers and destroyers, including the Polish remnants that had escaped to Britain in September. Much the same happened with the navy of Greece after that country was overrun in 1941. The Swedish Navy, while not large by global standards, was modern and well-equipped, and its existence was a major factor in Sweden's preservation of its neutrality and territorial integrity amidst war-consumed Europe. The navy of Spain, of similar size to that of the Netherlands, was, like the rest of the country, left reeling by the terrible convulsions of the Civil War. Therefore, while the sympathies of Spain's new leaders were clearly with the Axis powers, the navy's role was restricted to the policing of the country's stated neutrality.

The Merchant Marine

While not equipped with reckonable ocean-going naval forces, other neutrals – Norway, for instance – still maintained sizable merchant fleets whose survival would become bound up by the vicissitudes of Allied and Axis dominance. Some merchant vessels changed ownership a number of times. In 1939, Britain still held a clear superiority in her merchant marine. In percentage of worldwide tonnage, she held nearly twice that of her nearest competitor, the United States, with 26.4 per cent to 13.6 per cent. Japan had 7.5 per cent, Norway 6.9 per cent, Germany 6.3 per cent, Italy 4.9 per cent, France and the Netherlands each 4.3 per cent of global tonnage. The world's merchant fleets would be one of the most unsung factors in the war at sea, suffering casualty rates never lower than their naval counterparts and frequently much higher. As a strategic element of the war, the attack and defence of trade shipping would, on balance, occupy the energies of the world's navies on a hitherto unprecedented scale.

The Outbreak of War

The war at sea began with a friendly visit. The elderly German battleship *Schleswig-Holstein*, anchored off Polish Gdańsk, had arrived some days before on a mission of reassuring goodwill. But in the half-light of the early morning of Friday, 1 September 1939, while the city slept uneasily, her eleven-inch main armament swung round to face inland. At 04.45 she opened fire on nearby Polish fortifications. Overhead, German bombers violated Polish airspace on their way to destroying shipping in a series of knockout blows along the Baltic coast. Only a handful of Polish destroyers got away to Britain. Outside the port city, five Polish submarines fought a desperate rearguard until forced to seek shelter in Sweden and Britain. So began a conflict which would develop into global maritime struggle.

When war finally broke out in Europe, none of the major combatant navies were caught unprepared. While the period from September 1939 until Germany invaded Norway in April 1940 was called the 'Phoney War' on the western land front, no such calm existed at sea. As the Germans quickly and ruthlessly emasculated Poland and shared its remains with the USSR, the Royal Navy began to gear up its mobilization. British naval planners also set to work quietly considering ways to protect the Middle East from any Soviet threat supported by Germany. The Royal Navy was immediately busy at sea and needed men to fuel its eventual eight-fold expansion. Manning had always been one of the biggest problems of mobilization; Hostilities-Only men were recruited to plug the gaps in the ratings and petty officer ranks, Reserves were plundered and volunteers carefully sifted for useful officers. Experienced petty officers were drafted in from Dominion navies, often returning to bases and routines familiar from their pre-war training.

Not yet a nation of infantrymen, Britain turned to its senior service to provide assurance that the forces of Nazism would be checked. There followed large scale operations – and one battle which became legendary – as British and French forces set about dealing with the long-range German raiders already at large. Two *Panzerschiffe* (known as 'pocket battleships' to the British, on account of their heavy armament carried on a light displacement of 10,000 tons), the *Deutschland* and the *Admiral Graf Spee*, had been ordered to sea from Wilhelmshaven in August 1939. Now roaming in the South Atlantic and into the Indian Ocean, and supported by the supply-ship *Altmark*, the 11-inch gunned *Graf Spee* sank nine merchantmen in two months before being caught off Montevideo in December by a Commonwealth cruiser squadron under Commodore Henry Harwood. Fearful of a powerful British fleet reportedly gathering off Montevideo, Langsdorff preferred to scuttle his ship and commit suicide rather than fight his way through the damaged cruisers outside.

In fact, German 'pocket battleships' had originally been conceived to fight the USSR in the Baltic, but their size, long range and gun power made them natural commerce raiding platforms. The German Navy believed it needed more of them were it to make much impact on British trade shipping. And from March 1940, the Germans also made use of nine 'auxiliary cruisers' – merchantmen converted to carry 6-inch guns – some of them notching up impressive tallies of sinkings on worldwide cruises. Though they caused significant disruption and material loss – the *Widder* alone sank ten ships of nearly 60,000 tons between May and October 1940 – they could not survive for very long out in the open oceans with British hunter groups in pursuit. It was a risky business for the lone raider; every surface contact they made with a British merchantman or landfall resulted in potentially useful intelligence for the Admiralty plotters. The German support ship system, which worked very well in the early months, was broken at considerable expenditure of time and resources on the part of British and Dominion cruiser forces dotted around the Atlantic, but the raiders remained a nuisance to Britain until 1942. All the while, the Royal and Dominion Navies were also occupied escorting convoys of Canadian, Australian, Kiwi and Indian troops to the European war.

The Clash in Northern Europe

Simultaneously, the *Kriegsmarine* was put to work in the spring of 1940 to support German army operations on a broad front throughout western and northern Europe. Unable to interfere in the German annexation of Denmark, the British resolved to pre-empt German activity in Norway. This campaign was an early and very grim testing ground for the British against the Germans in combined arms.

The British aim was to cut off Swedish iron ore supplies to Germany, which were being conveyed through the Norwegian port of Narvik, protected by Norway's stated neutrality. The rugged country was also important to Hitler as a launching pad for the *Luftwaffe* against British targets and against the Royal Navy's traditional surface blockade instituted on the outbreak of war. Thus the British eyed Norway with concern. In February, much propaganda value had been made in Germany by apparent British violation of Norwegian territorial waters, when the *Altmark*, holding captive British crews taken off the merchant vessels the *Graf Spee* had sunk in the South Atlantic, was boarded in a fjord by the destroyer HMS *Cossack*. While Goebbels set to work to exploit ambivalent international attitudes towards the incident, Hitler ordered extra U-boats to Norwegian waters to stave off an expected Anglo-French invasion. The British mined the route north from the Baltic and their ships came under attack for the first time from modern aircraft. During this mining operation, the heavy cruiser *Admiral Hipper* was rammed by the British destroyer HMS *Glowworm* which had stumbled across the German ship en route to support landings at Trondheim. Despite a forty-metre gash in her side, the large German cruiser destroyed the intrepid but hopelessly outgunned *Glowworm* and carried on to fulfil her support mission. Then, on 8–9 April, in Operation *Weserübung*, German paratroopers and seaborne troops landed in key towns and harbours along the coast of Norway. They met particular resistance in the capital Oslo where the heavy cruiser *Blücher* was sunk and the 'pocket battleship' *Lützow* damaged by Norwegian coastal defences. The cruiser *Karlsruhe* was also sunk off Kristiansand in the Skagerrak and the *Königsberg* was bombed by Fleet Air Arm dive-bombers in Bergen the following day. Further north, between 10 and 13 April, in two daring actions the Royal Navy (the battleship *Warspite* accompanied by eight destroyers) sank ten German destroyers at Narvik for the loss of two of their own. Over the next five days, British troops landed at Narvik and near Trondheim, but were repulsed in early May; Narvik was recaptured by the British at the end of the month but was evacuated again as the Netherlands, Belgium and France fell victim to Hitler's *Blitzkrieg*.

During the withdrawal from Norway in June the British aircraft carrier HMS *Glorious* was sunk by the battlecruisers *Scharnhorst* and *Gneisenau*. *Glorious*, converted from one of Jacky Fisher's large light cruisers, was spotted over 25 miles away by a lookout in the foretop of the German 11-inch gunned battlecruisers, came under very accurate

fire, was hit and set ablaze. She capsized and sank with most of her ship's and flying crew. In a letter home, one airman survivor reported, 'When we were in the raft the Germans came up, had a look and then went straight away. I have a real hatred for the Germans now.'

At the time of the attack, the carrier was escorted by only two destroyers, *Acasta* and *Ardent*, which made smoke and counterattacked with torpedoes, one of which hit and damaged the *Scharnhorst* and forced her to return to base at Trondheim, out of action for more than six months. Only three destroyer men survived the attack, but the action undoubtedly saved the British troop convoy in the offing. At the start of the Norwegian campaign, the British battlecruiser *Renown* had attacked *Scharnhorst* and *Gneisenau* and disabled the fire control of the latter; but *Gneisenau* was far more seriously damaged when she was torpedoed by the British submarine *Clyde* on 20 June, at the end of the campaign.

Having won access to North Atlantic and Arctic waters, and gained firmer control of the resources of Norway, the Scandinavian campaign was a strategic victory for Germany. But tactically speaking the *Kriegsmarine*'s balance sheet looked grim. German losses from *Weserübung* were three cruisers, ten destroyers and four submarines and a badly damaged battlecruiser. After their brushes with the Royal Navy in the first eight months of the war, the *Kriegsmarine* could field just one heavy cruiser, two light cruisers and four destroyers. No German cruisers were laid down during the war to replace those lost. Likewise, few destroyers were built to replace those lost in the Norwegian campaign. Thus by the beginning of the summer of 1940, the British had destroyed several German warships which might conceivably have played a part in any execution of Operation Sealion – the planned invasion of Britain. But Norway was ultimately a catastrophe. Allied warships had come under savage air attack and anti-aircraft provision was largely found wanting; losses from the Norwegian campaign were one aircraft carrier, two cruisers, nine destroyers and a sloop, with others heavily damaged.

The Collapse of France

Meanwhile, failed counterattacks in France and Belgium had rapidly turned to disaster for the British Expeditionary Force and the bulk of the French army. Chased back to the Channel coast by the surprisingly speedy advance of German armour, and with their fighting front narrowing to focus on a few towns still in Allied hands, another British withdrawal across the sea became inevitable by the end of May. As Calais made its last stand against the panzers, covered by the last vestiges of the French First Army, the amphibious evacuation of 338,000 Allied men from Dunkirk and other Channel seaports was begun by the Royal Navy and Allied warships, aided by a motley collection of tenders, tugs, sailing barges, fishing boats, coastal steamers, private motor boats, pleasure craft and sailing yachts – the so-called 'Little Ships'. Another 200,000 men were evacuated from Atlantic French ports such as St Nazaire.

With France and Belgium out of the fight and Norway and Denmark overtaken by events, and with Germany's eastern and southern borders secure, Hitler could turn to the proposed invasion of Britain. Operation Sealion had been contemplated for several months, and with the Channel ports now in German control, an invasion force estimated at nearly 4,000 landing craft, tank transports, barges, tugs, Siebel ferries, fishing craft and motorboats was assembled and kept at ten days' readiness throughout September. This force could have landed 70,000 men on the first day. But bad weather added to German difficulties: command of the air was not won from RAF Fighter Command however much Goering made boastful predictions; Britain had rescued the core of its professional army from Dunkirk; and most of all, the Royal Navy was almost certain to wreak complete devastation should any Channel crossing be attempted, no matter what forces the Germans could throw into supporting the precarious amphibious craft. In October the operation was suspended indefinitely.

Outbreak of War in the Mediterranean

Meanwhile, German attempts to interfere in the Mediterranean by sending three U-boats past Gibraltar ended in failure. Italy, biding its time, had not been keen to support German activity against the British on its own doorstep. However, with the rapid fall of France, on 10 June 1940 Mussolini decided that Germany had won, and declared war on France and Britain himself.

The key to British strategy was the ability to leave the Italians and the Mediterranean to the French Navy. The Royal Navy could – just about – fight Germany and Japan. This whole strategy would collapse like a pack of cards with the defeat of France and the near-simultaneous entry of Italy into the war. A hostile fleet – including more than a hundred modern submarines – now sat astride the shortest British imperial route. But Italy, almost a maritime economy wedded to the continent, also suffered from some of the problems already faced by the British. She was deficient in raw materials and supplies and relied upon seaborne trade to bring much of these necessities in. Thus Italy was susceptible to contrary British pressure in the Mediterranean. The supply lines to her East African colonies adjoining the Red Sea were controlled by British warships and Anglo-Egyptian control of the Suez Canal. But there was no denying the vulnerability of the British position: Admiralty planners knew that in order to get warships and convoys through the Mediterranean to Malta and onwards to British ground forces in North Africa, given Italian hostility, would require a comprehensive fleet in support. Should the Germans become involved, British difficulties would multiply.

In pre-war talks, the western Mediterranean was agreed to be the responsibility of the French, with the eastern portion the charge of the Royal Navy. As long as the French fleet remained active in the western theatre, the Italian Navy was inferior to the Allies' overall combination. The Italians knew this. From September 1939 until June 1940 Italy had

sensibly chosen to remain a non-belligerent, saving itself from any Anglo-French naval offensive. But with the French knocked out by June, the British Mediterranean Fleet could no longer count on the *Marine Nationale*.

With fleets and bases strategically located at Gibraltar at the western entrance and Alexandria in the east (over 1,800 miles apart), the British under Admiral Andrew Browne Cunningham were at once divided and exposed. It was impossible for the two British fleets to be combined without losing dominance at one or other end of the Mediterranean. The key to this and other Mediterranean strategic fundamentals was the island base of Malta. Situated as a staging post on the lateral convoy route between the two main British bases and astride the north-south Italian routes from Sicily to her colonies in Libya, it was also close to the narrow, 30-mile channel between Cape Bon in French-held Tunisia and the Italian island base of Pantelleria south of Sicily. It was thus the fly in the ointment of Axis operations in North Africa, and the Axis would spend much time and effort attempting to neutralize it.

Thrown increasingly onto the back foot as it was, the French Navy had played little part before the Armistice on 22 June. Its offensive successes were confined to an initial rash of submarine and mine attacks on Italian merchant ships, operations in the Dodecanese islands and bombardment by its heavy cruisers of the western Italian coast. Free of this threat by the summer, the Italians ran convoys to Libya and built up ground and air forces there in order to over-run British and French North African territory. The overall Axis plan was to roll east and then to swing northwards into the oil-rich lands of the Middle East.

North Africa and the Mediterranean

Both the British and the Italians had great difficulty supplying their armies in North Africa. British convoys to Egypt were sent on the long sea route around the Cape of Good Hope. This entailed a much longer transit and in effect used more shipping. Italian convoys to Tripoli were harassed by British surface and submarine forces. Emergency supplies were sent by submarine to Italian positions in Libya, while the British used their own submarines to bolster fuel supplies to Malta and go looking for Italian shipping to attack. But large British submarines of the 'O', 'P' and 'R' classes, designed and built in the 1920s and 1930s to fight the Japanese in the open waters of the Pacific, proved unwieldy and vulnerable to Italian anti-submarine destroyer and air attacks. Three were lost within a month of hostilities with Italy. Five hundred British crew would be killed before the smaller and more handy 'U' class coastal boats were put into service with the First, Eighth and Tenth Submarine Flotillas.

Italian submarines had numbered over 110 in June 1940, about half of which were coastal types and the rest longer-range oceanic vessels, compared to a British force of around ten. Compared to U-boats, Italian submarines were of inferior design, manned by older crews and generally performed much less successfully.

In September 1940 the Italians invaded Egypt and, eager to imitate Hitler's successes, pushed into Greece in October. They were ejected from Greece and seen off by Wavell's British army in Egypt, with naval bombardments proving useful in dislodging Italian camps. While both sides suffered from the distances of operations from their main bases at Tripoli and Alexandria, signals intelligence helped the British ameliorate this with advantageous planning. Perpetually convinced of the impenetrability of their naval Hagelin codes, the Italians were vulnerable to British code-reading in the Mediterranean. Meanwhile, after the signature of the Tripartite Pact with Germany and Italy, Japan started its southward move into northern Indochina, a French colony.

Thrown off the European mainland and acting alone, the British looked to the Mediterranean as the only theatre they could operate in successfully for the time being. This relied upon seizing the initiative away from the Italians, depending on Gibraltar and Alexandria instead of Malta and exploiting their valuable aircraft carriers and well-honed ability to fight at night.

After Operation Sealion had been abandoned, the German Navy was forced to re-evaluate its plans. The *Kriegsmarine* continued to see the North Atlantic as its primary theatre and the Mediterranean as a distraction. But the failures of the Italians led first the German Army to be dragged in to support operations in North Africa, then the *Luftwaffe* (*X Fliegerkorps*) to support the Italian Navy, and finally the German Navy, which was ordered to redirect U-boats from the key North Atlantic theatre. All of these moves were opposed by the respective arms of the German forces, but they were over-ruled by Hitler who saw the Mediterranean war as an opportunity to damage British power more quickly with less effort.

The Question of the French Fleet

The fate of the *Marine Nationale* after the armistice with Germany had remained a vexatious question to the British, in particular to Prime Minister Churchill. A modern, powerful fleet, equipped with a number of battleships in some cases superior to their German counterparts, lay dispersed – and virtually intact – at three main bases around the Mediterranean: Toulon, on the southern French coast; British Alexandria, in Egypt; and at Mers el-Kebir on the coast of French Algeria. The incomplete battleship *Richelieu* was at Dakar in Senegal, and the *Jean Bart* was berthed in Casablanca in French Morocco. There was also a squadron of cruisers and *contre-torpilleurs* at Bizerte in Tunisia.

A small number of French destroyers, sloops and submarines were already lying in British naval bases, and these units were easily taken under British control though not without bloodshed. But it was one of British naval strategy's anxieties that the major French forces still at large should fall into German or Italian hands, as to do so would tip the balance firmly in favour of the Axis navies not only in the Mediterranean but in nearly all European seas, and by extension thence into the Atlantic. Article 8 of the Franco-German armistice stated that the French fleet 'shall be collected in ports to be specified and there demobilized and disarmed under German or Italian control'. The British high command resolved that, however difficult and rancorous the task, the remainder of the French fleet had to be taken under control or, if necessary, incapacitated.

Orders were issued to Admiral Cunningham in command of a powerful British squadron off Alexandria, and to Admiral Sir James Somerville at Gibraltar with Force H, to offer the French commanders the choices of sailing into internment in Britain, or to the West Indies and American control; to continue the fight against Germany; to dimilitarize their ships immediately; or to scuttle them. Cunningham negotiated successfully with the French ships at Alexandria and found a solution which did not require violence. Somerville was unable to achieve a similar outcome at Mers el-Kebir, and on 3 July was prodded by a nervous and expectant Admiralty to carry out 'one of the most disagreeable and difficult tasks that a British Admiral has ever been faced with'. The British squadron opened a heavy and mostly accurate fire on the French warships desperately trying to raise steam to escape

the harbour: the battleship *Bretagne* was blown up; the new battlecruiser *Dunkerque* and the battleship *Provence* ran aground, damaged, the former to be further damaged a few days later by a Swordfish torpedo attack. Further assaults likewise aimed at picking off the remaining French heavy units at places like Dakar. The deed was done with customary decisiveness. The French were outraged: 1,299 French sailors were killed and the rest had witnessed their ships being violated by an erstwhile ally. The *Strasbourg* managed to escape to Vichy-held Toulon, chased by the British battlecruiser *Hood*. Stunned by this act, Vichy France was pushed ideologically closer to the Axis. With its North African empire still loyal, Vichy was still a factor in the Mediterranean balance of power. But for the British, the danger of the Axis taking control of one of the most potent fleets in Europe had been averted, and British political and military resolve was plain to see around the world, most importantly visible to America but also impressive to the wavering Spanish. Encouraged, the United States signed a crucial 'Ships for Bases' agreement with Britain, handing over fifty elderly destroyers. Already cognisant of the fact that the survival of Great Britain was central to the security of the United States, in the face of a largely isolationist public attitude Roosevelt authorized the Two-Navy Ocean Expansion Act in July, ordering 1,300,000 tons of warships and 15,000 naval aircraft to be built.

The Beginning of the U-Boat War

As in World War One, to access the open seas of the world the German Navy had to negotiate the physical barrier posed by the British Isles. The Royal Navy sought to block the exits: the Channel and the North Sea, and further out, the UK-Iceland-Greenland gaps. The Home Fleet at Scapa Flow resumed its focus on the northern exits, but it could not cover everywhere and already there were a number of German raiders at large. British cruisers were stretched thinly. Fifty-six fast passenger ships were thus requisitioned by the Admiralty, equipped with 6-inch guns and a rudimentary AA outfit and sent around the world, operating out of Commonwealth or Allied ports. In the first few months of the war in 1939, thirteen of these armed merchant cruisers (AMCs) were used to patrol the North Atlantic gaps, suffering heavy losses to surface and submarine attack: the sinking of the 6-inch gunned *Rawalpindi* by the *Scharnhorst* and *Gneisenau* 11-inch-gunned battlecruisers in November is a famous case in point. But the biggest threat posed to all British ships came not from the surface units but from the *Luftwaffe* and the U-boats.

Germany entered the war with fifty-seven U-boats, of which twenty-six were of an ocean-going type. Of these, only eighteen U-boats were operationally available to the Germans for Atlantic operations on the outbreak of war. Their initial impact as a *guerre de course* weapon was limited: by the end of 1939, surface raiders and mines had accounted for roughly twice as many merchant sinkings as had U-boats. Against warships in this period, the U-boats performed more impressively: the British carrier *Courageous* and the battleship *Royal Oak* both fell prey to skilled U-boat attacks, the latter's loss particularly disturbing to the Royal Navy because it was perpetrated inside the Home Fleet anchorage at Scapa Flow.

French Capitulation and the U-Boat War

From Christmas 1939, average monthly losses of Allied and neutral shipping ran at a steady 80,000 tons. Pre-war British estimation of the U-boat threat – and of British ability to shrug it off – had so far been proven largely accurate. But the British anti-submarine situation in 1939 became worse with the conquest of Denmark and Norway in April 1940, and was made very much the graver in May and June with the fall of France. Almost at a stroke Germany gained unfettered access to French Atlantic ports, in particular Brest, La Rochelle, Lorient, St Nazaire and Bordeaux. Against this new disposition, a secure British anti-submarine blockade was totally impossible. With their effective range increased in a quantum leap, taking them out beyond the endurance of British convoy escorts, U-boats' scores began to rise accordingly: up to nearly 240,000 tons per month from July to late October 1940. The Royal Navy lacked the means to securely shepherd its own trade let alone impose a counter-blockade. Air power had long made close blockade impossible. Most of the Royal Navy's pre-war destroyers were designed to operate with the fleet rather than in anti-submarine and convoying work, though a major conversion programme had been started pre-war. With German forces on England's doorstep, provision also had to be made to prevent any attempted invasion, and this meant keeping destroyers in home waters. Also, half the modern fleet destroyers were stationed in the Mediterranean – and many ships had been damaged in early operations, from Norway to Gibraltar.

Organizing the assembly, disposition and timings of warships and convoys and the issuing of sailing instructions relied on an immense volume of information being flashed around the airwaves. That this radio traffic could be intercepted was largely unavoidable. The key was to make it as secure and encrypted as reasonably possible without creating gross inefficiencies. At the outbreak of war the Germans had quickly begun to read British merchant signals, giving them time to position U-boats to interdict not only unescorted singletons but also the early convoys out in the Atlantic. Facing only a small number of U-boats, mostly acting alone but beginning to use novel *Rudeltaktik* ('wolf-pack' tactics), British mercantile losses were growing increasingly worrisome but were not yet disastrous.

However, the Submarine Tracking Room set up at the Admiralty had little to go on except reports from foreign-based agents, radioed contacts from vessels at sea and marginally discernible patterns of losses. Existing hard-pressed escorts could not be everywhere at once, and the defence of convoys against U-boat attack – usually at night, and increasingly from more than one assailant – was weak and essentially negative. Unable to take the fight to the lurking U-boat until it had shown itself, British convoys had to rely primarily on evasion.

Compared to the volume of shipping which needed convoying, the Royal Navy possessed far too few dedicated escorts, and so hastily built corvettes to supplement its elderly 1918-vintage destroyers and a few sloops already labouring under the strain of convoy duties. Based on a classic commercial whaler design, these 'Flower' class corvettes did not boast much superiority over their quarry; with a top speed of 16 knots and a 4-inch gun, they were inferior to a surfaced Type VII U-boat by one knot and therefore unable to catch a fleeing opponent. They were cramped and had a tendency to roll in any kind of seaway. But they were cheap and quick to build, and seaworthy enough to operate out in the Atlantic, two-thirds of which was now accessible to U-boats that could be refuelled at sea by replenishment vessels. In time, brand new escorts would have to be built, quickly and in large numbers, and more sophisticated tactics had to be developed to counter the growing confidence and skill of Germany's submarine arm. But as a bandage to stanch the steady bleeding of British merchantmen, the corvette was indispensable in British and Canadian use.

The German U-boat Arm was the proud domain of Admiral Karl Dönitz, a leading light of the *Kriegsmarine* and a loyal Nazi. The lynchpin of the German U-boat force was the Type VII U-boat. Over five hundred boats were commissioned during the war. Of 750 tons displacement and armed with fourteen torpedoes, they could transit at 17 knots on the surface, easily fast enough to reposition and overhaul most convoys at night. The Type VII was joined by a larger design, the ocean-going double-hulled Type IX. Two hundred and fifty-two feet long, displacing over 1,100 tons, and with a capacity for twenty-two torpedoes with four tubes forward and two aft and fitted with a 105 mm gun, the newer class was also a capable submarine design, conceived to extend the range of U-boat influence across the Atlantic, despite the Type VII possessing adequate capabilities in this area, as the British merchant marine would find out to its almost ruinous cost in the coming months. The Type IX was able to menace shipping in the South Atlantic and Indian oceans too. Both types were equipped with the standard G7e electrical torpedo, capable of 5,500 yards at 30 knots.

To combat the threat posed by modern torpedo-armed submarines, Asdic (the name taken from the initials of the Anti Submarine Detection Investigation Committee), or sonar as it later became known, had been further developed in Britain in the 1920s to augment passive hydrophones and take the offensive in active detection of submarines. A major breakthrough had come in the mid-1930s with the development of the Asdic Range Recorder, which by means of an echo memory and a visual display could show a rudimentary fire-control solution. Too much faith was placed in this technology (by Britain but also by German submarine theorists) such that even by 1939 modern submarines were largely invulnerable to it, for the simple reason that most submarine attacks were delivered on the surface at night or from well outside the range of early Asdic (500 yards). Escort vessels could fire star shell, which illuminated the scene for a few seconds, but only once the escort had been made aware of the presence of the U-boat – and by definition an attack had usually been made by then. Assuming an escort could locate the source of the attack at night, and could catch up with the perpetrator, only then would Asdic be of use in a depth-charge attack.

The Diverse Threat to British Shipping

Other weapons threatened British coastal and oceanic shipping lanes. By March 1940 over 400,000 tons of British shipping had been sunk by magnetic mines. Sown by ships, aircraft and submarines around Britain, they caused a significant amount of dislocation of coastal shipping in the North Sea and especially in the approaches to the Thames, prompting Churchill to demand tighter precautions. In November 1939, two destroyers out of Harwich and a dozen merchantmen had all been lost to magnetic mines. All traffic out of the Thames was stopped, and Admiralty pressure on the RAF led to the raising of the first barrage balloons for the protection of harbours. In a war at sea which would increasingly be dominated by the application of rival technological ingenuities, one of the first steps would be to make improvements in minesweeping gear and the fitting of ships with degaussing coils. These small countermeasures went a long way to neutering the threat over the winter of 1939–40, by which time the insufficiency of German stocks had prevented their having a decisive effect; though by the war's end a staggering 10 per cent of overall merchant losses would be attributed to mines.

German motor torpedo boats – *Schnellboote* to the Germans, 'E-boats' to the British – caused havoc in the same waters, raiding coastal convoys and inshore traffic almost at will as British defences found their feet. These heavily armed, high-speed diesel boats would remain unmatched until the appearance of the later British Fairmile MTB designs.

Part of Dönitz's combined strategy for prosecuting the submarine war on trade involved maritime patrol aircraft. Four-engined *Luftwaffe* Focke-Wulf 200 Condors began to operate west of Ireland, attacking ships and spotting for U-boats. Though never as co-ordinated with U-boats as Dönitz had intended, they remained a threat into 1941 when they were largely chased from the skies by Allied shipborne fighter aircraft.

By the end of the first fifteen months of the war, nearly 3.5 million tons of trade-carrying shipping had been lost to bombs, torpedoes and mines. Sixty per cent of these losses were of unescorted vessels to U-boat attack, the Royal Navy having decided it would not convoy merchant ships whose speed fell outside the limits of 9–13 knots. Germany also attacked the shipping of neutral countries and these merchant fleets volunteered to be run under British control. Such appropriations meant that the nominal total tonnage under the British 'red duster' increased by an extra 2.5 million tons to 20 million between 1939 and 1941. And by the end of 1940, Canadian efforts had resulted in an extra fifty corvettes built for Atlantic service. Added to this much-needed boost from Canadian shipyards, twenty-four minesweepers and six destroyers were also acquired from the USA via Canada; all were signed over to Royal Naval control.

With only six destroyers, acquired from the Royal Navy for battle fleet and coastal defence roles and unsuited to anti-submarine work, the Royal Canadian Navy was under-trained in Asdic. Furthermore, in the early months it was wedded to a premature concept of offensive anti-submarine work which differed from the British policy of 'the safe and timely arrival of the convoy'. But through force of necessity, the slow transatlantic convoys would become a Canadian speciality.

The Italian and British Battle Fleets

Meanwhile, in the confined waters of the almost tideless 'middle sea', small convoys with light escorts crossing south from Italy and crawling along the Libyan coast constituted the main type of Italian operations. Occasionally, powerful battleship and cruiser forces ventured out to flex their muscles and to deter interference from the British.

The first contact between the Italian and British battle fleets was the result of operations around just such an Italian convoy bound for North Africa. An Italian force of two battleships and heavy cruisers covering a convoy carrying tanks for intended use against the British in Libya and Egypt was intercepted off Punta Stilo (Calabria) in July 1940 by a heavy British force under Cunningham, itself ostensibly covering a staged withdrawal of non-essential personnel from Malta to Alexandria. During the contact, co-ordination between the *Regia Marina* and the *Regia Aeronautica* was appalling: 2,000 bombs were dropped from medium level on friend and foe alike as the two fleets diverged, with many near-misses but few hits. Both British and Italian convoys reached their destinations unmolested. But all British heavy ships except the *Warspite* had been outranged by their Italian counterparts and the chaotic air attacks had rattled the British crews. Meanwhile the Italians had worn out many of their ships' engines while pushing for higher speeds, had proved unable to concentrate their fire to any effect despite numerical advantage, and overall felt relieved that it had not been worse. The probable usefulness of a few squadrons of capable dive-bombers was also noted.

Four months later, November would see two further actions between the Italian and British fleets: one at Taranto would demonstrate the decisive use to which air power could be put by an aggressor equipped with aircraft carriers; and the second off Cape Spartivento would reinforce the Italian battle fleet's growing feeling of frustration at being unable to seriously challenge the British battle fleet for command of Mediterranean waters.

The Readjustment of the British Naval Approach

By the end of 1940 the first tentative British steps had been taken towards measures which would achieve the eventual containment of the U-boat. The first surface-search radar in an escort destroyer was fitted to HMS *Verity* in June 1940. Laboratory refinements to Asdic equipment were fed back to the ships on anti-submarine duty. Operational experience was quickly analyzed and lessons promulgated. By the end of the year, RAF Coastal Command had adopted depth charges in place of useless anti-submarine bombs, had trialled Leigh searchlights mounted on Wellington bombers, and tested early forms of airborne radar. British shipyards were gearing up to provide replacement tonnage, and new warships, laid down before the war, were commissioning. Britain was surviving alone against Germany and Italy. In the South Atlantic and in the Mediterranean, battle honours were firmly in the Royal Navy's favour; but it was increasingly clear to the Admiralty (though not yet the *Kriegsmarine*) that it was under the sea where Germany would be hardest to beat.

The sinking of HMS *Royal Oak*

The most dramatic German success of the first few months of the war came in mid-October 1939 when *U-47* penetrated the British base at Scapa Flow and sank the battleship *Royal Oak*.

Scapa Flow: Lamb Holm and Kirk Sound

A *Luftwaffe* aerial reconnaissance photograph of Lamb Holm and Kirk Sound, one of the entrances to Scapa Flow, taken in early 1941, just over a year after *U-47*, commanded by Lieutenant Gunther Prien, had slipped between the blockships in Kirk Sound to torpedo HMS *Royal Oak*, which was lying at anchor. The photograph shows several key elements of the defences developed after the attack, including two anti-aircraft batteries west of St Mary's; a military camp to the east; and coastal gun batteries on Burray and Lamb Holm. Also evident are the blockships, including additional ones that were sunk after the attack. Subsequent to this photograph being taken barriers of concrete blocks (referred to as 'causeways' because they were built using Italian PoW labour, which was not permitted on military installations under the Geneva Convention) were built across Kirk Sound and other entrances to Scapa Flow.

U-47 returns to base from Scapa Flow

U-47 returns to a hero's welcome after her successful mission to Scapa Flow. The Type VIIB U-boat had already sunk three merchant ships under Lieutenant Prien, and went on to sink another twenty-seven before being rammed and sunk with all hands by HMS *Wolverine* in March 1941.

Rendering safe a mine on the east coast of Britain

Throughout the war, one of the most dangerous and unsung of tasks facing naval personnel was the disposal of mines. Some were dropped by aircraft in shallow coastal waters; others broke free of their moorings and drifted ashore. All had to be made harmless, either by removing the fuse or, if this was impossible, by blowing them up. Mine disposal was a job that had a high fatality rate.

Navies in exile: Poland

When Germany attacked Poland many units of the small Polish Navy escaped to Britain. Among them were three of the navy's four destroyers: *Burza* ('Squall'), *Blyskawica* ('Lightning') and *Grom* ('Thunder'). The fourth, *Wicher* ('Hurricane'), was sunk in action with German forces off the southern Baltic port of Gdynia. *Blyskawica* and *Grom* were brand new and amongst the most powerful ships of their type in service anywhere, and they were a significant addition to the strength of the Royal Navy.

Grom was bombed and sunk with heavy loss of life off Norway in May 1940, but the other two fought on through the war, alongside other ships and submarines that had escaped and more that were transferred from the Royal Navy. *Blyskawica* is now preserved as a museum ship at Gdynia.

Gun cleaning on ORP *Blyskawica*
Gun crew at work cleaning the single 120 mm AA gun on board *Blyskawica* on 13 September while the destroyer was in port. The curved frames are to prevent the gun accidentally being fired into any part of the ship while being trained towards hostile aircraft. Note the helmets hung up around the gun position, and the twin 40mm Bofors mounting in the background. Both *Blyskawica* and *Grom* had been built at White's shipyard at Cowes, Isle of Wight, and in May 1942 *Blyskawica* was able to use her guns to help defend the yard when it was subjected to a heavy air raid while the ship was there for a refit.

Sailors on the quarterdeck of ORP *Grom*
Clearly mustered for the camera's benefit, the reality is that the sailors' faces betray the strain and unhappiness of their overall situation and that of their homeland.

The Battle of the River Plate

Before the outbreak of war, the German 'pocket battleship' *Admiral Graf Spee* was ordered to proceed to the South Atlantic. Her mission as a commerce raider was to sink merchant ships and draw Allied naval units off their assigned stations in other parts of the world. In this last regard she was highly successful with twenty-two British and French ships dispatched to search for her. After taking nine merchant ships, she was tracked down by a British squadron comprising HMS *Exeter*, HMS *Ajax* and HMNZS *Achilles* under Commodore Henry Harwood on 13 December. During the Battle of the River Plate that ensued, *Graf Spee*'s captain, Hans Langsdorff, decided to concentrate his ship's fire on the *Exeter*, which, after suffering heavy damage, was forced to break off and retire to the Falklands.

Rather than pursue the *Exeter* or continue to engage the two other cruisers, the *Graf Spee* made for the neutral Uruguayan port of Montevideo in the mouth of the River Plate to effect repairs. Indecisive and increasingly in fear of a British aircraft carrier and other heavy units reportedly in the offing, on 17 December Langsdorff sailed *Graf Spee* into international waters, took off the crew, and blew up the ship. The following evening in Montevideo he shot himself.

This episode – welcomed in Britain as perfectly in keeping with the Royal Navy's traditional success in the south Atlantic against German raiders – was an early example of the influence that misinformation and perceived British fighting superiority could have on otherwise well-planned, successful German naval operations.

View from *Achilles*
A photograph of poor quality, but much historic interest, taken by a Royal Marines sergeant on board Achilles. It shows, 'Ajax firing her foremost turrets at 07.40 as *Graf Spee* was on a bearing of approx. Green 35 degrees. *Ajax* is making high speed, and is approximately 600 yards away.' Note the anti-splinter protection in the foreground.

The end of the *Admiral Graf Spee*
The *Graf Spee* burning after being scuttled in the estuary, 4 miles off Montevideo. The water was only 4 fathoms deep, and so as the ship settled on the bottom much of the wreck remained above the surface.

HMNZS *Achilles* arrives at Buenos Aires

Achilles sailed into Buenos Aires after the battle, and was given a great reception by the crowds on the quayside. Note the flags flown at half mast – four of her crew had been killed. In Montevideo off-duty men from the British ships had ended up drinking with men from the scuttled *Graf Spee*.

HMS *Exeter* at Port Stanley

This photograph shows the damage sustained by *Exeter*, taken while she was undergoing temporary repairs in Port Stanley in the Falkland Islands. In the first ten minutes of the battle both her forward turrets were hit and put out of action, while splinters killed or wounded most of the personnel on the bridge. In all, over sixty men were killed and 120 wounded – over a quarter of the ship's crew.

The captain then conned the ship from aft, while the one remaining turret, also aft, continued in action, controlled by an officer standing on the roof shouting instructions to the turret crew inside.

(left) Churchill addresses the crew on *Exeter*
Exeter was welcomed back to Britain by the First Lord of the Admiralty, Winston Churchill. He joined her in the Hamoaze before docking, and later addressed the assembled ship's company on the quarterdeck. Note how the wartime censor has indicated that the battlecruiser *Repulse*, tied up alongside in the background, be removed from the photograph before publication.

(above) HMS *Exeter* returns home
Devonport dockyard workers crowd every vantage point along the quayside, as well as on harbour craft, as *Exeter* arrives back home on 15 February 1940. Devonport was *Exeter's* home port. She had been built there a decade previously, and would now go into dock to repair the extensive damage suffered in the Battle of the River Plate, as well as to receive modifications to her armament. Note, compared to the photograph opposite, how the dreadful damage done to her forward gun turrets has been repaired, albeit temporarily. The crow's nest on the foremast has also been removed, but the splinter damage to the front of the bridge has simply been painted over, while that on the bridge wings and funnels has been left, presumably so as to still give the ship an appropriate 'battle scarred' look.

(above) HMS *King George V*
The youngest members of the crew of the new Royal
Navy battleship *King George V*, all aged sixteen, are perched
on an enormous anchor chain while receiving instruction
from an 'old hand' petty officer, likely a veteran of World
War One. Boys could enter the service at fifteen.

(right) The rum issue on HMS *Rodney*
The custom of issuing a ration of rum to sailors in the
Royal Navy dates back to the eighteenth century. Here,
men crowd round the rum barrel for the noon-time issue.
An eighth of a pint of Jamaican rum was doled out to each
rating, to be diluted with two parts water: petty officers
were allowed to drink theirs neat.

(opposite) HMS *Rodney*
Royal Marines in their smart uniforms are lined up for
inspection after Divisions on board the battleship *Rodney*.

The struggle for Norway

In a European maritime war, Norway is strategically located with access to the Atlantic and in the early months of the war it was a conduit through which iron ore could be transported to fuel the German war effort. In April 1940 the Germans launched Operation *Weserübung* – the sea, land and air invasion of Norway – with the intention of capturing key Norwegian ports and ore fields under the auspices of an armed protection of Norway's neutrality. Opposing them were partially mobilized Norwegian land and naval forces along with British and French troops, transported to Norway by ships of the Royal Navy. So began the first clash between Allied and German combined forces.

The village of Bjerkvik, at the head of Herjangen Fjord, opposite Narvik, burning after naval gun bombardment in support of the Allied landing, which took place here in the early hours of 9 May 1940. The apparent brightness of the flames indicates that the photograph was taken at a wide aperture, commensurate with the low light levels of early morning. The landing, by French troops supported by the British battleship *Resolution*, the cruisers *Effingham* and *Vindictive* and eight destroyers, resulted in Allied troops reaching Rombaks Fjord, and eventually capturing Narvik. While the operation was taking place Hitler was launching his *Blitzkrieg* in the west, and Chamberlain's government was falling: within a fortnight the decision was taken to withdraw from Norway. (The previous month, during the Second Battle of Narvik, when the outcome of the Norwegian campaign was much more in the balance, a Swordfish floatplane catapulted from HMS *Warspite* had bombed and sunk *U-64* in this location.)

British ships at Harstad

An AA gun manned by troops from Exeter, Devon, in a makeshift emplacement, covering shipping out in the fjord at Harstad, 14 May 1940.

British arrival in Norway

A deceptively peaceful view of the town and harbour of Harstad, 14 May 1940. However, the warship out in the harbour is not a unit of the Norwegian Navy, but the British cruiser *Effingham*, covering the landing of part of the Norwegian Expeditionary Force to re-take the port of Narvik.

HMS *Effingham*

Two views of HMS *Effingham* at anchor in a Norwegian fjord on 16 May 1940, two days before she hit a rock at over 22 knots while transporting British troops to Bodo. Her hull was ripped open 'like a giant tin opener' according to one of her officers: casualties were nil, but the ship was declared a total loss and had to be sunk by the British to prevent capture by the Germans. Note the Bren gun carriers stowed on the cruiser's upper deck – most of the army equipment was lost with the ship.

Although *Effingham* was fifteen years old, she had been completely modernized only a few years previously to bring her into line with the newer cruisers coming into service. She played a very active part in the Norwegian campaign, and would doubtless have been equally busy for the rest of the war had it not been for this accident.

(opposite) The torpedoing of HMS *Eskimo*

During the Second Battle of Narvik, the 'Tribal' class destroyer *Eskimo* had her bow blown off by a torpedo. She limped back to Skelfjord in the Lofoten Islands for temporary repairs. Surviving aerial bomb attacks, she was finally made ready for sea on 27 May 1940 and made it back to Vickers-Armstrong Yard in Barrow in northern England on 4 June for a rebuild.

British ships being bombed, Norway

While the British emerged from the Norwegian campaign tactically victorious on the surface, their vulnerability to determined aerial attack had been exposed. German land-based air power gave the Royal Navy a rude shock, showing the British that their anti-aircraft mix was not as effective as hoped. 4.7-inch guns with a maximum elevation of 40 degrees were known to possess only a limited capacity against torpedo-planes and none at all against dive-bombing Ju 87 Stukas. But the British had expected their four- and eight-barrelled 2pdr 'pompoms' to do better. These could engage high-angle targets but had insufficient range and there were never enough of them. More 20mm Oerlikon automatic AA guns were fitted in increasing numbers after Norway.

On this occasion while eight bombs were dropped there were no hits. The ship in the centre of the picture is HMS *Vindictive*, once a sister-ship of *Effingham* but by this time serving as a repair ship.

(above) Dunkirk on fire after German bombardment
This view, looking south-west, shows the inner harbour on the afternoon of 31 May. The large, fairly open area of quayside to the right is the Quai Félix Faure, from where much of the final, desperate stages of the Allied evacuation were to take place over the days to come, while the famous beaches at Malo-les-Bains, La Panne and Bray lie to the east, behind the photographer.

The photograph was taken by F/Sgt Lloyd Bennett from Lockheed Hudson N.7230, part of 220 GR (General Reconnaissance) Squadron flown by P/O Pedersen and operating from RAF Bircham Newton in Norfolk on 'Sands Patrol' covering the evacuation of the BEF (British Expeditionary Force) from Belgium and France. The following day they had to return to Bircham Newton on just their port engine after losing the starboard one to fire from an enemy Heinkel. Two days later the same happened again, this time due to AA fire off Texel, but again they got home.

(below) HMS *Javelin* off Dunkirk
The destroyer *Javelin* pictured off Dunkirk on 30 May 1940, with the port burning in the background. Prior to the onset of the *Blitzkrieg* in western Europe *Javelin* had been involved in convoy escort, but she then joined the First Destroyer Flotilla, engaged in cable-cutting operations off the Netherlands. On 27 May, together with her sister-ship *Jaguar* and another destroyer, *Grenade*, she joined the evacuation operations, picking up survivors from SS *Abukir*

and rescuing some 1,400 soldiers from Bray beach. On 29 May, with *Grenade* one of three destroyers having been sunk, and *Jaguar* being among another half dozen damaged, Admiral Ramsay was ordered to withdraw all the modern fleet destroyers from the evacuation. A tough decision, it deprived Ramsay of his best ships, but it saved them for future operations, where their value was to be proved again and again. Of the eight ships of the 'J' class, *Javelin* was one of only two to survive the war.

Chaos at Dunkirk and deliverance in Dover

There were repeated scenes like these at Dover, Ramsgate and the other ports in south-east England as destroyers, passenger ships and other vessels returned loaded with troops from the Dunkirk evacuation between 26 May and 4 June 1940. Of the 338,000 men rescued, over 100,000 were brought back by the Royal Navy's destroyers. The retrieval of ten times the initial estimate of men during Operation Dynamo was deemed a miracle by those in power desperate to put a brave face on a disastrously untenable position on the continent. A victory in no sense other than a well-brought-off strategic withdrawal, this point probably marked the nadir of British power on the continent until 1944.

Admiralty Pier, Dover

Troops crowd the Admiralty Pier at Dover after disembarking from the destroyers that had brought them back from Dunkirk. All rifles were collected before they boarded trains at Dover Marine railway station. Today the site shown in this photograph is a terminal for cruise ships.

Disembarking from the destroyers

In this photograph, four destroyers are lined up abreast against the quayside to allow the troops to gain access to the shore.

HMS *Codrington*

Troops preparing to disembark at Dover from the destroyer *Codrington*. Note how the ship is listing to port as the men crowd to one side. In the background, beyond the passenger ferry and sailing barges, is Dover Castle, under which, within the Napoleonic-era tunnels, Admiral Ramsay masterminded the evacuation. *Codrington* was bombed and sunk in the harbour two months later; the wreck remained lying on the beach until it was broken up in 1947.

Dunkirk, 4 June 1940

In striking contrast, these views show the sea front at Dunkirk immediately after the completion of the British evacuation earlier in the day. They were taken by Hermann Weper, a troop commander, wireless operator and official photographer with *Motorensturm* 13.M52 (52nd battalion, 13th Mobile Assault Unit). Others he took at about the same time show French prisoners already employed in shifting abandoned equipment, being interrogated, or being marched off into captivity, as well as many more of the victorious *Wehrmacht*. Later he photographed occupied Paris, and the Russian front during 1941 and the winter of 1941–2.

Arrival of German troops
The brilliant weather just serves to heighten the air of utter unreality as German soldiers of *Motorensturm 13* stand around in the sunshine next to their equipment and vehicles, staring out to sea at the wrecks of some of the Allied ships that failed to escape. There is little obvious elation at victory – if anything everyone looks vaguely stunned.

Stranded French submarine chaser
Motorensturm 13 soldiers examine the beached French submarine chaser CH.9 at low tide at Dunkirk. The ship had been completed only a few months previously, and had been beached after being bombed on 21 May. The damage that led to this stranding is clearly visible halfway along the port side. In the foreground a British Universal Carrier and a bicycle lie abandoned, half buried in the oil-streaked sand.

Wreck of a French destroyer

Cyclists attached to *Motorensturm 13* rest on the beach at Dunkirk. Other troops take advantage of the low tide to investigate the wreck of the French destroyer *L'Adroit*, which had been struck by a stick of three bombs from a Heinkel, which came over at 100-metre altitude just before midnight on 21 May. Two of the bombs landed alongside, but the third penetrated between the first two funnels. The ship was beached at Malo les Bains and the crew evacuated, but a serious fire started in a fuel bunker and touched off the forward magazines at 5 a.m. the following morning. More wrecked shipping can be seen further out to sea.

Makeshift pier

Although not part of the same series, this photograph shows another scene that would have met the German troops. In an effort to facilitate the evacuation, the British created two artificial piers extending into the sea by parking their lorries down La Panne beach at low tide. Under sporadic shelling, these were topped with decking lashed tightly against the breaking waves to provide a footway, and from them small boats were loaded with men before rowing back out to the larger ships.

The fate of the French fleets

At Alexandria, a mixture of diplomacy, deviousness, and the implicit threat of force – no doubt helped by the good relations resulting from the British and French fleets sharing the same harbour and operating as one on a regular basis until just days previously – resulted in the peaceful demilitarization of the French warships there.

But at Mers el-Kebir in French North Africa things did not work out nearly so well. On a blisteringly hot summer's day an appalling catalogue of missed chances, mistakes, misunderstandings, poor (or non-existent) communications, stubbornness, and simple bad luck eventually resulted in the ships of Admiral Sir James Somerville's just-created Force H opening fire on Britain's erstwhile ally, with tragic consequences. Gunfire, bombs and torpedoes left the *Bretagne* blown up and sunk and the flagship *Dunkerque* and the *Provence* run aground, seriously damaged.

For the Nazis it was a stunning and completely unexpected propaganda coup – 'the greatest act of scoundrelism in world history' as one newspaper put it – which they quite understandably exploited to the full. Recruitment to de Gaulle's Free French forces was dealt a severe blow. Reaction within France itself was one of horror and outrage, although, as time passed under Nazi domination, attitudes became more mixed. In the Royal Navy, and in particular among the officers and men of Force H, there was utter dismay, although those who expressed this were firmly put in their place. Churchill got what he wanted – if he couldn't have the French fleet continuing to fight alongside the British, or at least out of enemy hands, then he needed the most dramatic demonstration possible to the rest of the world, and to the USA in particular, that Britain was determined to fight on. In truth, with the exception of Captain Collinet of the *Strasbourg* and his comrades who extracted their ships from the maelstrom with such skill, none of the major players in the debacle came out of it particularly well. As a result of their actions, 1,297 French sailors lost their lives.

French sailors under fire
A scene on one of the French warships at Mers el-Kebir. Sailors stand, apparently stunned and bemused, on the smoke-filled deck while the British Mediterranean Fleet's shells land in the harbour and among the French targets.

Mers el-Kebir, 3 July 1940
The French fleet, awnings spread, at their moorings at Mers el-Kebir near Oran before the bombardment by Force H on 3 July 1940. From left to right are *Commandant Teste*, *Bretagne*, *Strasbourg*, *Provence*, and *Dunkerque*. Other ships were anchored out of shot, to the right. Note the smoke rising from the funnel of the *Dunkerque*.

The photograph may have been taken from one of the reconnaissance aircraft sent up from Force H to keep an eye on the French ships while negotiations were underway, an action which unfortunately just helped to increase French indignation.

***Strasbourg* escapes**
The *Strasbourg* getting underway as British shells fall beyond the breakwater. To the left, *Provence*, which did not escape, has her forward main turrets trained to return the British fire. *Strasbourg* made it to the Vichy-held port of Toulon.

Operation Catapult, Portsmouth

Operation Catapult, to neutralize the French navy, began peaceably enough. As the first stage, French ships in the British ports of Portsmouth and Plymouth were boarded on 3 July. At Portsmouth these included the torpedo boats *La Melpomène* and *La Flore*. In this photograph showing *La Melpomène*, the French tricolore is still flying; but no members of the French crew are visible, suggesting this photograph was actually taken on 3 July. Both vessels were returned to France in 1945.

French *contre-torpilleurs* at Portsmouth

Other ships seized at Portsmouth included the *contre-torpilleur Léopard*, the colonial sloop *Savorgnan de Brazza*, and a number of small submarine-chasers of the *CH.5* and *CH.11* classes.

A convoy at sea

Often proven since the seventeenth century to be the best way of protecting merchant shipping, convoys were quickly reintroduced upon the outbreak of war, but their outnumbered escorts found it difficult to protect their charges, especially after the U-boats were able to use French bases. This convoy is in the process of executing a turn, probably on exercise as practice for when it might be required in response to U-boat attack.

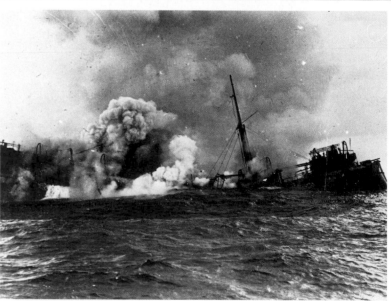

Another British merchant ship is sunk

The Elder Dempster Line's *Apapa*, on fire, her back broken, and steam rising as sea water comes in contact with her boilers, sinks in the Atlantic, November 1940.

A British escort vessel at sea
It wasn't just German U-boats, surface raiders and long-range aircraft that merchant ships and outnumbered escort vessels and their crews had to cope with. The Atlantic ocean was at least as fearsome a foe.

Shipbuilding on the River Clyde

An RAF aerial photograph taken on 11 July 1940, showing the famous John Brown Yard at Clydebank, Dunbartonshire, viewed from the south east. The yard is a bustle of activity, clearly illustrating how the British shipbuilding industry rose to meet the demands of the wartime Royal Navy. In the fitting-out basin can be seen the massive form of the recently launched battleship *Duke of York*, her superstructure just starting to take shape. Next to her are two destroyers, probably *Nerissa* (shortly to become the Polish *Piourun*) and *Nizam*, and the depot ship *Hecla*. Other vessels of various types are under construction on the building slips to either side, including the aircraft carrier *Indefatigable*. To the bottom right a tramp steamer and coasters lie alongside the quays of the commercial Rothesay Dock.

(opposite) US destroyers arrive in Britain

The first of the ex-US flush-deckers after arrival at a British port. The censor has blocked out the hull number of the ship in the foreground, Note the cramped and cluttered layout of the ships, and that her starboard side propeller guard has been removed.

Destroyers for bases

In exchange for the British naval bases at Newfoundland (not then part of Canada) and throughout the Caribbean, fifty old 1918-vintage *Wickes* and *Clemson* class flush-decked American destroyers were supplied to the Royal Navy to help ease the growing strain upon British convoy escort resources. These are the US destroyers *Twiggs* (DD127), *Philip* (DD76), *Evans* (DD78) and *Yarnall* (DD143), awaiting transfer to the Royal Navy. *Yarnall* went on to serve under three flags – the Royal Navy, the Royal Norwegian Navy, and the Soviet Navy.

Operation *Seelöwe* (Sealion): the invasion that never was

Preparations

This series of photographs, believed to have never been published before, were taken during September and October of 1940 by Volkmar König, then a nineteen-year-old *Fähnrich* (midshipman) in the *Kriegsmarine*, who had just finished his training near Kiel. Like others in his class he had then found himself placed in nominal command of the civilian crews of assorted inland and coastal craft – in König's case a barge and two fishing vessels – which proceeded to make their way from Germany by rivers and canals across northern Europe as far as Dunkirk. From there they travelled along the coast to the ports of the Pas-de-Calais, to prepare for the invasion of south-east England. König had the misfortune to injure his ankle landing on a coil of rope while jumping aboard one of his fishing vessels, and so was transferred to the staff ashore at Boulogne. There his duties consisted primarily of keeping a record of the numbers of different vessels in the harbour.

Some 2,000 barges, tugs, fishing vessels, ferries, motor boats and other craft, together with a small number of specialized assault craft, were gathered together in the harbours, from where they sailed to practise landings on the nearby coast of occupied France. The largest concentration was at Boulogne; other ports used were Calais, Dunkirk, Le Havre, Antwerp, Rotterdam and Ostend. While the barges were in harbour the soldiers were happy to lounge around on deck (image 4), where many of them got sunburnt, while at sea on exercises they tended to get sea-sick, even in the calmest conditions.

The preparations for the invasion were rushed, with very few specialized assault craft available, and the conversion of existing vessels was to a large degree extemporized. Parts of the barges' bows were cut off to enable embarkation and disembarkation, wooden planks being installed to prevent them flooding with water (images 1–3).

Image 5 shows a tug towing two barges, one motorized, one unmotorized, towards an 'invasion beach' south of Boulogne. When they arrived off the beach the two motorized vessels swung off to either side and continued to the beach on their own; meanwhile two other, smaller, motorized craft such as fishing boats would come alongside the unmotorized

4

2

3

5

barge and propel it forward to the beach. In the meantime, storm troopers would have embarked from the tug into special high-speed motorboats (propelled using an outboard motor with the propeller on the end of a long shaft and steered by simply turning this entire assembly) to lead the first assault on the beach (image 6).

However, the majority of the disembarkation took place using ramps placed over the open bows of the barges, a slow and most precarious operation even during exercises. Images 7–10 show this, complete with the tricky manoeuvre of landing a gun carriage. König remembers that though the troops rolled up their trousers, the sea came over the tops of their boots, so they still got thoroughly cold and wet.

All this König captured on his Leica camera. Even at the time, looking at how primitive it all was, he shared the misgivings of many of his fellow officers about the feasibility of the plan. Years after, especially comparing it to the Allies' preparations to invade Normandy four years later, he couldn't help but wonder if Hitler had ever really planned to invade Britain at all.

6

7

8

9

10

Death of an Italian destroyer

The heavily damaged Italian destroyer *Artigliere* lies disabled under the guns of the Royal Navy's 8-inch gunned cruiser *York* following the night action between an Italian torpedo-boat force and the British 6-inch light cruiser *Ajax* off Cape Passero (above). The British cruiser finishes her off with a 21-inch torpedo (right).

The British Mediterranean Fleet at Sea
In the early months of war between Italy and Britain, both navies' battle fleets were keen to bring about an engagement; the Royal Navy in particular worked hard to provoke a battle, often firing on Italian coastal fortifications and bases with the aim not only of inflicting damage but also of drawing out the Italian battle fleet. Here, units of the Mediterranean Fleet are on their way to bombard Fort Capuzzo and Bardia, 22 October 1940.

Force H from HMS *Sheffield*
Ships of Force H (probably *Berwick*, *Barham* and *Glasgow*) during a sweep through the Mediterranean in November 1940, seen over the 21-inch torpedo tubes of the cruiser *Sheffield*, as a member of the cruiser's crew looks on.

The British attack on Taranto

While the Italian fleet emerged from port quite frequently in the early months of the Mediterranean war, seeking a decisive victory, it suffered from over-restrictive control by the *Supermarina* command ashore, and from poor co-ordination with the *Regia Aeronautica*. The frequent result was that the Italians at sea rarely knew exactly where the British battle fleet was, or how it was composed. British admirals were keen to get to grips with the Italian battle fleet, and therein lay a problem for the British – how to inflict some decisive damage on their opponents and remove the threat from an Italian fleet-in-being. Air power provided the solution. Despite being outnumbered three to one in the Mediterranean, the balance of power was swung towards the British in November 1940 when torpedo-armed Swordfish biplanes launched from the recently arrived *Illustrious* flew at wave-top height into heavily-defended Taranto harbour and knocked out three Italian battleships, the *Conte di Cavour*, *Littorio* and *Caio Duilio* at anchor. The attack, delivered at night, showed precisely how air power had begun to eclipse the big gun. This was British naval air power in full flow: integrated with the battle fleet (instead of separate, as in the later incarnations of American and Japanese doctrines), aircraft could reach out and take the battle to a reluctant or fleeing enemy. This methodology would later be repeated in the action to sink the *Bismarck* and at Matapan. The immediate effect of the attack was the withdrawal of the Italian fleet to Naples, giving the British greater freedom and even allowing two battleships to be released to other campaigns. Thousands of miles away, Japanese Admiral Yamamoto took a keen interest in the lesson the Fleet Air Arm had taught the Italians. Original war plans – for a Japanese fleet to drive south to Taiwan to meet US naval intervention expected from the direction of Pearl Harbor – were constantly evolving during 1940–41 but the action at Taranto played its part in informing Japanese intentions of knocking out the Pacific Fleet at base rather than at sea. While British and Allied morale received a huge boost, Mussolini became even more cautious about committing his ships to battle – and already a lack of fuel was beginning to have a limiting effect on Italian naval operations.

Conti di Cavour in Taranto harbour
The most heavily damaged of the Italian battleships, the *Conte di Cavour*, lies settled on the harbour bottom.

Conti di Cavour is raised
The *Cavour* was raised the following year, but she was never put back into service. Captured by the Germans after Italy's armistice, she was sunk for a second time by Allied bombers at Trieste in February 1945, and the wreck was broken up after the war. This view shows her in floating dry dock in 1941, with her main armament removed.

The *Caio Duilio* and *Littorio*
The other two battleships, *Caio Duilio* (left) and *Littorio* (below left) were less badly damaged, but were still out of action for some time. Prime capital ships had been battered into submission by a small number of archaic and slow biplane aircraft.

The Battle off Cape Spartivento
The same month as Taranto, the limits of actions based around slow battleship forces were highlighted as British and Italian fleets met off Cape Spartivento, south of Sardinia. Of the British heavy units, only the *Renown*, a battlecruiser, was able to reach a favourable position to attack the speedier Italian battleships. But once again, the Italians turned away and as 1940 gave way to 1941 the Royal Navy regained temporary command of the Mediterranean. This photograph shows the cruisers *Trieste*, *Bolzano* and *Pola* making headway against a steep sea in November 1940. Having escaped damage on 'Taranto Night' they fought a high-speed running battle with British cruisers off Cape Spartivento.

Germany Enters the War in the Mediterranean

For the British, the arrival of German forces in the Mediterranean spelled big trouble. Italian reverses encouraged Hitler to send submarines and aircraft, which severely curtailed British freedom of movement and engendered a number of crises. Heavy attacks on the British base at Malta were mounted from January 1941 by the German air forces newly arrived in Sicily. On one day, the dockyard and the carrier HMS *Illustrious* – in port because of six bomb hits sustained at sea – were attacked by over eighty Ju 87 Stuka dive-bombers. Assaults like these brought to reality the long-held fear of the non-viability of Malta-based forces in the face of concerted air attack (which the Italian air force, operating mostly at high level, had been unable to deliver to ships at sea). British air defences were swamped on the ground and in the air. Debate would surround the question of whether Malta – and the entire Mediterranean strategy – was worth the cost to the Royal Navy. In fact, in pre-war calculations Malta had been considered indefensible, especially by the RAF, but the island, its garrison and the Maltese population held out under great stress, was never taken and its light forces – cruisers, destroyers and submarines – instead played a leading role in disrupting Axis operations in North Africa.

During 1941 four major British convoys were successfully run to Malta through the gauntlet of submarines, minefields, E-boat raids and air attacks flown from Sardinian and Sicilian bases. Safe arrival at Malta was a contradiction in terms: once in harbour at Valletta or offshore, ships were subject to yet more intense bombings. Methods of swift offloading, refuelling and rearming of vessels in the face of air raids became vital. But steadily, the British position was being reinforced.

Meanwhile, submarines and mines continued to make a mark on both fleets as transports crisscrossed the central Mediterranean. Supplied by ongoing reinforcements sent around the Cape between December 1940 and February 1941, British General Wavell achieved great successes against the Italians in Libya and began his Abyssinian campaign; but in February 1941 Rommel arrived in North Africa, and so began a seesawing series of important battles in the sand and rock of Libya and Egypt.

The British and Italian Battle Fleets Meet

Despite being bolstered on all its original fronts by the arrival of crack German units, for the Italian Navy their first year of fighting produced almost continual defeat at the hands of the outnumbered British Mediterranean Fleet. Force H, on the offensive, was even able to sail right into the Gulf of Genoa, bombard the city, sow mines and launch bombing raids on the fleet base at Leghorn in February 1941.

The following month, the battle of Cape Matapan vindicated the British Navy's training in night-fighting. Lessons from the battle of Jutland in 1916 had prompted the postwar Royal Navy to pay special attention to its close-range night-fighting capabilities. In contrast, the Italian Navy, lacking radar and flashless powder and unwilling to engage on unfavourable terms, had decided to avoid night actions where possible. But springing a trap, the British very efficiently defeated an Italian heavy cruiser force off the coast of Greece at night. Radar and air power played a leading part as once again a fleeing force – of one Italian battleship and eight cruisers, plus escort – was caught and damaged by Swordfish-launched torpedoes. The cruiser *Pola* was stopped by Swordfish flying from *Formidable*; her sister-ships came back to assist her, unaware of their proximity to the big guns of the British battleships *Warspite*, *Barham* and *Valiant*. The *Pola*, *Fiume* and *Zara* were hit at close range by the battleships and all three were sunk as a result. Meanwhile, the brand-new 35,000-ton battleship *Vittorio Veneto*, already struck by an aerial torpedo, managed to withdraw as the British battleships closed in. Two Italian destroyers completed the British tally.

Two of the three battleships torpedoed by Swordfish at Taranto took about six months to repair; the third was never fully repaired; and now the *Vittorio Veneto* had to repair the torpedo damage sustained at Matapan. This left only the old but modernized *Cesare* and *Doria* in service. The Italian surface fleet had been totally outfought, such that it was unable to intervene when the Royal Navy came to evacuate British troops from Greece and Crete later that year.

Where the Italians (and the Axis navies in very broad terms) could justifiably claim superiority was in their genius for 'asymmetric warfare' weapons. The *Decima Flottiglia MAS* (officially Tenth Anti-Submarine Motor-Boat Squadron, but in reality Tenth Assault Craft Squadron) launched an explosive motorboat attack on HMS *York* in Suda Bay, Crete in late March, resulting in the British cruiser being disabled and later sunk in May during the German invasion. Human torpedo attacks occurred elsewhere as the Italians pioneered the use of these stealthy but powerful weapons; meanwhile their two remaining expensive battleships languished under friendly air cover at their moorings.

Axis Success in the Eastern Mediterranean

On land, the German-Italian forces fared better. By April, Rommel had recovered Cyrenaica in eastern Libya. German conquest of Yugoslavia and Greece in the same month proved disastrous for British forces rushed there from North Africa, but worse was to come. The loss of Greece prompted another British withdrawal, to Crete.

The island of Crete was over four hundred miles from the nearest British base at Alexandria; the British had minimal air cover from land-based aircraft and the limited resources of only one carrier, *Formidable*, to call on. The German *VIII Fliegerkorps*, tasked with covering the German invasion, had over five hundred medium bombers, fighters and dive-bombers in its arsenal. Italian bombers also joined in. The aerial bombardment of Crete began in earnest. The Royal Navy stationed itself to the north of the island, on the lookout for incoming Axis invasion vessels. At one point standing only twenty miles off the Greek coast, the British chased an Axis invasion force back to port and came under intense dive-bombing. Desperate manoeuvres were called for as a relentless air attack poured down. During one two-hour period, sailors aboard one British cruiser counted 181 bombs dropped on their ship. With wave upon wave of German dive-bombers attacking a divided force of cruisers and destroyers, and then quickly refuelling and rearming at nearby Greek airfields to resume the attack within half an hour, it was difficult enough for the British ships without attempting to stop and pick up survivors from already-bombed ships. The aerial attacks of 22 and 23 May constituted the most costly two days of the war so far for the Royal Navy, with two cruisers and four destroyers sunk, and two cruisers and four destroyers seriously damaged. To make matters worse, a surprise counterattack by aircraft from *Formidable* on the Axis airfield at Scarpanto was pressed home but at the cost of serious bomb damage to the carrier. With German paratroopers soon in control of Crete's only usable airfield at Maleme, and with virtually uncontested Axis superiority in the air, the British had no choice but to attempt to evacuate the same forces from Crete that had been snatched from Greece only a month before.

The first stage of the evacuation operation met with renewed aerial attack and casualties were extremely high among the defenders. When the cruiser *Orion* limped into Alexandria harbour, her crew exhausted, she had only two rounds of six-inch shell remaining, and more than 250 dead and 300 wounded aboard. The second stage of the withdrawal passed off more smoothly with less attention from Axis bombers, and by contrast was deemed a miracle, with almost 17,000 troops evacuated in five days. Overall, losses were terrible: three British cruisers and six destroyers sunk, all by Axis air power; three battleships, an aircraft carrier, six cruisers and seven destroyers received damaged. Two thousand Allied sailors were killed, and over 13,000 men captured, wounded or killed on the island.

It seemed that the lesson was stark and indubitable: that ships, unless heavily armoured and with ample sea-room, could not operate safely where enemy aircraft held air superiority. Shattered British crew morale seemed to bear this assumption out. Anti-aircraft measures had not proved very successful, with fire control still a hit-or-miss affair exacerbated by a lack of enough adequate high-angle guns to take down dive-bombers overhead. But in fact the Axis aircraft, despite overwhelming numbers and continual attack, had scored a remarkably low hit ratio; in many cases warships had been able to stay in the fight despite air attacks spanning entire days on end.

The Growth of Allied Participation in the North Atlantic

In the Atlantic theatre, Britain and Canada together faced Germany. Only nine of the obsolescent US destroyers passed to the Royal Navy were found to be serviceable by February 1941, and due to destroyer shortages, convoy escort was largely limited to only two warships per convoy, which in the face of increasingly co-ordinated U-boat and Luftwaffe attacks, was little more than a token presence. Discussions between American and British Commonwealth naval officers, begun in 1937, were formalized at the first ABC (American-British-Canadian) negotiations in Washington in January and February 1941. Here the Allies worked out much of the basic strategy that would govern operations during the war. In March 1941, the Lend-Lease Act was passed in Congress and American supplies to the Allies increased, helping alleviate that spring, Roosevelt authorized the transferral of a quarter of the US Pacific Fleet to the Atlantic, as his nation moved from neutrality through the non-belligerency of 1940 towards eventual co-belligerency, careful to place the onus of the outbreak of hostilities on Germany. As early as October 1939, Grand Admiral Erich Raeder, Commander-in-Chief of the *Kriegsmarine*, had pressed for unlimited submarine warfare against all trade inbound to Britain – including American ships – but Hitler had demurred, aware that a knockout blow against the US could not be delivered before American naval power joined the British. At the end of March, Roosevelt had ordered that all Italian and German shipping in American harbours be seized, and US Navy participation in the areas south of Iceland and Greenland – both islands having been occupied by American forces, relieving earlier British garrisons – was stepped up, to the chagrin of Raeder.

At first the convoys outward-bound from Britain had been given Royal Navy escorts to about 15° West longitude. This was then extended by another 10° westward, and extended again until by the middle of the year convoys were shepherded right across the ocean by relays of escorts operating from Britain, Iceland and Newfoundland. This extension of the policy of convoy escort stretched the Royal Navy even more thinly, and increasingly involved the Canadian Navy, which had to be trained at the Royal Navy's working-up bases.

Thus Canadian corvettes became increasingly valuable to British convoy planners. In the late spring of 1941, Canada took over the duty of convoying merchantmen east out of Newfoundland to the Mid-Ocean Meeting Point south of Iceland, whereupon the Royal Navy would resume responsibility for the escort. Forming the Newfoundland Escort Force with their slow corvettes, the Canadians were joined by swifter American destroyers in the western Atlantic. They agreed to divide slow and fast convoys between them accordingly. Hard to manoeuvre round waiting wolf-packs, slow convoys and their mixed-experience Canadian escorts were particularly vulnerable to concerted night attacks.

In March, the U-boat arm had suffered its first bad month. Three of the leading U-boat aces – Shepke, Kretschmer and Prien – were sunk by British escorts. But the success of the Allies' strategy of Atlantic convoying was measured not by battles won or U-boats sunk, but by the safe arrival of merchant vessels at their destinations. In the first four months of 1941, nearly two million tons of shipping had been lost, exacerbated by a lack of air cover and sufficient numbers of trained escorts despite the introduction of newer types such as the bigger, more capable 'Castle' class corvettes. Shipyards in Germany, France and the Low Countries were assembling U-boats at an increasing rate. Wolf-pack tactics were becoming better understood by the Allies but they had no breathing space to implement a counter-offensive. By mid-1941, the British and Allied merchant marine and its crews were steadily being bled white in the Atlantic during what the U-boat crews would come to call their 'Happy Time'. The avoidance of looming defeat in the Battle of the Atlantic became the most critical priority of the British navy and merchant marine.

Allied Countermeasures in the U-Boat War

Allied ingenuity was called upon and resulted in a number of new measures to counter the immediate U-boat and *Luftwaffe* threat. Greater quantities of small seaborne radar sets were developed for use aboard escort ships, making submarines theoretically detectable on the surface from beyond visual range. Equally importantly, German VHF signals

were detectable by High-Frequency Direction-Finding (HF/DF) equipment which could provide approximate triangulation fixes to build up a plot of U-boat positions across the Atlantic. It became possible to fit light HF/DF systems aboard escort vessels for tactical use, helping to locate wolf-packs as soon as they signalled an attack on a convoy. The policy of using signals intelligence to steer convoys away from contact with U-boats was actually very successful, particularly so when the convoys were fast-moving troop convoys and high-speed transatlantic passenger liners such as the *Queen Mary* and *Queen Elizabeth*, whose cruising speed was as high as 27 knots and troop capacity a staggering 16,000 men.

But signals intelligence could play only a small part. To aid defence, merchant ships were fitted with more AA guns and in some cases catapults to launch single-shot modified Hawker Hurricanes for anti-reconnaissance air defence. These Catapult-Armed Merchantmen (CAM ships) were quite successful, though launching an aircraft destined to be ditched was clearly a desperate measure designed to prevent more powerful forces descending on a convoy. Later the concept was taken further, resulting in the Merchant Aircraft Carrier (MAC ship), usually a flat-decked tanker or cargo vessel converted to launch and recover a small number of aircraft. All these helped alleviate the dire need for carriers (which in any case could hardly be spared from fleet duties), even if equipped only with a few low-performance Swordfish. Indeed, this was the only type that could have comfortably operated off such vessels. Continuous near all-weather air cover prevented submarines from operating on the surface with impunity. The British also introduced the 'River' class frigate, a significant improvement on the 'Flower' with double the endurance, more weapons and 4 knots more speed.

Behind the frontline, industrial capacity was being expanded by Britain and Canada, but particularly in the United States. By mid-1941, six months before the United States entered the war as a full belligerent, Allied shipping losses were being outstripped by new vessels joining the available active tonnage. British naval dockyards almost stopped new construction in favour of repair and maintenance; meanwhile, the systematic clearing of congestion and the repair of temporarily laid-up hulls in British west-coast and Scottish ports helped reintroduce more ships. Looking at this war of attrition, some historians contend that Germany could only have won the Battle of the Atlantic in 1941; having missed the chance to strike a decisive blow to Britain's Achilles heel, Germany had no hope once the events of December 1941 came to pass. But while new ships might be on the stocks, the immediate effects of the loss of cargoes was another matter. Concentrating in the mid-Atlantic would help the Germans to maximize their forces and increase their stranglehold on the free movement of essential supplies across the Atlantic sufficient to seriously affect Britain's ability to stay in the fight. If the British public were feeling the pinch, the sailors aboard some merchant vessels experienced something not seen since the introduction of antiscorbutics to victuals in the nineteenth century – an outbreak of scurvy.

The *Bismarck* Action and Progress in the North Atlantic

Even without the burdens of the Mediterranean, the constant grind of Atlantic convoying, and devoting resources to the training of the eager Canadians, the spring of 1941 was a difficult period for the Royal Navy, stretched to its tolerable limits. The *Bismarck* chase and engagement is a case in point: Force H (*Ark Royal*, *Sheffield* and *Renown*) had to come from Gibraltar, while big convoys sailing from the Clyde and Liverpool were denuded of escorts to free up heavy ships such as the *Rodney* to join the hunt from the ever-pressed Home Fleet.

With the German battlecruisers *Scharnhorst* and *Gneisenau* perched at Brest, the British had plenty to worry about in May 1941 even before the pride of their fleet, the fast, powerful and unmodernized battlecruiser *Hood*, was blown up on 24 May in the North Atlantic by a salvo from the *Bismarck*. All but three of *Hood*'s crew of 1,419 were lost in very deep water. Sunk after only eight minutes of action, her destruction was a massive shock to the Royal Navy and the British public; but it sounded the death-knell on the first and only sortie for the brand-new 15-inch gunned German battleship. The British battleship *Prince of Wales* – new and not yet properly worked up – had scored a 14-inch hit on the *Bismarck* and as she steamed on in company with the heavy cruiser *Prinz Eugen* she was down at the bow and leaking fuel. Worse was that a thousand tons of oil could not be pumped from the bow.

The psychology of confidence and the expectation of success – or the opposite – were very important to a fighting service's psyche and could influence operational performance to a degree. Just minutes after the *Bismarck* had sunk the *Hood* and seen off the *Prince of Wales*, *Bismarck*'s Admiral Lütjens broadcast a message exhorting his crew to prepare to go down gallantly, indicating an underlying conviction of inevitable demise. (Similar sentiments were expressed, perhaps more understandably, within the U-boat arm; poetry and letters written by crewmen reveal that eventual death at the hands of the enemy was expected and even sentimentalized in advance.)

Galvanized by the sure belief that the *Bismarck* had to be sunk at all costs, the Royal Navy set to its task, employing cruiser screens joined by carrier forces from Force H and the Home Fleet to harry the fleeing *Bismarck*. Battleships *Rodney* and *King George V* finally caught up with the crippled German battleship on 27 May and sank her in a hail of heavy shellfire and torpedoes. The destruction of the *Bismarck* had diverted a huge amount of Royal Naval resources but the neutralization of the threat to British convoys was more than adequate recompense to the Admiralty. To the shocked German high command, it was another example of the folly of building prestige battleships which could apparently be hamstrung by a couple of torpedoes dropped from archaic biplanes. From June 1941, only German armed merchant raiders continued operations in every sea except the Arctic.

Three weeks prior to the destruction of the *Bismarck*, a far smaller-scale and totally unpublicized operation had taken place that would help to build a picture whose resolution would have even greater strategic consequences. During the first half of the year, the British made deliberate efforts to capture German ships out at sea. And on 9 May, the British destroyer *Bulldog* had captured *U-110* and, with it, an Enigma cipher machine along with code books, rotor settings and supplementary documentation. With this key to German naval signals, particularly the complex 'Hydra' U-boat codes, now in the hands of British cryptographers at Bletchley Park, U-boat movements could to some degree be unravelled in advance. Teamed with HF/DF, this combination of near real-time knowledge of German intentions almost immediately reduced losses, and despite future code changes and the introduction of more sophisticated encoding methods and equipment by the Germans later in the war, the quiet intelligence contribution to victory was significant.

A further step-change in Allied anti-submarine defence at sea came in June with the launch of HMS *Audacity*, the prototype escort carrier. Built on merchant hulls, escort carriers were originally conceived as aircraft transports, but they soon adopted more warlike roles, including anti-submarine, anti-air and amphibious support functions. In the autumn, *Audacity* was the first vessel to down a Focke-Wulf Condor at sea, using her US-built Grumman Martlet (Wildcat) fighters.

The Soviet Union Enters the World War

On 22 June, having failed to act on the plan to invade Britain twelve months before, and with the Balkan and Greek flank secured, Hitler broke the non-aggression pact signed with Stalin in 1939 by invading the USSR. Hitler calculated that by securing a quick military victory over the USSR, he could force an agreement on Great Britain, whose hopes he saw pinned on the USSR and a United States which would be distracted by an unencumbered Japan. But by embarking on Operation Barbarossa, Hitler started on the long road to defeat on the steppes of the Soviet hinterland. By this time the Soviet Baltic Fleet, based at the Kronstadt, had grown to two battleships, two cruisers, nineteen destroyers, sixty-five submarines and large numbers of torpedo boats. In those confined waters, warships were especially vulnerable to air attack and minefields. On the outbreak of hostilities between Hitler and Stalin, German mine barrages in the central and eastern Baltic immediately put paid to a Soviet destroyer and damaged a second along with a cruiser. Indiscriminate sowing by both navies led to casualties from their own mines. E-boats and U-boats added to the efforts of dedicated German minelayers, and also had success against Soviet patrol boats and submarines. Within three weeks the German army had secured a bridgehead across the sea on Finnish soil and had cut off Russians fighting to the north. The relief and eventual evacuation of this trapped corps occupied the Soviet Baltic fleet until the end of the year, during which operations nearly eighty Soviet ships were dispatched by mines and *Luftwaffe* bombers and many thousands of men were killed.

A similar scene unfolded hundreds of miles away to the south-east in the Black Sea. There, the Soviet fleet, based on the yards at Nikolayev and Sevastopol, found itself trying to relieve and eventually evacuate besieged Odessa. By the autumn, Sevastopol itself was invested: naval gunfire and naval brigades were thrown ashore in a desperate campaign to dislodge the German and Romanian armies encircling the fortress-port. Forced to flee its main bases, the Black Sea Fleet had to repair and rearm itself much further to the east while German aircraft bombarded Soviet ships unable to escape the inferno at Sevastopol, sinking a cruiser and two destroyers and several transports.

Back in the Baltic the siege of Leningrad dragged on, with Soviet warships heavily engaged in the defence of the city. Ships' crews were formed into naval infantry brigades much like the British of the nineteenth century, while men remaining aboard the fleet manned the big guns of the elderly battleships *Oktyabrskya Revolutsiya* and *Marat*. Even the old, protected cruiser *Aurora* – which fired the first shots of the October Revolution of 1917 – was pressed into the defence, as a headquarters ship for trawlers, while her dismounted guns were used ashore as artillery. The *Minsk* – a 2,000-ton destroyer leader of the 'Leningrad' class, the first large ships built in Russia after that revolution – was sunk in Kronstadt harbour by dive-bombers, though later salvaged. Reliant on widespread defensive mining, subject to the icing sea and tied to the land in resisting German occupation along the Baltic coast, the Soviet Baltic fleet was stuck in the waters between the Kronstadt and Leningrad and firmly on the back foot.

The Arctic Convoys

Waking the sleeping Soviet giant would ensure that Germany would eventually be defeated on land. But the entry of the USSR had already increased the British burden at sea, as Churchill agreed to institute convoys to Russia via the Arctic route as a substitute for the 'Second Front' requested by Moscow. As German offensives on the Eastern Front destroyed more and more materiel, captured oilfields and absorbed precious raw material sources, the Soviet Union grew ever more in need of essential supplies and equipment if it was to regroup and fight back. Over the course of the war the majority of supplies to the Soviet Union would flow through the Persian Gulf or across the Pacific, but from a political standpoint a northern route from Britain was a necessity. Arctic convoys from British ports thus began in the summer of 1941. Summer and winter convoys took different routes according to the extent of the polar ice edge. In the summer, the White Sea port of Archangel was the destination, reached by going north about Jan Mayen and Bear Islands, keeping to the extreme limit of *Luftwaffe* range but threatened by U-boats in the perpetual daylight conditions. In the dark Arctic winter, with the sea ice much further south and the White Sea frozen, fewer U-boats operated but the more risky port of Murmansk had to be used. This route was much more vulnerable to German air attack from occupied Norwegian and Finnish air bases. All the while, German capital ships, holed up in Norwegian fjords to deter any Allied flanking movements, were deemed a significant threat to the convoys.

Thus, just as the British were becoming better armed and on a surer economic footing with unfettered American aid, large-scale diversions of weapons, equipment and supplies had to be sailed to the northern Russian ports, through the worst weather conditions in the world and with German submarines and aircraft lying in wait. What made the strain of the Arctic convoys harder to bear was the suspicion that it was comparatively a waste of effort, resources and lives – indeed, it is still a matter of debate whether the USSR was a burden rather than a help to the Allies for the first year of her fight against Nazi Germany. Certainly from a British perspective their sacrifices were met just as often with complaint and unhelpful silence in Moscow than with the gratitude they felt they was due. In time, of course, the intractable Soviet winter and the scale of Soviet manpower would defeat Hitler's armies and divert enormous German resources away from the west, which provided inestimable help to the western Allies' efforts in establishing a permanent bridgehead on continental Europe in 1944.

Despite the dangers, by the end of 1941, fifty-three ships had made it without loss to Russia in seven convoys, delivering 750 tanks, 800 fighters, 1,400 vehicles and over 100,000 tons of supplies. The Germans, hampered by a lack of reconnaissance, were unable to deliver co-ordinated attacks. With American entry to the war, the supply of materials to Russia would go up a gear – but so would German interest in interdicting it. As the ice closed in on Archangel in the darkening winter of 1941, the *Bismarck*'s sister battleship *Tirpitz* and the 'pocket battleship' *Admiral Scheer* were moved to Trondheim, ready to be unleashed.

In response to a failed U-boat attack on an American convoy escort, on 11 September Roosevelt gave permission for the US Navy to sink on sight any Axis submarines operating in proscribed American shipping lanes. The autumn saw the first fourteen of hundreds of Liberty ships launched from US shipyards, as American material assistance to Britain burgeoned. German planners accepted that war with America was unavoidable, and urged the Japanese to stay out of the war with the USSR so as to focus efforts against the western colonial powers in the east.

But while negotiations with the US continued through diplomatic channels, the Japanese Combined Fleet under Admiral Isoroku Yamamoto quietly prepared its ships for the most audacious operation ever mounted by the Japanese Navy.

The Struggle for Dominance in the Mediterranean

Pressed back from the Balkans and in reverse gear in North Africa, the British situation got steadily worse over the autumn of 1941. But so long as Malta could be kept in the fight, the Axis would not enjoy unfettered use of the sea. In November the Italian Navy attempted to run a convoy from Greece to North Africa to supply Rommel's siege of Tobruk. Seven transports, escorted by six destroyers, were intercepted off Cape Spartivento by a strong British cruiser force out of Malta and all bar one Italian destroyer were sunk. Controversially, the British 'U' class submarine *Upholder*, commanded by Lieutenant-Commander Wanklyn VC (awarded for sinking the 18,000-ton passenger ship *Conte Rosso* in May), then moved in and sank the last remaining Italian destroyer as she stopped to rescue survivors.

Italian timidity and British fighting confidence were again evident at the First Battle of Sirte in December, when the main Italian battle fleet was driven away from a British convoy by its escort, consisting of just three cruisers and a handful of destroyers. But Italian mines took a toll of two British cruisers and a destroyer attempting to harry coastal shipping upon arrival off Tripoli.

Meanwhile, German submarines had made their way to the Mediterranean in the autumn and, using a form of the Enigma code as yet unreadable to the British, they had a significant effect on the balance of power, sinking the British carrier *Ark Royal*. More U-boats were sent but many were sunk by Allied submarines and aircraft operating out of Gibraltar. However, the battleship *Barham* and the cruiser *Galatea* also fell prey to U-boats towards the close of 1941. The Mediterranean was never a 'target-rich environment' for Axis submarines; certainly not in comparison to the Atlantic, where targets were more numerous and proportionately less heavily defended. For the British submarine the opposite was true. Despite a gradual improvement in Italian anti-submarine countermeasures such as active sonar, extremely fatigued yet increasingly deadly flotillas of small and elusive British craft found their mark along the Italian convoy routes. British submarine *Urge* torpedoed the repaired Italian battleship *Vittorio Veneto* on 14 December, forcing her out of action for another four months. But later that same month, Italian human torpedoes returned the deed with interest by sinking the old battleships *Queen Elizabeth* and *Valiant* at anchor in Alexandria harbour, dealing a serious blow to the British Mediterranean fleet.

The 'Day of Infamy' and the Effects of American Entry

It is often unwise to highlight turning points in history to the exclusion of more subtle yet pervasive trends, but everything changed on 7 December, when the American Pacific Fleet base at Pearl Harbor, Hawaii, was attacked by Japanese carrier-launched bombers and torpedo-planes. By crippling the bulk of the American battleship fleet at anchor, the Japanese gained time and space to conquer South East Asia before again turning east to face the stunned Americans.

Though taken completely by surprise by the Japanese action, Hitler – initially encouraged by the speed of his advance into the USSR and latterly mindful of Raeder's desire to apply naval pressure in the Atlantic before it was too late – joined the Japanese in declaring war on the USA.

It is from this point that most historians agree that the Allied cause was saved. Indeed, Churchill later wrote of how he 'slept the sleep of the saved and the thankful' – privately, for a man and a service accustomed to Royal Navy pre-eminence, this tacit acknowledgement of reliance on American maritime capacity (and the power it could project) to guarantee British survival must have been a bitter pill to swallow.

It has been argued that without Pearl Harbor, and Hitler's declaration of war, the USA would have continued to stay out of the World War Two. It had been augmenting British and Canadian convoy escorts to the mid-Atlantic position for some months, but it is perhaps Winston Churchill's greatest contribution to the British war effort that he succeeded in securing American sympathy and support. The British Prime Minister had met the American President in Placentia Bay in Newfoundland in August 1941, aboard the *Prince of Wales*, and a church service with fraternal hymns was conducted underneath the big guns. The main point of business was the drafting of the Atlantic Charter, the firmest commitment by the USA to entering the war to defeat Nazism to have appeared thus far. But this was by no means a likelihood, far less the certainty Churchill prayed for. In the event, the US commitment to the defeat of Nazi Germany in Europe as its primary war aim, with Japan a close second (and Italy a distant third), was a great boost to beleaguered Britain. In the autumn of 1941 American naval power had stood tall: fifteen battleships, five carriers, eighteen heavy cruisers, nineteen light cruisers, 200 destroyers and 111 submarines. More ships – roughly equivalent to 50 per cent of the built fleet – were under construction. With American entry to the war, the British also gained access to crucial repair and rebuilding resources in the US ports on both coasts.

Thus in 1941 the European war turned into a world war. The Soviet Union and now America were thrown into battle. Churchill appreciated Japan's attack on the USA even more than Germany's attack on Russia, despite this adding Japan to the Axis war effort and leading, in short order, to a series of appalling losses to the British Empire and the Royal Navy in the Far East.

British Disasters in the Far East

For so long to her advantage while her enemies were European, and already mitigated to a large degree by the mobility of the submarine and aeroplane, the facts of geography turned against Britain when Japan joined the war. The fact that all three of the Axis navies were hostile at the same time stretched British sea power to its limit.

Despite the withdrawal of many British vessels from the Asiatic stations to bolster the Mediterranean and Atlantic in 1940, and despite the knowledge that by 1941 only the US Navy could effectively oppose the Japanese in the western Pacific, throughout the year Churchill had pressed for the sending of two capital ships and an aircraft carrier to the Far East as a deterrent against Japan. Naval staff at the time, and historians subsequently, questioned whether this small force (a far cry from the main battle fleet of 1930s war plans) would have carried any political deterrent value. Those in favour considered it a sound plan, reasoning that most of the Japanese Navy would be occupied against the US Navy, with their remaining forces being inferior to the powerful British units. In any case, 'Force Z', as it was known, arrived after the outbreak of hostilities in the east, and whatever peacetime deterrent value it had was swiftly negated by events. A lack of friendly air cover on the Malay peninsula

(and the grounding of the carrier *Indomitable* while working up in the Caribbean), allied with a tendency to underestimate the striking power of Japanese aircraft, contributed to the dramatic loss of the battlecruiser *Repulse* and battleship *Prince of Wales* on 10 December 1941 while they attempted to intercept a Japanese invasion force heading for Malaya. The gamble had failed spectacularly. During what the Japanese call the 'Battle off Malaya', these two prime capital ships were sunk during a sustained torpedo and bomb attack by land-based planes. The losses dealt a huge blow to British naval prestige in the Far East. It was another tragic lesson in the increasingly unavoidable reality that naval units without strong air cover were vulnerable as never before to skilled aerial attack, a tendency already demonstrated by British losses off Crete and which should have been obvious to the commanding officer Admiral Phillips. Despite violent manoeuvres and all AA guns thrown into defence, these two symbols of traditional naval power were sent to the bottom in just over two hours by weapons vastly cheaper and more numerous. The Prime Minister was grievously upset by the news.

The Allied Outlook

In the wide expanses of the Atlantic, in the second half of 1941, Allied losses to U-boats dropped to around 100,000 tons per month. However, U-boat construction programmes were producing a growing fleet and Dönitz was increasingly able to establish patrol lines right across the Atlantic, aided by almost continuous German codebreaking of low-level British convoy signals. By the end of the year, nearly 1,300 Allied merchant ships had been sunk. Only thirty-five U-boats had been sunk in return. Britain was ostensibly losing the Battle of the Atlantic.

However, there were small signs of hope for the Allies. American carriers had escaped the disaster at Pearl Harbor; so had US submarine facilities and fuel supplies. The massive industrial capacity of the American economy was now on an official war footing. A promising glimpse of the future of integrated air-sea convoy protection was afforded in December when a Britain-bound convoy, HG 76, of thirty-two ships from Gibraltar, made it home with only two merchantmen lost. By contrast the Germans had lost five U-boats over four days at the hands of the convoy's twelve escorts. Air cover – provided by *Audacity*'s Martlets – had seen off the circling Condors, given advance warning of lurking U-boats and served to guide the escorting destroyers to their work until *Audacity* was herself sunk by torpedo. But the template had been successful.

And as a taste of how the Allies would eventually re-enter the continental European fray, throughout 1941 Britain had conducted small-scale amphibious raids to damage installations and divert German resources. Combined operations became an important part of Allied strategy, as the British were forced to revert to their time-honoured expedients when faced by a dominant foe on the continent. The islands off Norway bore witness to no fewer than three such sea-launched British raids that year. These operations showed that well-executed amphibious assaults – delivered with strategic and tactical surprise against enemy shores – could reap substantial rewards. If the western Allies were to achieve their stated primary aim of defeating Nazi Germany on European soil, their first steps would have to be from the ramp of a landing craft.

The White Ensign sweeps the Mediterranean

As 1940 moved into 1941 the Royal Navy, which had played no small part in the British successes in the Western desert, bombarding Libyan ports and even sailing into the Adriatic to bombard Valona, carried on policing the Mediterranean. This photograph shows British destroyers patrolling off the Libyan coast.

War in the North Atlantic

During 1941 the Battle of the Atlantic reached unprecedented intensity with the U-boats making full use of the bases on the French coast. While merchantmen and escorts battled the inclement conditions, the most dramatic episode involved a German surface warship, the battleship *Bismarck*.

(right) Facing the elements
Officers dressed for the Atlantic weather on the open bridge of an escort.

(below) A British destroyer battles on
The deck awash, HMS *Milne* ploughs through heavy seas, in company with other destroyers. Note the tattered White Ensign.

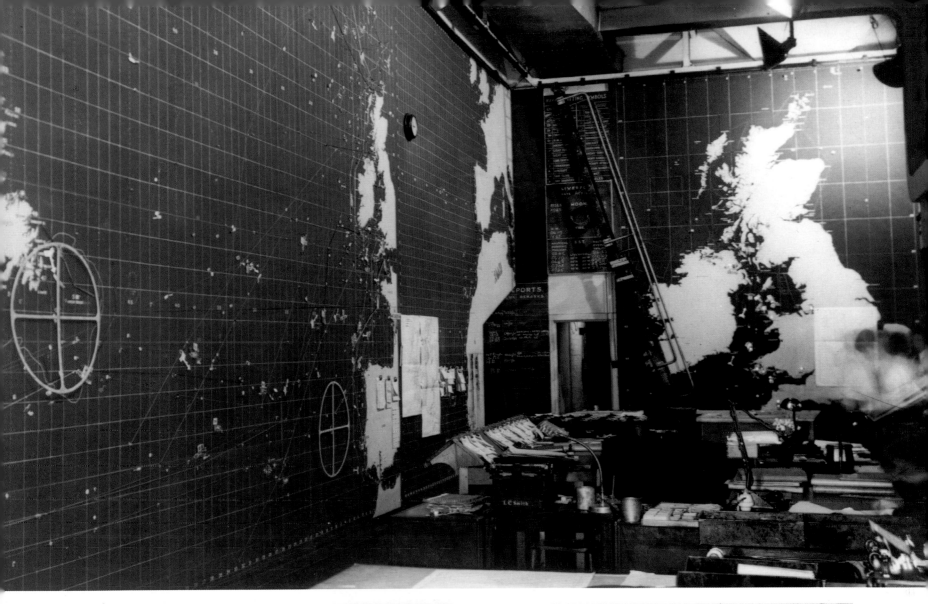

Western Approaches Command Headquarters, Derby House, Liverpool.

The Operations Room beneath Derby House, Liverpool, the Headquarters of Western Approaches Command. The main Atlantic plot is to the left, with the home waters plot in the background. On these were shown the movements of every convoy and escort, as well as (as much as possible) every straggler, and every U-boat. Admiral Horton's office overlooked the Operations Room.

The Lofoten Islands raid

In March the Lofoten Islands off Norway were raided by the British, the local fish-oil plant destroyed and eleven ships and 200 German prisoners captured. In August, large coal and oil reserves in the Spitzbergen archipelago were destroyed to prevent the Germans making use of them. Lord Louis Mountbatten became head of Combined Operations and launched a raid on Vaasgo in Norway in the December, destroying shipping and factories, capturing the garrison and thereby inflaming Hitler's growing obsession with Norway.

This is an official British photograph taken during the Lofoten operations, showing a well wrapped-up gunner manning the pom-poms of one of HM ships (possibly HMS *Legion*), silhouetted against the snow-covered mountains overlooking Kirke Fjord.

Mooring up
British crew mooring their destroyer to a huge buoy in the sea, some time during 1941.
This procedure, entailing intricate precision as well as brute strength in what was very wet
work, was necessary when mooring up in a harbour with no available anchorage or pier
space, or at readiness in the roads outside.

HMS *Prince of Wales*

The battleship HMS *Prince of Wales* was in service for fewer than eleven months – from 18 January to 10 December 1941 – yet played probably a more prominent part in the war at sea than all but a very few ships.

An April 1941 view from inside the port aircraft hangar of the *Prince of Wales* showing a Supermarine Walrus Mk.I aircraft on the ship's catapult. This particular aircraft, L2181, had originally been with the School Of Naval Co-Operation, was transferred to the Admiralty in May 1939 and was one of two which formed the ship's flight from October 1940 to December 1941.

Churchill on the deck of HMS *Prince of Wales*
During the course of 1941 the *Prince of Wales* took part in the *Bismarck* operations, scoring a vital hit on the German battleship although she was not yet fully worked up; took British Prime Minister Winston Churchill across the Atlantic for his historic meeting with US President Franklin D. Roosevelt; escorted a convoy to Malta; and finally was the flagship of the ill-fated Force Z sent to Singapore in a fruitless and eventually disastrous attempt to first deter, and then counter, Japanese aggression in the East Indies.

This photograph shows Churchill and Minister of Supply Lord Beaverbrook aboard the *Prince of Wales* while she was anchored in Placentia Bay, Newfoundland, in August 1941. In a series of conferences on the ship, the principles of the Atlantic Charter were drawn up with Roosevelt and his staff, berthed in the cruiser USS *Augusta*. This was the first summit of many between the two leaders during the war, and important to the British in that it garnered the firmest support so far for US participation against Nazi Germany.

Maritime patrol aircraft
The Short Sunderland flying boat, brought into RAF service just before the outbreak of war, turned out to be of immense value to Coastal Command for convoy escort and anti-U-boat patrols. This particular Sunderland is a GR5 of 201 Squadron.

HMS *Suffolk* in the Denmark Strait

Gunners man one of the quadruple 0.5-inch Lewis anti-aircraft guns situated amidships aboard HMS *Suffolk*, on a patrol of the Denmark Strait between Iceland and Greenland in 1941. Ice flows can be seen in the background. The northern part of the Denmark Strait lies within the Arctic Circle, though the drift ice extends a good deal further south.

Suffolk and her sister-ship *Norfolk* spotted *Bismarck* and *Prinz Eugen*, and shadowed them for nearly 1,000 miles through ice, frequent mist and heavy squalls of snow and sleet prior to the Battle of the Denmark Strait during which the *Bismarck* scored a hit on HMS *Hood* and the battlecruiser exploded.

Naval aircraft on HMS *Suffolk*

A Supermarine Walrus aircraft of *Suffolk* is hoisted aboard while on patrol in the Denmark Strait, May 1941.

The pursuit of *Bismarck* following the loss of *Hood*

Shadowed on her journey south by the radar-equipped cruisers *Norfolk* and *Suffolk*, the German battleship *Bismarck* was struck and partially slowed by torpedoes launched by Swordfish flying from *Victorious*, forcing Admiral Lütjens to turn back towards St Nazaire. *Ark Royal*, making full speed in company with *Renown* in a pincer movement up from Gibraltar, launched her own Swordfish in response to a sighting of the German flagship by an RAF Catalina on 26 May, and the torpedo attack jammed *Bismarck*'s rudder. She was narrowly caught only a day away from land-based friendly air cover, and eventually dispatched on the morning of 27 May by the guns and torpedoes of *King George V*, *Rodney* and company. There were just 110 survivors from a complement of over 2,300 men.

(left) The last photograph of HMS *Hood*
Taken from HMS *Prince of Wales*, shortly before they went into action against the German ships. Note the spray covers over the ends of the gun barrels; the turrets are still trained aft so as to reduce the ingress of water while the ships travel at high speed in heavy seas.

(above) The 'mighty *Hood*'
HMS *Hood* viewed between two 16-inch guns belonging to HMS *Rodney* after the former had returned from the Mediterranean. HMS *Repulse* can be seen to the left.

Bismarck attacks the *Prince of Wales*
An iconic shot of the battleship *Bismarck* taken from the heavy cruiser *Prinz Eugen* shortly after the sinking of the *Hood*.

(opposite) The evacuation of Greece
Exhausted troops on the foredeck of the cruiser *Phoebe* during the evacuation of British forces from Greece. The loss of Greece and the withdrawal to – and subsequent evacuation of – Crete, resulted in a horrendous ordeal for the Royal Navy – perhaps its most trying single episode of the entire war.

(left) HMS *Kelvin* at Alexandria
An officer and seamen prepare a depth charge on *Kelvin* ready for use at sea in June 1941.

(below) HMS *Kipling* with HMS *Kelly*'s survivors
Travelling at full speed in the Kithera Channel between Greece and Crete on 23 May 1941, Captain Louis Mountbatten's command, the *Kelly*, was hit and sunk. The survivors were rescued by *Kipling*, but on her approach to Alexandria, she ran out of fuel and had to be replenished by another ship before she could enter the harbour. In this photograph her arrival is being cheered by the ship's company of HMS *Kelvin*.

HMS *Furious* in the Mediterranean
Rough seas breaking over the decks of HMS *Furious*
during 1941 (photograph taken from the cruiser HMS
Sheffield). At least one of *Furious*'s crew seems completely
unconcerned. Originally built as a battlecruiser during
World War One, *Furious* was one of two ships – *Argus*
being the other – to serve as an aircraft carrier in both
conflicts. These two were also the only British carriers
in service in 1939 to see out the war: the other five,
completed or converted between the wars, had all been
sunk by the late summer of 1942.

HMS *Sheffield* and German supply ship *Friedrich Breme*
On 12 June 1941 in the North Atlantic, HMS *Sheffield* intercepted the German supply ship *Friedrich Breme*, full of fuel and provisions for U-boats, and sank her with gunfire. The German crew abandoned ship and were taken prisoner. In this photograph, empty shell cases litter the deck around the aft 6-inch turrets of HMS *Sheffield* after the encounter.

Burial service
The burial service being read on board HMS *Sheffield* for two of the crew of *Friedrich Breme* who were killed by shell splinters during the shelling of the tanker. The service was attended by the ship's company of both ships.

The sinking of HMS *Barham*

Of all the British images of the war at sea, 1939–45, some of the best known are the dramatic and horrifying last moments of the British battleship *Barham*. A veteran of World War One, when she had played a major part in the Battle of Jutland, by November 1941 the old (though modernized) ship had chalked up a not inconsiderable combat record in World War Two, including the bombardment of Dakar, the Battle of Matapan and the evacuation of Crete. She had been torpedoed by a U-boat, and damaged by bombs and by shellfire, had accidentally rammed and sunk the destroyer *Duchess*, and towed the cripped battleship *Resolution* to safety after the Dakar debacle. But on the afternoon of 25 November 1941, while the Mediterranean Fleet was operating off the coast of Libya, she was hit on the port side by three or four (reports vary) torpedoes fired by *U-331*. Even a modern ship would have been unlikely to survive such blows, and *Barham*, mortally wounded, immediately began to heel over and sink. Four minutes after the first hit, as the ship reached a 90-degree angle, she blew up.

The subsequent Board of Enquiry concluded that it was probably a secondary magazine that had expoded, igniting in turn the after main magazine. When the appalling cloud had cleared, the battleship was gone, together with 862 of her crew, including Captain G. C. Cooke. Astonishingly, given the speed with which *Barham* turned over, and her cataclysmic end, some 396 men, Vice-Admiral Sir Henry Pridham-Whipple among them, survived to be rescued by accompanying ships. One survivor recalled checking that all his limbs were still in place as he was flung through the air; after hitting the water he was then bowled over and over by the shock wave of the explosion. Admiral Cunningham, on board the flagship *Queen Elizabeth*, described it as 'a horrible and awe-inspiring spectacle'.

(*U-331* was sunk, together with thirty-two members of her crew, by an Albacore aircraft from HMS *Formidable* just under a year later.)

Coming at possibly Britain's, and the Royal Navy's, lowest point in the war, *Barham*'s loss was initially kept secret. But on board HMS *Valiant*, the next battleship in line, was John Turner, a Gaumont British News camerman. He had joined the organization in 1936, and had filmed many of the notable events of the last years of the decade for the news that was shown in the cinemas of the day. At the outbreak of the war he had become a naval war correspondent. At the time *Barham* was torpedoed Turner had just two minutes' worth of film left in his camera, so what he filmed was a series of moments from the ship's loss, rather than the entire event. The film was subsequently impounded until the war's end, even after the Admiralty had admitted the battleship had been sunk, Cunningham saying that it was 'not in the interests of the war effort or of the Royal Navy' for it to be shown.

Turner went on to cover the invasions of Sicily and Normandy, and the Japanese surrender at Singapore, and enjoyed a long and successful career after the war, becoming a news editor for Pathé after the demise of cinema news reels and of Gaumont British News. His film of the destruction of *Barham*, and the numerous stills that have been made from it, have meanwhile gone on to provide some of the best known images of the war, even though the film sequences in particular are frequently used to 'illustrate' other events such as the loss of *Hood*, and even the three British battlecruisers sunk at Jutland, twenty-five years previously.

The Soviet Navy on the defensive

When Germany invaded the Soviet Union the Soviet Navy became heavily involved in the desperate struggle to stem the advance, supporting the Red Army ashore and assisting in evacuations of troops and civilians alike. At Leningrad the ships and their crews played their full part in what became one of the great sieges of history.

(above left) **The battleship** *Oktyabrskaya Revoliutsya*
Anti-aircraft guns on board the *Oktyabrskaya Revoliutsya*, which remained at Leningrad throughout the siege, helping to defend the city against land and air attack. She was damaged by artillery on 16 September 1941, and by bombing on 4 April 1942.

(above) **The cruiser** *Kirov*
On board the cruiser *Kirov* during the winter of 1941–2. The first major warship to be built since the Revolution, the handsome *Kirov* was completed in September 1938, and had participated in the opening attacks of the Russo-Finnish War. In 1941, after evacuating Riga and Tallinn, *Kirov* was caught between shoals and German minefields. Her crew desperately tried to lighten the ship and the *Kirov* successfully made a hair-raising passage back to Leningrad, and took up position to resist the German besiegers.

(left) **The battleship** *Marat*
In the autumn of 1941 German armour advanced on Leningrad. Battleships and cruisers, many of elderly design yet mounting powerful guns, proved very durable against German field artillery. *Luftwaffe* air strikes were called up and on 17 September the battleship *Marat* was hit by dive-bombers, her forward magazines exploded, and she sank to the shallow harbour floor, her main guns unaffected. This photograph shows the wreck of *Marat*'s forward superstructure.

The icebreaker *Molotov*, under camouflage at Leningrad
The Soviet Navy had only a few icebreakers of its own, but with the outbreak of war all icebreakers were taken under naval control and were armed. With the Gulf of Finland normally freezing for four to five months each winter, icebreakers were vital, but no fewer than ten were sunk in the Baltic during 1941.

The destroyer *Storozhevoj*, heavily camouflaged
The Type 7-U destroyer was one of the most modern Soviet destroyers of the period. Torpedoed by a German MTB in the Irben Straits in June 1941, she was towed to Leningrad for repair. This resulted in a new bow and updated armament. She re-entered service in 1943.

The submarine *M-172*
Commander I. Fisanovich aboard his submarine, the small, 200-ton coastal vessel *M-172*. From July 1941 German U-boats and Soviet submarines began to operate in the same deep waters of the north-eastern Norwegian fjords and Barents Sea. On 21 August, *M-172* sneaked into Petsamo Fjord undetected by the German guardboat and fired torpedoes into a merchantman tied alongside a pier. *M-172* made her escape having heard explosions, but in fact her torpedoes had missed the ship and struck the pier instead. In mid-September she found her mark against the hull of a Norwegian steamer, and again in November 1941 sank a ship which the captain claimed was of 8,000 tons. In fact she was the *Vesco* of only 331 tons. Soviet submarines claimed thirty-two ships of a total of nearly 96,000 tons sunk in northern waters in 1941. According to German figures, only twelve ships of 28,000 tons were lost, and only three of these ships of 6,400 tons are attributable to Soviet submarines. The rest were sunk by a pair of British submarines operating from Polyarnyy until December 1941.

The *Josif Stalin*
The passenger ship *Josif Stalin*, pressed into service as a transport, is shown here sinking in December 1941 after being damaged by mines during the evacuation of Hangö. Some 7,000 men were aboard: 1,850 were taken off by Soviet vessels, over 2,000 were taken prisoner by the Germans, and nearly 3,000 perished.

Free French submarines

(below and opposite) *Surcouf*

Two views of the mighty French submarine *Surcouf*, in Dry Dock No. 2 at Portsmouth, New Hampshire, on 1 September 1941, giving an impression of this remarkable vessel's immense size. At 360 feet long and some 4,200 tons submerged displacement she was the world's largest submarine: her dimensions were not exceeded until the completion of the first of the giant Japanese aircraft-carrying submarines of the *I-400* class in 1944. *Surcouf*'s appearance in 1931 not surprisingly caused consternation in other navies: equipped with a pair of 8-inch guns, ten torpedo tubes and even her own scouting aircraft she was a *tour de force* of submarine technology. Yet she was far from an unqualified triumph, the sheer ambition of the design being beyond what French industry and technology of the time could really deliver; she also represented something of a tactical dead end, and as a result remained unique.

In July 1940 *Surcouf* was one of the vessels taken over by the Royal Navy at Plymouth, and was one of the few where there was resistance, with the result that two British and one Frenchman lost their lives. It then proved difficult to find a proper job for her, and in the end (ironically in the light of the fact that she had been designed as a commerce raider) *Surcouf* spent much of the next eighteen months escorting convoys across the Atlantic. She proved awkward to crew, requiring a larger number of highly skilled personnel than were easily available to the nascent Free French Navy. There were also problems of discipline. Finally, in February 1942 she was lost with all hands in somewhat mysterious circumstances, apparently rammed by an American merchantman off Panama.

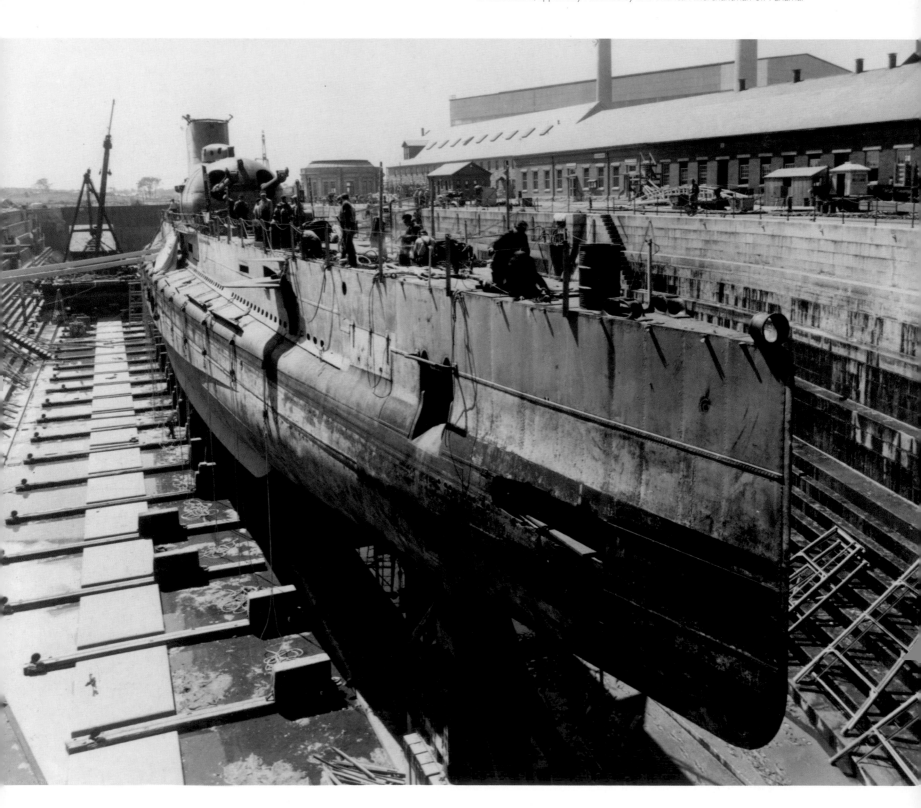

(below) *Rubis*

In contrast to *Surcouf*'s less than glorious wartime career, that of the little *Rubis* (pictured after the war at Toulon) was one of outstanding success. Less than a quarter of the size of her giant sister, *Rubis* served throughout the war, first with the *Marine Nationale*, and then after July 1940 with the *Force Navale Française Libres*. Operating mainly from Dundee and Gosport, she carried out twenty-eight patrols and minelaying sorties, laying 683 mines and being responsible for the sinking of twenty-two enemy vessels and damaging two more. This one small submarine was credited with doing more damage to the enemy than any other French warship during the six years of war. In 1941 *Rubis* survived a nerve-shredding episode when attacking a German convoy off Norway: she torpedoed a freighter at such close range that the shock of her torpedoes exploding damaged the submarine's batteries, preventing her from diving and necessitating a three-day return passage across the North Sea on the surface. Fortunately it was high summer, the weather was calm, and *Rubis* made it home, although one man was washed overboard. Her dedicated, tightly knit (only five out of forty-four had elected not to join the Free French forces) and extrovert crew amassed an impressive collection of decorations (both British and French) between them, perhaps none more popular or deserved than those awarded to Bacchus, the stout, endlessly cheerful, short-haired mongrel dog that was her mascot.

US escort

Even before the attack on Pearl Harbor the US Navy was becoming increasingly committed to the war at sea; during 1941 there was growing involvement of US destroyers in escorting convoys against the U-boats, and as a result they began to suffer losses. This photograph shows USS *Drayton* (DD-366) under way at sea off the US West Coast in about October 1941. The photograph is taken from a navy SNJ aircraft, whose starboard wing is in the foreground. Note *Drayton*'s camouflage, which was the source of her contemporary nickname 'The Blue Beetle'.

The loss of *Ark Royal*

In the late autumn and winter of 1941, the Axis stepped up its pressure in the Mediterranean. Struck by torpedoes fired from *U-81*, the *Ark Royal* sank on 13 November 1941 about 30 miles east of Gibraltar, with the crew being taken off by destroyer.

Hangar on US aircraft carrier

American aircraft carriers featured capacious hangars. This is a view of one of USS *Enterprise*'s three elevators which moved aircraft to and from the flight deck to the hangar deck below. Note the off-duty sailors lining the hangar deck bulkhead.

The attack on Pearl Harbor

Pearl Harbor was hit by Japanese carrier-launched bombers and torpedo-planes in a startling *coup de main* reminiscent of the British aerial attack on the Italian fleet at anchor in Taranto, but far more devastating in its power and consequence. Five US battleships were sunk and three destroyers lost; and three other battleships and two cruisers were damaged, with over two thousand American deaths. The primary purpose of the attack was to prevent the USA from executing Plan Orange once the Japanese 'moved south' by sending the US Pacific Fleet at Pearl Harbor against its 'open flank'.

An aerial view of the Naval Operating Base, Pearl Harbor, looking southwest on 30 October 1941. Ford Island, with its Naval Air Station, is in the centre, with the Pearl Harbor Navy Yard just beyond it, across the channel. The airfield in the upper left-centre is the Army's Hickam Field. The ships moored in 'Battleship Row' are to the left of the island, with an aircraft carrier occupying the southern-most berth — it was the fact that the carriers were all away at sea on 7 December that was one of the reasons why the Japanese attack was fundamentally a failure. Cruisers and destroyers are moored out in the harbour towards the bottom of the photograph.

The Japanese assault commences
A Japanese Navy Type 97 carrier attack plane ('Kate') taking off from a carrier to attack Pearl Harbor as the ship's crew cheer 'Banzai'. The ship is either *Zuikaku* or *Shokaku*. Note the light tripod mast at the rear of the carrier's island, with a Japanese naval ensign.

US battleships on fire
A view looking along 'Battleship Row' on 7 December 1941, after the Japanese attack. USS *Arizona* (BB-39) is in the centre, burning furiously after her forward magazines exploded. To the left of her are the damaged USS *Tennessee* (BB-43) and the sunken USS *West Virginia* (BB-48).

View from Ford Island
This is often claimed to be the moment of the explosion on board the USS *Arizona*.
In fact the photograph has been taken from the other end of the island from where
the battleship was moored, and the huge fireball erupting beyond the two-engined
Consolidated PBY-5 Catalina is most likely that from the destroyer USS *Shaw*, hit by bombs
and practically destroyed while lying in dry dock. The masts and funnel of a battleship that
are visible beneath the cloud of smoke and flames belong to the USS *Nevada*, which in an
outstanding piece of seamanship was got underway and attempted to escape out to sea,
only to be ordered to be beached rather than risk being sunk in the main entrance to
Pearl Harbor.

The sinking of HMS *Prince of Wales*

Not surprisingly very few photographs were taken during the destruction of Force Z at the hands of Japanese aircraft, and this is by far the best known, giving an idea of the pandemonium as the *Prince of Wales* began to sink on 10 December 1941. Smoke is rising from midships, evidence of damage below decks; while members of the crew, some still dressed for battle in anti-flash clothing and tin helmets, others now in life jackets or even stripped down to their underwear in anticipation of having to make a swim for it, are lining the ship's side and beginning to make the perilous crossing to the destroyer *Express* (from which this photograph was taken)

alongside the battleship's starboard quarter. Such a manoeuvre required skilled seamanship to minimize the risk of damage from collision, as well as to give every chance to those who were attempting to cross from one ship to the other – any who fell into the gap in between the vessels would have little chance of survival. Of the 1,612 on board *Prince of Wales*, 1,285 were saved. The less robust *Repulse*, which sank more quickly, lost 513 out of 1,309. Admiral Phillips, and Captain Leach of the *Prince of Wales*, were not among those rescued by *Express* and two other destroyers, *Electra* and the Australian *Vampire*.

materialization of the expected major thrust aimed at Midway using almost the entire Japanese fleet. Intelligence also indicated a simultaneous feint north-east towards the Aleutians.

On the morning of 4 June, a land-based PBY Catalina flying-boat from Midway sighted the Japanese invasion support force but mis-reported it as Admiral Nagumo's carriers. But thorough enough was the US intelligence picture that the commanders of the American carrier force, assembled and lying in ambush, knew to disregard the incorrect sighting. The Japanese, still confident that no American force was there to oppose them, flew off a hundred bombers to attack the Midway archipelago. Information gained from a second aerial sighting was relayed to *Enterprise* and *Hornet*, waiting in ambush to the north east of Midway, and they turned in towards Nagumo's carriers; 150 miles away from the Japanese, US task force commander Admiral Spruance decided to launch his attack, hoping to catch the Japanese carriers recovering their strike aircraft, when they would be at their most vulnerable. Admiral Fletcher on the *Yorktown*, recalling the relatively wasteful attack on the *Shoho* at Coral Sea, launched his dive-bombers and torpedo planes sixty minutes later, hoping to get a clearer picture first of the exact location of the most important Japanese targets. Meanwhile, as it re-armed its planes for a second attack on Midway, Nagumo's force received intelligence from a scout plane indicating the presence of American ships to the north. The Japanese had no idea that the US carriers were at sea and in the area until a floatplane found 'what appears to be a carrier' later that morning.

Admiral Yamaguchi, in command of Carrier Division 2 (*Hiryu* and *Soryu*), signalled Nagumo to suggest they attack the American carriers immediately, but Nagumo, hesitating, preferred to retire slightly to the north east to re-arm and re-fuel, as his planes were still armed with weapons designed to attack land targets and not ships, and he would need to re-arm them with torpedoes.

At this crucial point the first American carrier-based attacks began, but aircraft launched separately from the *Yorktown*, *Hornet* and *Enterprise* fared badly; all three torpedo squadrons found the Japanese and attacked but they had become separated from the dive-bombers and the majority of their escorting fighters. *Hornet's* squadron of torpedo-bombers were entirely shot down by fighters and AA fire. *Enterprise's* squadron lost ten of its fourteen aircraft in the attack. Twelve torpedo aircraft from the *Yorktown* were lost, with no hits scored (though their fighter escort from VT-6 brought down six Zeroes for one loss). But crucially, the Japanese fighter patrol, its attention focused on the low-level fight with the *Enterprise's* torpedo and fighter planes, failed to notice the arrival of Douglas Dauntless dive-bombers from *Yorktown* and *Enterprise* at high altitude. Unmolested by Japanese fighters, the dive-bombers swooped down on the Japanese carriers and scored between eight and ten devastating hits on the *Akagi*, *Kaga* and *Soryu*, which were swiftly engulfed in explosions and flames.

Despite being harassed by American fighters, retaliatory strikes by planes from *Hiryu* managed to deliver two torpedo and three bomb hits to the *Yorktown*, causing heavy damage and necessitating her being towed to Pearl Harbor for repair, though she never arrived there. During the voyage home she was sunk by a Japanese submarine – but not before dive-bombers from both her and *Enterprise* completed the rout of the Japanese carriers by sending the *Hiryu* to the bottom with four bomb hits late on 4 June. At the cost of one carrier, the US fleet had sunk at a stroke four Japanese carriers, destroyed 270 enemy aircraft, defended Midway and their rearward lines of communication, and secured their first major victory of the war.

The Strategic Effects of Coral Sea and Midway

Was Midway a decisive victory which decided the outcome of the Pacific war? In the sense that an American victory in the Pacific was almost inevitable given her vastly superior shipbuilding, munitioning and manpower capacity vis-à-vis Japan (six times more capacity in 1941), Midway was by definition not a decisive victory. But in a contemporary battle-by-battle mindset, Midway proved to be a major signpost in the direction of US triumph. Japanese offensive power, so far largely unstoppable, had been stretched and then beaten. The Imperial Japanese Navy was still a force to be reckoned with, but Midway denuded it of enough of its experienced air component to allow the process of American counter-attack to begin.

By the spring of 1942, the Allies, on the back foot everywhere, had needed a signal strategic victory. The Americans, at Midway, provided it. The tactical lessons of Coral Sea and Midway in the late spring of 1942 seemed obvious: that gun power no longer decided the fate of fleets, but that the aircraft carrier could deliver crushing blows across hundreds of miles of sea space far beyond the range of conventional battleship influence. But in reality these battles also reminded naval staffs of the vulnerability of carriers to exactly the style and weight of attack that they could deliver; thus a crushing knockout strike was the essential objective. At Coral Sea, the Americans had lost half their carrier force and none of the remaining carriers on either side were fit to stay in the battle; but at Midway, the Japanese lost three quarters of their force to the first overwhelming strike launched from the American carriers.

Furthermore, at the Battle of Midway, over 60 per cent of the participating American aviators had completed their training in 1941 or later – evidence of the first fruition of an enormous training programme which produced thirty thousand navy and marine aviators a year in seventeen new training centres across the USA. Two years before, flying men made up only 16 per cent of all American line officers, but by Midway there were two-and-a-half times as many aviation officers than all other specialities combined. In marked contrast, Midway severely damaged Japan's elite carrier fleet and permanently removed perhaps one third of its very experienced pilot strength. Furthermore, Japanese naval aviation was also deeply harmed by the loss of large numbers of trained mechanics, armourers and other support personnel, killed when the carriers were lost.

A new Japanese Third Fleet was brought into being, based around the surviving carriers and escort vessels, but the lost squadrons and crews were harder to replace. Unlike the Americans, the Japanese did not establish carrier replacement air groups, which brought substantial benefits to the efficiency of American combat-ready carriers and the standards of their trained aviator force. The Japanese did not rotate their experienced combat pilots away from front-line duties, but preferred to keep them in their squadrons aboard ship where they could provide training for newer pilots. This left them exposed to defeats like Midway which could seriously weaken the experienced core of aviators and diminish aggregate combat effectiveness. And as the Japanese corps of experienced naval aviators crumbled away, American strength grew.

America on the 'Offensive-Defensive' in the Solomons

The US Navy could take the 'offensive-defensive' to the Japanese diaspora after Midway. By the middle of July, the Americans could call on four fleet carriers – *Enterprise*, *Hornet*, *Saratoga* and *Wasp* – while Japan could field two fleet carriers and three light carriers of which *Junyo* and

Hiyo – available at the end of the month – were virtually fleet carriers in terms of capacity.

First the Americans landed marines at Guadalcanal in the Solomon Islands on 7 August. Operations intensified as both sides sought to gain the upper hand. The Solomon Islands would be the scene of the Pacific's lengthiest and most bitterly fought naval campaign. Mutual attempts over the course of fifteen months to interfere with each others' reinforcements led to a series of a dozen large air and sea battles, including the campaign in the vicinity of Guadalcanal itself.

Within two weeks of the US invasion, a carrier battle was fought in the Eastern Solomons, the Japanese losing the carrier *Ryujo* and the Americans suffering severe damage to the *Enterprise*. In October, while attempting to attack the American-held airfield on Guadalcanal, the Japanese won a tactical victory at the Battle of Santa Cruz by delivering a well co-ordinated dive-bomber and torpedo attack against US carriers, in particular the *Hornet*, which was knocked out and eventually sunk (though by US and Japanese torpedoes fired from destroyers). Once again, fighter defence, along with better damage control and improved AA gunfire, was critical in limiting the damage sustained from a well-aimed carrier strike. But this time, American fighters were unable to stem the Japanese tide, while their own bombers were shot down often many miles away from their targets. While radar existed aboard American carriers, it was not always utilized properly. Escorting the *Enterprise*, the battleship *South Dakota* had used her modern batteries of AA guns to destroy twenty-six aircraft. The mighty battleship was playing second fiddle to the flat-top and its tiny aircraft.

Japanese naval aircraft were of superior quality to all other combatants' in 1942. The Mitsubishi A6M2 Type 00, or 'Zero', was a fast and very manoeuvrable fighter aircraft and the first carrier-borne plane to outclass its land-based counterparts. In the hands of well-trained Japanese pilots, many of whom had acquired hundreds of hours of flying and battle experience over China, it was a formidable challenge to American and British types in the Pacific theatre and provided the Japanese with the leading edge to its air superiority. The Japanese also produced world-leading torpedo and dive-bombers, including the Nakajima B5N2 Type 97 'Kate' and Aichi D3A1 Type 99 'Val'. American aircraft – the Grumman Wildcat fighter, the Douglas Dauntless dive-bomber and Grumman Avenger torpedo-bomber – were usually slower, less manoeuvrable and of lower range, but were more rugged and capable of carrying heavier payloads.

New American aircraft – for example the Chance-Vought Corsair, Grumman Bearcat and Curtiss Helldiver – would later remove Japanese qualitative superiority, but in 1942 what the US Navy really needed to improve was its fighter direction and air-combat tactics to counteract Japanese technical superiority. Leading American fighter aces had begun to formulate new formation-based tactics (such as the 'Thach weave') which had already been proven to cut away much of the Zero's superiority at Midway and Santa Cruz.

While their plane losses roughly equalled those of the Japanese, American aircrew losses were only one-sixth of the Japanese at the Battle of Santa Cruz. More US pilots survived being shot down. So while the Zero might be a superior aeroplane, there were increasingly fewer experienced pilots to fly it as the war of attrition over the Solomon Islands ground away much of the remaining experienced Japanese aviation force. Periodic American attacks on Rabaul demonstrated that while an airborne strike force was away from its carrier, this did not automatically mean that the carrier was itself vulnerable to attack,

providing it retained sufficient fighter aircraft to defend against land-based aerial counterattack. This was something the British, with fewer carriers and no dedicated high-performance carrier-borne fighter aircraft, had been unable to achieve in the comparatively narrow seas of the Mediterranean.

With the impetus of continual advance stripped away, the Japanese had lost the ability to follow up their victories in a meaningful way, and during 1942 Japanese carrier aircraft losses were double the numbers constructed as replacements. However, with the loss of *Wasp* to a Japanese submarine in September the US Navy was down to two fleet carriers until the new *Essex* class and the converted light fleet carriers entered service in mid-1943. There was even talk of borrowing a British carrier at one stage. With the commissioning of *Hiyo* in the autumn the Japanese Navy had four fleet carriers and one light carrier.

Over the next three months, the Americans, with control of the airfield on Guadalcanal, held sway during daylight hours, but with incredible determination the Japanese managed to deliver troops and supplies to their position on Guadalcanal during night hours, operations the Americans nicknamed the 'Tokyo Express'. By November 1942, both sides' exhausted carrier forces were withdrawn to regroup, leaving the Solomons struggle to their battleship groups and land-based aircraft.

On the night of 12–13 November, a Japanese force of two battleships, a cruiser and eleven destroyers was spotted approaching Guadalcanal. An American force of two heavy and three light cruisers and eight destroyers was handed the task of meeting and driving them off, as no US battleships were on hand to interfere. The two forces met unexpectedly and suddenly in the pitch black, and in the pell-mell battle that followed, the US cruiser *Atlanta* and four American destroyers were lost, with several other ships badly damaged. In return, the *Kongo*-class Japanese battleship *Hiei* had been disabled; eighty-five hits from cruiser shells, followed by air-dropped torpedoes and bombs dispatched her later, on the night of the 14th. Also that night, her sister battleship *Kirishima* with four cruisers and nine destroyers steamed into the area where they met the battleships *Washington* and *South Dakota* and four destroyers. Slugging it out, the *South Dakota* sustained 14-inch shell hits in her superstructure but her armour remained intact; however, the *Kirishima* was battered into a wreck by the Americans' 16-inch fire, and was eventually scuttled. Apart from the serious damage to the *South Dakota*, three US destroyers were sunk. Japanese losses in these and other November battles off Guadalcanal also included three destroyers, while the American Navy lost three cruisers and six destroyers, sunk by superior Japanese night-fighting skills. Nonetheless, appalled at their losses on land – where the war of attrition, it became increasingly clear, could not be won – the Japanese began to plan for their withdrawal from the Eastern Solomons by the end of December. The first of a string of US re-conquests had been achieved.

The Battle of the Atlantic and Signals Intelligence

Unlike the Pacific, the war in the Atlantic was one of no major set-piece engagements. Instead it was characterized by the ebb and flow of steady, grinding pressure applied through blockade and counter-blockade; a technological advantage here soon crossed out there; an unscathed convoy followed by a disastrous re-crossing; and so on. By far the majority of worldwide merchant losses continued to occur in the Atlantic, where the number of U-boat losses (thirteen) was far outstripped by new U-boat launches (108). Figures show that in the first six months of 1942, 585 Allied ships were lost, totalling 3 million tons – an unsustainable casualty rate for the Allies, and one which led Admiral

Raeder and Hitler to believe, as Dönitz always had, that the U-boat would be the decisive weapon in this theatre of the war.

Increasingly, the interception and analysis of German radio communications became essential to the defeat of the U-boat. All German U-boat operations were co-ordinated from a shore headquarters known as the *Befehlshaber der Unterseeboote* (*BdU*), and it was standard operating procedure for a U-boat to put to sea and there to receive its orders by radio signals. Likewise U-boats reported back to the *BdU* by radio transmissions. The Germans, committing one of the biggest failures of intelligence of the war, never accepted the logical possibility that their Enigma codes could be intercepted, broken and put to Allied use quickly enough to have an effect on their operations. Yet it was this constant flow of radio messages that gave the Allied operational intelligence commanders (but not the main Operations Rooms, who were kept unaware of the existence of Allied decryption for security reasons) the intelligence needed to defeat the U-boat threat during the Battle of the Atlantic, and the Germans never worked this out.

German messages between submarines, patrol aircraft (such as the Focke-Wulf Condor) and shore were intercepted and used in two crucial ways. First, to the contrary of German scientists' belief, German VHF signals were detectable by High-Frequency Direction-Finding (HF/DF) equipment. HF/DF remained unknown to the Germans throughout the war. Secondly, the intercepted encoded messages were sent to the Government Code and Cypher School at Bletchley Park, where a small team of talented mathematicians, programmers and intelligence experts broke the encryptions and sent the decoded messages to the Submarine Tracking Room at the Admiralty in London. The US Navy initially shared this intelligence and other HF/DF information, and later in the war assumed the lion's share of decoding a range of other German codes.

However, the Allied ability to read German codes, at great effort, secrecy and patience, and despite a multitude of unavoidable delays and disappointments, did not at all make U-boat operations transparent. For long periods the U-boat codes could not be decrypted. The British were unable to read any U-boat messages until January 1941. They then began to read, to January 1942, the 'Dolphin' encoded traffic, but on 1 February 1942 the Germans added an extra, fourth, wheel to the standard three-wheel Enigma encoding machine. This new Atlantic code, 'Triton' (called 'Shark' by the British), remained unbreakable through the 'Great Blackout' until December 1942.

But like other weapons, decryption was double-edged. The Germans were also active in their own signals intelligence war. From February 1942 to June 1943, when the Battle of the Atlantic would be at its height, a German staff team led by Heinz Bonatz had reached such efficiency that it was deciphering low-level British operational codes and the Admiralty's daily U-boat disposition signal within a few hours of dispatch. By this the Germans were able to forecast alterations in convoy routes, and to reposition their wolf-packs accordingly. As a 1946 British special report into wartime cryptographic activities ruefully reported: 'The patient and careful work of the submarine trackers was in fact being used against our own ships.' British high-level codes were generally secure for long enough until scrapped and replaced, but weakness lay in the fact that the messages were recoded to ships and stations using less secure wireless telegraphy, which could be broken and used to work back on the original transmissions.

However, even the best intelligence has its limits; it can be misused, ignored, misinterpreted and is subject to processing and analysis delays before it is even acted upon, 'correctly' or not. The physical realities of warfare – the men and machines tasked with the fighting – are always more important than any intelligence. Intelligence could, realistically, do little more than contribute to a war of attrition.

'The Second Happy Time': U-Boat Successes Reach Their Peak

It was at this time that Atlantic shipping losses were at their height; within the first four months of 1942, as much Allied tonnage was sent to the bottom as had been lost in the whole of the previous year. Some longer-range Type IX U-boats operated in the Indian and Southern Atlantic oceans, but the principle was obvious: most U-boats would concentrate in the area of greatest Allied shipping – and the North Atlantic became an even richer hunting ground when American coastal and transatlantic shipping became fully legitimate targets in 1942.

Upon the German declaration of war against the USA in December 1941, a large number of U-boats sailed west to attack comparatively unprotected and fresh targets off the east coast of America. Type XIV 'Milchkuh' supply submarines enabled the Type VII to operate this far away from home. The Gulf of Mexico was a particular hot-spot of Operation *Paukenschlag* ('Rolling Drums'); over fifty tankers and freighters were sunk in its waters in a six-month period between March and September 1942. Italian submarines also operated in American waters and further south in the Caribbean.

Focusing on the conveying of fast troopships in the Pacific, and believing a weak escort to be a waste of warships, Admiral King did not institute convoying along the American East Coast until May 1942. The effect of the delay was massively adverse: 1.2 million tons of American shipping – unescorted, sailing singly, openly radioing and with navigation lights undimmed – were sent to the bottom in the four months nicknamed 'The Second Happy Time' by U-boat crews. The US Navy was so short of anti-submarine craft that it was given a number of 'Flower' class corvettes by the Royal Canadian Navy and the British. Later it built dedicated coastal patrol craft, but by then, Dönitz's submarines had exacted their highest six-monthly toll since the war had begun. By August, when the most deadly phase of the Battle of the Atlantic was just beginning, over 3 million tons of Allied shipping had already been lost in American waters. British stocks of essentials were edging close to collapse. The *BdU* had recalled most of its U-boats to the mid-Atlantic which was swamped by wolf-packs sometimes numbering over thirty boats.

But despite the U-boats' gathering density, statistically only 40 per cent of all Allied convoys were ever sighted, let alone attacked successfully. A third of these sighted convoys subsequently eluded U-boat attack entirely. And only 9 per cent of all convoys lost more than four ships. Several important factors influenced the U-boats' variable strike rate: efficiency of communications; the weather conditions, including visibility; the skill of the U-boat crew's attack; and the abilities of the defensive forces – human and technological – arrayed against them.

Brilliant Allied minds were put to work fine-tuning Anti-Surface Vessel search radar, removing early glitches. Radar, particularly lightweight sets mounted in patrol aircraft but also increasingly aboard ship, could detect a surfaced submarine at a range of five miles, and sometimes pick up a periscope at half a mile. The significant night-time surface advantage enjoyed by the U-boat was negated by this electro-magnetic advance. In April, new escort-mounted centimetric Type 271 radar scored its first U-boat kill in concert with portable HF/DF – a sign of things to come, and not a moment too soon, as U-boat numbers reached 300 by late spring, with one third operational.

The key was either to attack and sink the submarine or to force it underwater. Here a U-boat's speed was much reduced to, at best, 7 knots (compared to a convoy speed of perhaps 10 knots, and escort sprint speeds of over 20 knots), and the submarine became detectable by Asdic sets mounted aboard escorts which could in turn be given precise directions by air cover. The efficacy of British Type 271 shipboard radar was partially demonstrated by the fact that slow convoys, run by Canadian warships carrying the less efficient SW1C Canadian-developed radar, suffered losses in excess of their share of convoy duties. Then again, while providing 35 per cent of Atlantic escorts, the Canadians were in charge in over half of all convoy combats with U-boats. With more than eighty corvettes in commission by 1942 but still only a handful of effective destroyers, they fought a disproportionate amount of battles with U-boats, all the while under-resourced and under-trained. By the middle of the year, it was clear (to the British at least) that the Canadian components of the Mid-Ocean Escort Forces were unable to compete effectively against the U-boat tactics, and the Canadian force was requested to withdraw to re-train and re-equip with Type 271 radar and new HF/DF gear.

The Tide Begins to Turn

Autumn saw the U-boat attack intensify further. Convoy ON 127 lost six ships totalling 44,000 tons and the Canadian destroyer *Ottawa* to attacks by over a dozen U-boats. Sinkings of independent sailers in the Caribbean and off South America remained troublesome. Large-scale *Rudeltaktik* operations were mounted in October. Convoy SC 104 lost nine ships of nearly 50,000 tons; SL 125 suffered twelve losses, of 80,000 tons; SC 107 lost fifteen ships of 83,000 tons. And by September, German scientists had developed the Metox radar warning receiver which alerted a U-boat to the presence of ASV I and ASV II radar. The technological pendulum had swung again. But while radar warning receivers fitted to U-boats enabled them to dive before an attack could be launched, to a convoy escort this was a very acceptable second best to an actual 'kill' as it threw the U-boat off track and could pin it underwater for hours on end, by which time the convoy was long gone and anti-submarine reinforcements called up if available.

A new British weapon, hurriedly introduced at the end of 1941, began to mature and prove its worth in 1942. The forward-firing mortar bomb thrower called 'Hedgehog' began to equip British escorts and was also adopted by the US Navy. Its twenty-four small projectiles detonated only on contact, and therefore did not require last-second fiddling with depth settings before firing, which improved strike efficiency and no doubt saved a few fingers too. For a variety of reasons it took time to be accepted in the Royal Navy, but was very popular with the Americans, and was a lethal submarine killer.

Maritime patrol aircraft would eventually prove to be key in combining reach, presence and offensive power. Not only could they force a transiting U-boat to dive and thereby lose its position vis-à-vis a convoy, but armed with depth charges and machine guns the patrol aircraft could take the offensive to the U-boats by attacking them upon and beneath the surface. Large land-based Very Long Range (VLR) aircraft, by extension, could provide an umbrella over a convoy for much longer. As VLR maritime patrol aircraft equipped only one squadron in RAF Coastal Command and none at all in the US Atlantic command, the Mid-Atlantic 'air gap' was still a major problem for the Allied

transatlantic convoys. U-boats would lurk in it, resupplying from 'Milchkuhe', reliant on Metox and largely safe from land-based air cover.

But over the course of 1942, the U-boat's growing destructiveness was checked. Between the spring and the autumn, the average number of U-boats per operation had increased from five to twelve. Statistics show that a greater number of U-boats were accounting for fewer merchant sinkings among them. Thus while the tallies for the second half of the year showed the highest overall total of Allied tonnage sunk, each U-boat was sinking less and less during this period – from 16,000 tons per U-boat per month down to 7,000 tons. And while this did not alter the fact that more merchant ships than ever were being lost, it meant that Allied measures were having an underlying effect. At the same time, more U-boats were sunk than ever before. From 1942 onwards, the majority of U-boat losses were administered by aircraft flying from new escort carriers, MACs and from land bases. The complexion of the Battle of the Atlantic was slowly changing.

The Tragic Risks of Arctic Convoying

Meanwhile, convoys had also to be run up in the Arctic, drawing heavily on British naval resources, morale and endurance. Convoy requirements were expensive for navies to continually attempt to meet, denuding other theatres and specific operations of much-needed naval support. Despite shipyards on both sides of the Atlantic churning out ever-increasing numbers of 'Castle' class corvettes, *Black Swan* class sloops, 'River' class frigates and American 'Destroyer Escorts', the workhorses of the Allied navies could not be everywhere at once. Experiments of sending merchant ships off unescorted and scattered met with higher losses, and were curtailed. The tragedy of convoy PQ 17 in July – when twenty-three out of thirty-three merchant ships were lost – demonstrated the difficult decisions facing those in command.

The catastrophic decision to scatter the convoy, taken by the First Sea Lord in fear of the German battleship *Tirpitz* in the offing, resulted not only in significant loss of life, ships and war materiel to marauding U-boats and dive-bombers, but also a temporary decline in the confidence of the Red Ensign in the White. Nearly 100,000 tons of supplies, and hundred of tanks and aircraft, and thousands of vehicles were lost to the Barents Sea. Two months later, PQ 18 lost 33 per cent of its ships. Hard as these losses were for the British to bear, the investment would eventually pay dividends.

The Baltic and Black Sea: Ice and Mines

Anxious to pin down Soviet submarines operating in the Baltic, once the winter ice had retreated the *Kriegsmarine* found itself unable to prevent a Soviet breakout in the spring, and suffered losses from mines laid by the Royal Air Force. More German and commandeered Swedish ships were sunk by Soviet submarines and minefields in the Gulf of Finland. Conversely, in the Black Sea, German minefields successfully warded off Soviet submarines and minesweepers attempting to interfere with supply shipping off the Bulgarian and Romanian coasts. And as the siege of Sevastopol entered its eighth month at the end of June, Hitler's summer offensive in Russia and Ukraine began. In the Crimea, the cruiser *Molotov*, six destroyers and two transports landed thousands of fresh Soviet troops into Sevastopol and fought at great cost to bring away wounded evacuees. By the first week of July, all four destroyers and both transports had been sunk from the air while the port of Novorossiysk was attacked by the Germans but saved by Soviet amphibious counterattacks. As the German offensive rolled east around the northern Black Sea shore and into the Caucasus, German air superiority made Soviet surface units very vulnerable and confined them to the eastern Black Sea ports of Tuapse, Poti and Batum as a consequence. Hitler's plan to seize the oilfields of the Caucasus – which could provide four times the quantity of oil that had been available to Germany in 1941 – came ever closer to fruition.

By August one of history's most intense sieges was under way some four hundred miles to the north east at Stalingrad. But on 19 November the Soviets launched their scything counterattack, leading to enormous blood-letting on both sides and a flattened city. The precarious Soviet situation was bolstered and the Germans were themselves surrounded, resulting in the surrender of von Paulus's decimated armies early in the new year. The Battle of Stalingrad hung over all other events of that winter simply by dint of the scale of the slaughter it involved. German and Soviet casualties numbered almost one and a half million – quite unlike anything the other belligerents ever encountered.

This was the strategic pivot of the year – Soviet Russia, at enormous cost, had stemmed the German tide on land and, buoyed by reinforcements sent via the sea, could now gather itself to the long task of ejecting the Nazi invaders and eventually deciding the outcome of war in Europe. It was the anvil upon which Hitler's *Lebensraum* dream was hammered into pieces. The Caucasian oilfields and the oil artery up the River Volga were preserved. Hitler's armies, unable to conquer the oil supplies they needed, would never make further such advances into the Soviet interior. Instead, Soviet doctrines of encirclement and deep battle would come to shatter over-stretched German armies.

The Fight for the Mediterranean Intensifies

In the Mediterranean and North African theatres, the Italians had been sidelined by the Germans, as a result of which the British army under Montgomery was firmly on the defensive. And at sea, the Italian battle fleet was able to show initiative on a par with its British opponents at the Second Battle of Sirte in March 1942. That month, British 'U' class submarines sank three Italian submarines.

The Italians revised their convoying policy in early 1942 and decided to provide each convoy with a battleship in close escort. This enabled a more secure transport of supplies to Rommel's force fighting the British Eighth Army, which would result in the German recapture of Benghazi and the fall of Tobruk, and the subsequent Axis re-invasion of Egypt.

Simultaneously, an increase in *Luftwaffe* strength in the arrival of *II Fliegerkorps* brought the fight over Malta to crisis point for the British. The Royal Navy was forced to leave the island base in April, the month of heaviest losses (four destroyers and four submarines bombed in the harbour, in dock or trying to leave), followed shortly by the submarines which redeployed to Alexandria. RAF forces on Malta comprised mainly outdated medium bombers and a few tired fighters. Forty-seven Spitfires had been flown off from the American carrier *Wasp* on 20 April, but within ten days only seven were left operational in the face of unrelenting aerial attack from Ju 87s, Ju 88s and Me 109Es. Axis supply lines were no longer hindered by Malta, and in the face of overwhelming German air superiority large British naval forces became compelled to turn back when nearing Sicily on eastbound escort duty.

The Relief of Malta

The British position in the Mediterranean was now tenuous at best, and for Malta to survive seemed an impossibility in the face of Axis preparations for amphibious and parachute invasion (involving Japanese

assistance in the early planning stages). But Hitler felt unable to trust the capabilities of the *Regia Marina*, which would have to be relied upon to keep a British attack away from the invasion transports, and was unwilling to divert resources away from the massively urgent priority of the Russian front, and secondarily from Rommel's campaigning in North Africa. Resistance on Malta was likely to be stubborn, he also calculated. This hesitancy was key.

A small number of British convoys were pushed through with mixed success. In August, the biggest Allied relief operation so far – Operation Pedestal – was launched from Gibraltar, augmented by naval units released after the PQ 17 disaster and by a reduced threat to the Indian Ocean after the American success at Midway. At the cost of a British carrier, eight other warships and nine merchant ships, a convoy of five remaining merchantmen was pushed through to Malta. Some revisionist historians have subsequently questioned whether this operation to sustain Malta – and the wider Mediterranean strategy – conducted at such cost to the Royal Navy, was worth it to the overall Allied war effort. But to the people on Malta and to Churchill, it was vital. And coming after the traumatic surrenders at Singapore and Tobruk, the loss of Malta would likely have had dire consequences to British morale, not to mention the Mediterranean military situation. In any case, the supplies Pedestal delivered enabled the island to hold out until the end of the year, by which time two more convoys had successfully arrived.

With the return of offensive British naval and air forces to Malta, pressure was renewed on Axis supply lines crossing on the north–south route from North Africa to Italian ports. Simultaneously, Axis air attacks began to decrease in numbers, ferocity and effect, with the Italians resuming the burden of the bombing and preferring to revert to higher-level tactics despite being supplied with Stukas. Never again would Malta be in such peril.

The Axis on the Retreat

The success of the Italian armies and Rommel's *Afrika Korps* were significantly affected by the aggressive patrolling of British submarines, though the British found the submarine war tough in the Mediterranean despite the Italian lack of radar; targets often hugged enemy-held shorelines and attacks in shallow, clear waters were difficult to pull off, especially in the face of local enemy air and submarine cover. But guided by Ultra intercepts, smaller 'U' and 'T' class boats and motor torpedo boats had a decisive effect upon Axis supply convoys to North Africa. Nearly five hundred merchant ships – a quarter of all Axis shipping sunk in the Mediterranean – and 169 warships would fall prey to British submarines. In 1942 these British craft helped create conditions by which the German position in North Africa was eventually rolled up and decisively defeated during 1943. The consequent loss of fuel supplies (estimated at two-thirds of its oil requirements) destined for Rommel's army helped Montgomery keep him at bay in early September 1942. Meanwhile, British supplies of tanks, munitions and troops continued to trek the long way round the Cape of Good Hope to reach Montgomery, giving him a growing material advantage over the increasingly cut-off German and Italian opposition. The Eighth Army secured victory over Rommel at the second battle of El Alamein at the beginning of November.

Freed momentarily from its convoy-covering duties, Force H went over to the offensive and looked south from its base in Gibraltar to its next employment. Coinciding with Montgomery's signal victory over Rommel at El Alamein and just as the Soviet armies began the bitter fight-back at Stalingrad, Operation Torch – the invasion of French North

Africa – was launched in Morocco by US and British forces comprising the biggest amphibious operation of the war to date. When German troops entered Toulon in November 1942, the French managed to scuttle seventy-seven of the eighty ships within the base. French naval power, trampled on by friend and foe, may have been at its lowest ebb but American and British strength was what mattered if France was ever to recover its bases and much else besides.

Unable to interfere with Torch, the *Kriegsmarine* did not have it all its own way in the Arctic. On New Year's Eve, the escorts of convoys JW 51A and JW 51B – two British 6-inch cruisers, *Sheffield* and *Jamaica* and six destroyers respectively – were confronted by a powerful German raiding force of the 'pocket battleship' *Lützow* and the heavy cruiser *Hipper* accompanied by six destroyers. Unaware of the presence of the British cruisers, the *Lützow* peeled off to investigate the incoming convoy JW 51B, while the *Hipper* and destroyers attacked the hopelessly outgunned British destroyers, which laid a smokescreen between the Germans and the convoy. The 4.7-inch armed *Onslow* was disabled and the *Achates* sunk while they battled to cover the retreating convoy JW 51B. Meanwhile the British cruisers appeared on the scene and opened fire, holing the *Hipper* below the waterline and sinking one destroyer. The Germans broke off the action and the convoy was saved. Hearing news of his ships failing to act decisively and being seen off by inferior forces, the incandescent Hitler famously ordered the scrapping of the *Kriegsmarine* surface fleet, an order he later reversed but not before Grand Admiral Raeder had been replaced by Dönitz as Commander-in-Chief of the *Kriegsmarine*.

End of the Beginning

In the spring of 1942 Hitler had been on the cusp of major victories. The British Commonwealth army fighting out of Tobruk had capitulated to Rommel; the Malta convoys were barely getting through; and Allied convoys to Russia suffered major losses, exemplified by the disaster of PQ 17. The Japanese had walked into most of East Asia and defeated American, British and Dutch naval forces along the way. But within six months of the Allied nadir in late spring, the picture now looked very different for the Axis. With Alamein, Midway and Stalingrad on the plus side of the balance sheet, the Allies moved over to the offensive. Hitler's strategy for 1942 – the conquest of the oil-filled Persian Gulf and Trans-Caucasus specifically; the quick defeat of the Soviet Union in general – remained forever unfulfilled. Hitler admitted that he did not know how to defeat the United States. Strategic initiative had passed from the Axis to the Allies.

For the Soviets, the first major victory over a massive German army showed the way towards a wider counter-offensive which would not stop until it reached the *Reichskanzlei*. The Japanese may have felt satisfaction in their swift and violent acquisition of an enormous new empire but had been shown to be materially and strategically at a growing disadvantage fighting against the USA. For the Americans, the carrier-based fight-back through the Pacific islands would be facilitated by the victories at Midway and Guadalcanal.

Throughout the year, American production had skyrocketed. Extravagant targets – 60,000 aircraft in 1942, 125,000 in 1943; 25,000 tanks in 1942, 75,000 in 1943; 20,000 AA guns up to 35,000 the following year; and most importantly, merchant shipping tonnage up from 1.1 million tons in 1941, to 6 million tons in 1942, 10 million tons in 1943 – were not only met but exceeded as the huge industrial capacity of the continental United States was harnessed and expanded.

For the British Commonwealth, which had been fighting alone for at least eighteen months by the turn of 1942, the victory at Alamein and the North African landings marked an important turning point in the war; it was, as Churchill put it, 'the end of the beginning'. American forces and strategic will increasingly became more involved in the European conflict; in the hushed back-rooms and offices, code-breakers were back in business with 'Triton'; and thanks largely to the efforts of US shipyards, Allied escort numbers climbed towards the 500-mark.

If Britain could be sustained through the climax of the U-boat onslaught then the planned Allied victory in Europe would be possible; without that, for the Allies the war would be America's burden in the oceans of the world and the Soviet Union's on land.

The US Navy in the Atlantic

Upon entry to the war, American warships assumed responsibility for anti-submarine convoying and patrolling in the western North Atlantic, joining the growing Royal Canadian Navy, which had been performing sterling service on behalf of Britain since 1940.

(opposite) USS *Memphis* in the South Atlantic
A superb view looking aft from the bow of the light cruiser *Memphis* (CL-13) underway, 1941–2. This photograph gives a very good impression of the ship's fine lines, and the unorthodox arrangement of her 6-inch guns with two in the forward turret and four more in single casemate mountings either side of the forward superstructure. This arrangement was originally duplicated aft, but two of the casemate guns were removed because the ships turned out to be overweight. Also visible here is the forward 3-inch anti-aircraft gun, behind the turret, and the rangefinders and other fire-control equipment on the tripod foremast. The crewmen are wearing the short 'Whites' popular in the tropics. *Memphis* was one of the ten *Omaha* class, and like her sister-ships served mainly in the Atlantic during the war (two that were in the Pacific, *Marblehead* and *Raleigh*, both survived serious damage from Japanese air attack, suggesting that those who criticized the original design as too lightweight were not altogether correct). In January 1943 she hosted President Roosevelt during the Casablanca conference – the ship's second brush with VIPs: back in 1927 *Memphis* had brought home Charles A. Lindbergh after his pioneering trans-Atlantic flight.

Landing Signal Officer on *Wasp*
On board the carrier USS *Wasp* (CV-7) in early 1942. The Landing Signal Officer and ensign assistants guide planes in to land. *Wasp* served in the Atlantic and Mediterranean during the first half of 1942, before being transferred to the Pacific.

Scout-bombers on USS *Ranger*
Douglas SBD 'Dauntless' scout-bombers on USS *Ranger* circa June 1942. *Ranger* was the only large US carrier to serve in the Atlantic throughout the war.

North Atlantic patrol
The wet and freezing cold at high latitudes attacked every exposed surface. Here USS *Trippe* (DD-403) is covered with ice in February 1942, after arriving at Portland, Maine. The ice had to be constantly chipped away by ships' crews, otherwise top weight increased considerably and stability was threatened.

Loading provisions
Crewmen loading the USS *PC-556* for a cruise off the Atlantic coast, 8 October 1942. This particular vessel was only five weeks old when this photograph was taken, and may well have been preparing for her maiden operational voyage. These small, 174-feet, 285-ton patrol craft were capable of 20 knots and carried one 3-inch gun and two depth-charge throwers and racks for coastal anti-submarine work. They were unable to counter the U-Boat Arm's Operation '*Paukenschlag*' in the first six months of 1942.

(opposite) Flush-deck destroyer
The US Navy retained use of seventy-one of the old flush-deck destroyers. Like those taken over by the Royal Navy, they were eventually re-armed and given up-to-date radar, and later many were converted for other tasks such as fast transports, minesweepers and seaplane carriers.

Life on board a British minesweeper, HMS *Sandown*

The 684-ton paddle steamer *Sandown* was an Isle of Wight ferry built in 1934. She was just one of many such ships requisitioned by the Admiralty in 1939 and converted into a paddle minesweeper. As such *Sandown* was typical of the thousands of small civilian vessels taken over for the countless unglamorous but essential duties of a navy at war. Based at Dover during 1940–2, she was then converted again, this time into an auxiliary anti-aircraft vessel, before being returned to her owners in 1944.

Crewmen and Spot the dog, after hosing down the decks.

Another, no doubt, much-loved ship's dog.

'In Sweeps': stowing the Otter, the kite-like device used to hold the sweep the correct distance from the ship's side.

Card game in the Mess Room, January 1942.

Cleaning Lewis guns in Dover harbour.

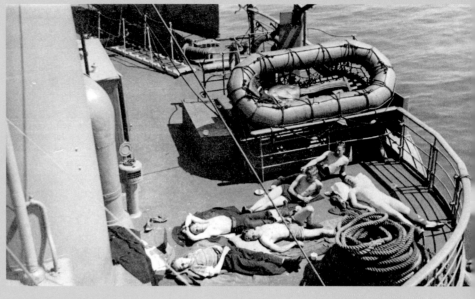

Sunbathing on deck.

IN SWEEPS

The command is given to haul in the sweeps.

Letter writing on the Mess Deck.

Operation *Zerberus*: the 'Channel Dash'

The *Scharnhorst* and *Gneisenau*, accompanied by a *Schnell-boot* (right), seen from *Prinz Eugen*, steaming up a typically grey and misty English Channel on 13 February 1942.

Three days prior to the loss of their premier Asian base at Singapore, the British had watched as the German battlecruisers *Gneisenau* and *Scharnhorst* and the heavy cruiser *Prinz Eugen* escaped from Brest and audaciously steamed in broad daylight up the English Channel and back to Cuxhaven. Three attacks were mounted, by MTBs, Swordfish and by four elderly destroyers to within 3,000 yards, but to little effect. However, both battlecruisers hit mines as they neared their destination, and while under repair *Gneisenau* was hit by RAF bombers and was so badly damaged that she never returned to service. (Some of her main guns were subsequently mounted for coastal defence in Norway, where they survive to this day.) The 'Channel Dash' was a serious embarrassment to the Royal Navy and RAF, and a dramatic propaganda success for Germany; however it was also a considerable strategic own-goal, removing at a stroke the threat of the big ships easily breaking out into the Atlantic, instead leaving them bottled-up in the Baltic.

The *Kriegsmarine* at war

Although the *Kriegsmarine*'s surface forces were never able to recover from the losses sustained during the Norwegian campaign, and the majority of resources were increasingly put into the U-boat campaign, it still had to carry out the same numerous routine tasks of a wartime navy as its bigger opponent across the North Sea. A number of warships that had belonged to the navies of captured countries were put into service to help accomplish this.

(top left) *Brummer*, former Norwegian minelayer
The minelayer *Olav Tryggvason* was captured during the German invasion of Norway in April 1940, and was employed by the *Kriegsmarine* under the names *Albatros* (1940–1) and then *Brummer* (1941–5, after the previous ship of that name had been sunk). She is seen here in the latter guise, underway during minelaying operations off a snow-bound Norwegian coast in 1942.

On 18 February 1942, *Brummer* was engaged in laying mines off Porsangen Fjord in Norway when she sighted, through thick fog, a Soviet submarine on the surface. Narrowly missing her while trying to ram, the German crew heard the submarine crew shout 'Russki!', the Soviets apparently thinking they had been attacked by a British vessel. An accompanying minesweeper then rammed the submarine, which submerged and made its escape – but not before her captain, his foot caught in the rapidly shut hatch, was left behind and rescued by the minesweeper. The *Brummer* and her ilk were frequently the target of Soviet submarines, though were rarely hit.

Depth-charge thrower
A sequence of three photographs showing depth charges being fired from a thrower on a German escort vessel. The *Kriegsmarine* had an abysmal record in anti-submarine warfare, achieving just one confirmed sinking during the war.

On board a British destroyer

A fine view looking forward from the crow's nest on the foremast of a British destroyer ('A'-'H' class) showing the layout of the open bridge (a concept favoured by the Royal Navy, because of the better view it gave, but not by most other navies), the forecastle, and 'A' and 'B' guns. A Royal Navy photograph officially dated 1942, the relatively low-tech appearance of the bridge, without the clutter of additional wartime equipment; as well as the red, white and blue air recognition roundel around the capstan, suggests an earlier date.

The ship is making slow way on a calm, sunny but not particularly warm day – the gun's crew relaxing in the sunshine next to 'B' mounting are still well wrapped up. The generally relaxed air also suggests that the ship is in a sheltered, safe stretch of water such as a harbour or anchorage. Note the assorted cables and other gear stowed, none too neatly, within the blast shield between 'A' and 'B' guns. Visible on the bridge are the compass, the pelorus (used for taking bearings), some of the many voice pipes for communicating with various parts of the ship, and the glass screen which gave a modicum of protection from the elements. Note also the rounds of ammunition stowed along the deck edges near the forward guns.

(opposite) Using a sextant

A 1942 photograph of a Royal Navy officer using a sextant, aboard one of the former American destroyers employed on convoy protection duty by the Royal Navy. This view is looking aft, and beyond the sextant can be seen one of the American 0.5-inch machine guns mounted on the roof of the ship's galley for anti-aircraft defence, surrounded by anti-splinter mats.

A Royal Navy signaller

A signaller operating an Aldis lamp on board a British warship during 1942. There were a number of different sizes of such lamps, which were operated by a shutter arranged like a Venetian blind that would open and shut to transmit Morse code. Although this might seem a rather low-tech method of signalling between ships, it had the immense advantage in that it could not be intercepted by the enemy. Signallers tended to be among the brighter or better educated seamen, for they had to become proficient in three distinct methods of signalling: by lamp; by semaphore using flags; and by use of signal flags hoisted from the masthead, and become immensely speedy and accurate in all three.

The Prime Minister and Lord Privy Seal visit the Home Fleet

An official photograph of Britain's leader for most of the war, Prime Minister Winston Churchill, with the Lord Privy Seal, Sir Stafford Cripps, and the Commander-in-Chief Home Fleet, Admiral Sir John C. Tovey, on the quarterdeck of Tovey's flagship, HMS *King George V* at Scapa Flow on 11 October 1942.

Admiral Tovey, who had a distinguished record in action from World War One, served as Commander-in-Chief of the Home Fleet during the immensely stressful years of 1940 until 1943. He then went on to serve as Commander-in-Chief Nore, as well as First and Principal Naval Aide de Camp to the King from January 1945. He was not averse to standing up to Churchill (other commanders learned to deal with him more diplomatically) and as a result their relationship was somewhat mixed. Cripps had been Solicitor-General in the second Labour government, but sat as an independent MP in the wartime coalition, serving as Ambassador to the Soviet Union during 1940–2. As Lord Privy Seal he was Leader of the House of Commons and at the time this photograph was taken had just had a major disagreement with Churchill over the overall planning of the war effort, and had in fact offered his resignation. Within a few weeks he moved to become Minister for Aircraft Production.

Anti-aircraft guns on board a battleship

An eight-barrelled 2pdr pom-pom anti-aircraft gun mounting on a battleship, possibly *King George V*. The gun layer in the further (right hand) enclosed position is looking through the fore- and back-sights. Such enclosed positions were not fitted as standard, and more often than not the entire crew mounting would be in the open, although a number of such modifications seem to have been used in various individual instances. The boxes to either side of the eight gun barrels are for the ammunition, while below the barrels can be seen the exit chutes for empty cylinders. The funnel-shaped object visible in the middle of the mounting is for cooling water for the gun barrels. In the background are two single 20mm Oerlikon mountings, again used mainly for anti-aircraft defence. Only one actually has the gun mounted.

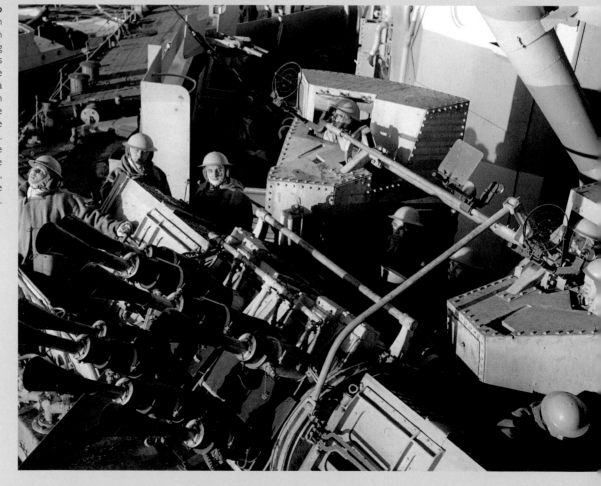

The Wrens

Women's Royal Naval Service (WRNS) units were attached to most naval shore establishments in Britain. During World War Two the Women's Royal Naval Service was expanded rapidly – from 3,400 to nearly 74,000 by the war's end. The main objective was for women to replace certain personnel in order to release men for active service in the fleet. A large number of women also served abroad in both the Middle East and the Far East. Some members of the service were employed in secret naval communications and transport flying duties.

Wren inspection
Vera Laughton Mathews inspects Wren chiefs and petty officers at the Royal Naval Barracks at Devonport in 1942. Daughter of eminent British naval historian Sir John Knox Laughton, Vera was the Director of the Women's Royal Naval Service from 1940 to 1946.

Western Approaches
Wrens working at a plotting table in Western Approaches headquarters, Liverpool.

Arctic convoys

The sea voyage to the north Russian ports of Murmansk and Archangel was the shortest route for sending Allied supplies to Russia. But it was also the most dangerous owing to the large concentration of German forces in northern Norway. The last convoy to reach Murmansk without loss, PQ 12, had arrived in early March. After this, convoys grew in size and urgency, as did German efforts to destroy them.

Convoy PQ 17

In June, the Admiralty received word that the next convoy to sail for Soviet Arctic ports would receive an all-out German assault. Despite this, on 27 June convoy PQ 17 set sail from Reykjavik, consisting of thirty-three merchantmen with a close escort and a battleship covering force giving an unprecedented seventy-seven warships in total. The covering force turned back on 1 July. On 4 July, two merchantmen were lost to air attack, and news of the German capital ships *Tirpitz*, *Scheer* and *Hipper* sortieing from Altenfjord near Tromso in Norway led to an Admiralty order to scatter the convoy. The next day, a further twelve merchantmen were lost to U-boats and air attack. The threat of the German heavy units distracted the attention of the covering and escort forces, despite the German ships never becoming involved in the action and returning to port in the evening of 5 July. Only ten merchant vessels eventually reached Archangel, guided in by Soviet destroyers.

This image shows escorts and merchant ships at Hvalfjord in May 1942 before the sailing of convoy PQ 17. Behind the destroyer *Icarus* is the Russian tanker *Azerbaijan*.

(below) Clearing snow from the flight deck of HMS *Victorious*

Men work hard to remove the snow after a storm on 24–27 March 1942 while the aircraft carrier was part of a force covering convoys to northern Russia. Beyond is the impressive bulk of the flagship, *King George V*. Note the puff of steam at the forward extremity of the flight deck – this was to indicate the direction of the wind.

(above) Witnesses to an explosion

An ammunition ship exploding, seen from on board an escort carrier on 19 October 1942. Of all the merchant cargoes most lethal to crew in the event of a torpedo or bomb strike, ammunition ranks with petroleum as the worst. The possibility of escaping a stricken ship was difficult enough in most circumstances, but the detonation of onboard munitions made the likelihood of survival terribly slim, if not impossible. Crews abandoning ship in the Arctic also had to contend with seas so cold that their survival was a matter of just minutes at most.

These pictures show aspects of life aboard a typical U-boat, on a typical war patrol, during the summer of 1942. The story of the photographs themselves, however, is far from typical.

U-564 was a Type VIIC U-boat, not only the most common class of U-boat, but the most numerous of any class of submarine ever built, some 572 being produced. Between 11 July and 19 September 1942 she sailed from Brest, where she was based as part of the 1st U-boat Flotilla, via Lorient and then across the Atlantic to operate in the Caribbean, where she sank sank five Allied merchant ships, returning home undamaged, despite depth-charge and air attacks.

Commanded by *Kapitänleutnant* Reinhard 'Teddy' Suhren, who had become one of the *Kriegsmarine*'s top U-boat 'aces' (as well as acquiring a reputation as an outspoken, almost rebellious commander), U-564 had on board forty-five officers and men. One of these was an extra to the usual U-boat crew: *Propagandakompanie Maat* Meimes Haring was a war correspondent who had been attached to the boat for the duration of the patrol to record the daily life aboard one of the 'grey wolves'. Using both cine and stills cameras, Haring did just that, for the benefit of German cinema audiences and for Goebbels' Propaganda Ministry's publications such as *Signal* and *Die Kriegsmarine*.

However, the majority of the photographs, some 561 of them, did not make it back to Germany and remained in Brest. When the port was besieged and eventually recaptured by the Allies in 1944, they were discovered and 'liberated' by a member of one of the Royal Navy teams engaged in the massive clear-up of the shattered port, taken home to Yorkshire, and then forgotten about. Unearthed again in the spring of 2000, they now reside in the safe keeping of the Royal Navy Submarine Museum in Gosport, Hampshire, providing a remarkable insight into the daily lives of a few of Germany's submariners.

U-564 did not survive the war. She was sunk with twenty-eight of her crew – including six who were serving during the patrol shown here – by British aircraft in the Bay of Biscay less than a year later. In fact, in retrospect these images represent the last days of the U-boats' 'Happy Times', before new equipment and techniques enabled the Allies to decisively gain the ascendancy in the Battle of the Atlantic. However, both Suhren and Haring did survive the war, as well as twenty-six others out of the forty-five on board at the time these photographs were taken.

Lookouts on the bridge

Four lookouts were stationed permanently when the submarine was on the surface, each being responsible for one 90-degree quadrant, and each on duty for a four-hour watch. In the centre of this view, looking aft, is the attack periscope; the spiral around its base was designed to reduce both vibration and the tell-tale wake when in use. The upright object to starboard is one of the U-boat's two machine guns, carried primarily for anti-aircraft defence. Each crewman did not have his own wet-weather gear. There were only enough for those on the bridge at any one time.

The *Funkraum* (Radio Room)

Oberfunkmaat (Radio Petty Officer) Willi Anderheyden on duty. He received and sent signals to and from headquarters, using the 'Enigma' coding machine. On the hull frame over Anderheyden's right shoulder is the voice pipe running to the U-boat's bridge, while the pad in which he is taking notes is resting on the boat's gramophone: this, together with a small radio enabled the radio room to double as U-564's entertainment centre. The main *Telefunken* Type E radio receiver can be seen above Anderheyden's left arm.

Supper in the forward torpedo compartment (*Bugraum* or bow-room)

Twelve bunks and twenty-five men were crammed into this compartment along with ten torpedoes and all their associated handling equipment. Even then it was only with the firing of torpedoes that space became available for the lowest tier of bunks to be used. There was practically no room to move about; men were only allowed a bare minimum of spare clothes, and those attempting to rest while off duty could find torpedo maintenance going on next to them.

Fresh air
Off-duty crewmen crowd the U-boat's *Wintergarten*, enjoying the sunshine as the submarine cruises on the surface out of range of Allied aircraft. Nevertheless, the lookouts continue to scan the horizon, although now dressed for rather different weather. The dreadfully cramped conditions, poor sanitation, damp and foul atmosphere of the interior of a U-boat, even when running on the surface, meant that every bit of time above decks was valuable.

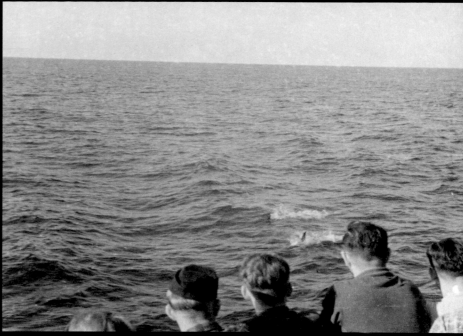

Dolphin-watching
Crewmen enjoy the company of two dolphins as *U-564* cruises on the surface.

Maintenance on the U-boat's diesel engines
Maschinenobergfreiter (Diesel Stoker) Walter Labahn and *Obermaschinist* (Diesel Chief) Hermann Kräh wrestle with a recalcitrant cylinder head that is in need of changing. The engine room was even more cramped than the rest of the boat, making all work, including photography, extremely difficult.

Preparing cakes in the petty officers' mess
The U-boat's cook, Herman Hausruckinger, helped by an off-duty Anderheyden and *Obermechanikermaat* (Torpedo Mate) Gerhard Ehlers, put the finishing touches to some cakes for a party to celebrate a successful attack on convoy OS 34, when *U-564* sank two merchantmen and survived a fearsome depth-charge attack by the escorting British warships. Such culinary events helped to keep up morale, and were possible because the U-boats always received the best quality rations.

(above) Lookout
One of *U-564*'s officers, possibly Suhren himself, scans the horizon on a tranquil Caribbean evening. Haring was clearly a talented and skilful photographer, able to compose striking and even beautiful images from the most unpromising of raw materials.

(above right) The crew of *U-564*
On her way home after a successful patrol, *U-564* received news that Suhren had been awarded the Oak Leaves with Swords to the Knight's Cross (the second highest German military honour), and promotion to *Korvettenkapitän*. Haring extensively recorded the event for posterity and Suhren (centre) made sure that as many as possible of his men were able to appear in the posed group shots. Somewhat remarkably, this appears to be all but five of the crew; the others being presumably Haring himself and the four bridge lookouts.

(right) Gunnery practice with *U-564*'s 8.8cm deck gun
The ammunition had to be brought up from below manually, through the conning tower, and from there delivered to the foredeck via a chute, which can be seen with a shell sitting in it on the left-hand side of the picture. The crewmen standing-by with ammunition ready to load into the breech of the gun include Herman Hausruckinger, the cook – multi-tasking was commonplace among a U-boat's crew. The cable dangling from the gun barrel was attached to the water-tight tampion, which was used to keep the sea out of the barrel when the gun was not in use.

U-boats at Kiel

Type VIID U-boat *U-218*, together with *U-226* and *U-227*, on 17 August 1942, at Krupp's Germania Werft shipyard, Kiel, where all three were built. The latter two boats had only been launched in June and July respectively and were still fitting out. Both were lost the following year, with all hands. *U-218*, on the other hand, having been commissioned at the start of 1942, survived the war, although she didn't have a particularly successful career, laying mines that were responsible for the sinking of just three small vessels while being damaged three times herself. However, she did have one unique claim to fame: one of her victims, the fishing vessel *Kned*, sunk on 10 July 1945 by a mine laid off the Lizard, was the last British ship to be lost to enemy action during the war. Like many of the U-boats at the end of the war, *U-218* was to be sunk as part of Operation 'Deadlight', but instead she foundered under tow to her designated sinking area.

The huge steel and glass hangar over the building slips, which dominates this photograph, had been part of Krupp's investment in the yard at the beginning of the twentieth century, allowing work to continue in all weathers, a precursor to the covered shipbuilding facilities of the modern era. Allied bombing during the war removed most of the glass, but by that time the need for U-boats was such that they were being built in the open anyway. Germania Werft built over a hundred U-boats between 1935 and 1945, yet was one of the smaller builders of these vessels. Alongside the quay in the background is the cruiser *Prinz Eugen*, which had been forced to return to Kiel in May for repairs after having her stern nearly severed by a torpedo from the British submarine *Trident* off Trondheim on 22 February.

On board a Royal Navy destroyer in northern waters
An official photograph, dated 15 March 1942, captioned: 'A destroyer receives the
signal saying an enemy air attack can be expected. Gun crews are standing by their
guns watching and waiting.' The ship is probably a 'Tribal' class destroyer, but beyond
that the salient impression, from the manner of dress of the men around the guns –
well wrapped up but with not a tin helmet in sight – is that they are rather more
concerned about the cold than being attacked. This suggests that the ship is serving
somewhere in northern waters.

Survivors of the *Laconia*

Survivors of the torpedoed liner *Laconia* cling to an upturned lifeboat just prior to being rescued. In an incident that was long kept secret the *Laconia*, serving as a troopship but also carrying Italian prisoners of war, was torpedoed by *U-156* on 12 September 1942 off west Africa. Realizing this, the U-boat's commander, Werner Hartenstein, signalled in plain language for help in rescuing as many as he could, resulting in other U-boats as well as Vichy French warships coming to his aid. Tragically an American aircraft also arrived and attacked *U-156*, resulting in the breaking off of the rescue. Although over 1,000 lives were saved, 1,600 more were not.

Ships of the Home Fleet guarding the northern trade routes

Taken from the destroyer HMS *Wheatland* in Icelandic waters, en-route to Scapa Flow, 26–29 May 1942, the photograph shows the 'Hunt' class destroyers *Middleton*, *Lamerton* and *Blankney* in line ahead rolling through choppy seas. For most of the participants in the war at sea, this is what it was like much of the time.

The Second Battle of Sirte

The Italian battle fleet was able to show initiative on a par with its British opponents at the Second Battle of Sirte on 22 March 1942. The battleship *Littorio*, supported by three cruisers, inflicted damage to a British force of four *Dido* class cruisers and 'Tribal' destroyers protecting a small convoy heading for Malta from Alexandria. Pressing home the attack despite British smoke screens and evasive action, and suffering from excessive salvo-spread, the *Littorio*'s main armament found its mark among the British destroyers. Delayed by the battle, upon finally reaching Malta the British transport ships were sunk by air attack and one destroyer was lost to a mine.

Admiral Vian's British cruisers in action against the Italian battle fleet. HMS *Cleopatra* throws out smoke (dark from her own boilers, white from a smoke float dropped astern) to shield the convoy as HMS *Euryalus* elevates her forward 5.25-inch guns to shell the Italian fleet.

Salvaging *Breconshire*

Three photographs taken in August 1942, showing salvage work taking place on the wreck of the *Breconshire*, one of the British supply ships sunk by bombing after the Battle of Sirte. The diver is salvaging cases of goods from the sunken ship, which is lying on its side. The men supporting the diver are in fact perched on an AA gun, now lying parallel with the surface of the sea. The salvage parties worked on the side of the hull, the items retreived being taken ashore in small boats. Oil was also pumped from the ship into drums and then taken ashore in harbour craft.

Italian operations in the Mediterranean

In contrast to the Royal Navy's travails in attempting to continue running supplies into Malta, in the early months of 1942 the Italian Navy was able to escort substantial convoys to North Africa, reinforcing Rommel for his next offensive. Rommel was able, by the end of the month, to occupy Benghazi.

The cruiser *Montecuccoli*
Like all Italian cruisers the *Montecuccoli* was very fast, but unlike most of the others, she survived the war. In 1952 she visited London, the first Italian warship to visit Britain since before the war. She is photographed here from on board the *Duca d'Aosta* in April 1942.

Firing practice
Anti-torpedo-bomber firing practice onboard the cruiser *Montecuccoli*, 1942. Note the fingers in ears!

Launching a new anti-submarine motor launch
The launch of the *VAS-225* at the Celli yard, Venice, 5 March 1942. Note the blessing.

Italian torpedo boat *Lince*, at Piraeus, Greece
Built as a result of a clause in the Washington Naval Treaty which permitted unlimited building of ships below 600 tons displacement, *Lince* was one of the 'Spica' class of warships closer in size and role to destroyer escorts; their principal prey were submarines. The same month as this photograph was taken in August 1942, the British submarine *Porpoise* was attacked and damaged by the *Lince* off Derna, Libya. A year later, *Lince* was sunk by the British 'U' class submarine *Ultor* in the Gulf of Taranto.

Pearl Harbor, March 1942

If any evidence was needed of the tactical blunder of not launching a second attack on Pearl Harbor and of concentrating on the port facilities rather than the ships, these photographs taken at the base less than four months later would have amply provided it. Already most of the damaged ships had been sufficiently patched up to make their way back to the mainland United States for full repairs, and even the first of those sunk were afloat again. But what makes these scenes particularly telling is that they not only show major work being carried out on a ship that was not one of the victims of the Japanese attack, but major work that had already been planned and was being done as part of a routine programme. It was business as usual at Pearl Harbor, and America was already flexing the vast industrial muscle that would soon begin to crush Japan.

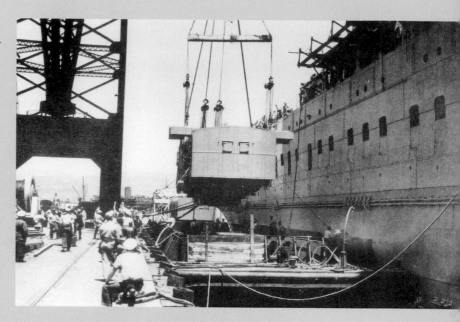

USS *Lexington*

The ship shown in these photographs is the aircraft carrier *Lexington*, one of the ships that had the good fortune to be at sea that fateful December Sunday. The work being carried out is the removal of her eight 8-inch guns in twin mounts. These had been part of *Lexington*'s equipment since she first entered service – like other fleets, the United States Navy had originally envisaged its aircraft carriers possibly having to defend themselves against surface attack. As carrier doctrine developed during the 1930s this view had become less and less fashionable (the Royal Navy being the first to effectively recognize this, replacing HMS *Furious*'s original surface armament with dual-purpose guns in 1939),

and by the middle of 1941 the decision had been taken to replace *Lexington*'s 8-inch guns (and those of her sister *Saratoga*) with new 5-inch dual-purpose weapons.

Both photographs were taken on 30 March 1942. They show 8-inch mount No. 3, having being rigged for removal from its position to the rear of the funnel, being lowered into a transport barge alongside. With fear of invasion of the Hawaiian islands understandably high, the guns were utilized as coast defence batteries. In the event, *Lexington* never got her new armament, being sunk in the Battle of the Coral Sea a little over a month later. The 8-inch guns were never called on to repel invasion either, and were taken out of service and scrapped after the war.

The Battle of the Coral Sea

Haphazard aerial reconnaissance and over-zealous reporting led to confusion and mis-targeting, and both fleets failed to locate each others' main forces for almost an entire day on 6 May 1942; the Americans thought they had hit one of the main Japanese fleet carriers but had instead sunk a light carrier from the Covering Group, the *Shoho*. The main Japanese strike was mistakenly launched against the American oiler *Neosho* and her escorting destroyer, both of which were sunk; a second strike was attempted in the late evening against the US carriers, only to be repulsed with heavy losses by American fighters supported by radar aboard the *Lexington*. Confusion reigned: some Japanese aviators mistook US carriers for their own and American anti-aircraft fire was accidentally aimed at US planes.

US Navy torpedo planes attack the Japanese light carrier *Shoho* during the Battle of the Coral Sea on 6 May 1942. At least four aircraft can be seen in this photograph.

Death of the USS *Lexington*

Converted from the hulls of unfinished battlecruisers and permitted by clauses in the 1922 Washington Treaty to exceed the tonnage limitations applied on new carriers, the *Lexington* (CV-2) and her sister *Saratoga* (CV-3) were the 'super-carriers' of their day. At the Battle of the Coral Sea, the *Lexington*, less able than the accompanying *Yorktown* to take evasive action and having mis-co-ordinated her Combat Air Patrol, suffered hits by three bombs and two torpedoes. Fires were not entirely brought under control and two large internal explosions in the following hours prompted her crew to abandon ship, whereupon she was sunk by an escorting destroyer.

(below) USS *Morris* goes to *Lexington*'s aid
Photographed from on board an accompanying cruiser (probably USS *Minneapolis*), *Morris* and another destroyer are seen alongside, taking off the carrier's crew.

(above) Abandoning ship
Crew gathering on Lexington's flight deck in preparation to abandon ship on 8 May 1942.

(above) Climbing to safety
Survivors climb aboard another vessel. The rescue effort
was superbly carried out, and although 216 men lost their
lives aboard the *Lexington*, 2,735 were rescued.

(left) Smoke and debris as the carrier explodes
Lexington explodes as the fires reach the aviation gasoline
storage. She was the first large carrier to be sunk in the
Pacific, but over the next three years sights like this would
be seen time and time again by men serving in the US and
Japanese Navies.

The Battle of Midway

The Japanese Navy expected its picket line of submarines outside Pearl Harbor to give Admiral Nagumo plenty of advanced warning of an American sortie. Adherence to radio silence meant that Admiral Yamamoto – at sea in the battleship *Yamato* – was unable to give instructions to Nagumo of what to do in the event of encountering American carriers. The Japanese had to wait an hour for the confirmation that at least one of the ships was a carrier. During this time, Nagumo's carriers came under attack from Midway-based aircraft, but sustained no hits and beat off much of the attack using the Zero fighter cover. US Navy dive-bombers fared better, sinking four Japanese carriers.

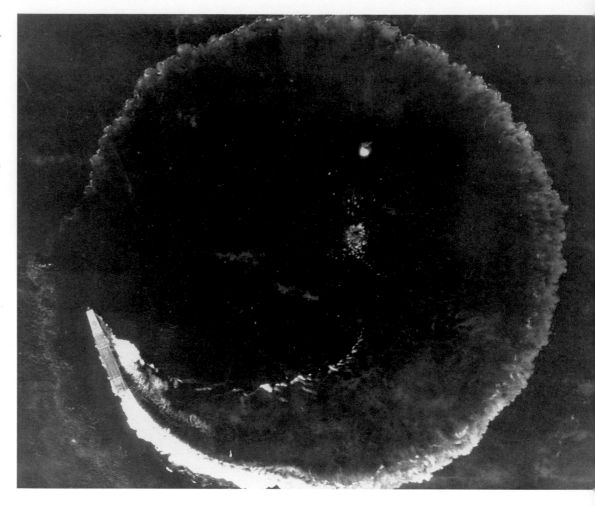

***Soryu* takes evasive action**
Soryu, of Carrier Division 2, circles while under high-level bombing attack by USAAF B-17 bombers from the Midway base, shortly after 8 a.m. on 4 June 1942. This attack produced near misses, but no hits.

Destruction from the air
One of the iconic photographs of the war at sea. The Japanese heavy cruiser *Mikuma*, photographed from an SBD aircraft during the afternoon of 6 June 1942, after she had been bombed by planes from *Enterprise* (CV-6) and *Hornet* (CV-8). Note her shattered midships structure, the surviving crew members huddled on her stern, and wreckage atop her number four 8-inch gun turret.

Japanese prisoners of war under guard on Midway
The survivors of the sunken aircraft carrier *Hiryu* were rescued from an open lifeboat by USS *Ballard* (AVD-10) on 19 June 1942. After being held for a few days on Midway, they were transferred to Pearl Harbor on 23 June aboard USS *Sirius* (AK-15), arriving there on 1 July. Note the marine guard in the centre background, armed with a M1903 'Springfield' rifle.

Sand Island pier, Midway
The heavy cruiser USS *Pensacola* (CA-24) alongside the Sand Island pier, disembarking Marine reinforcements for the island on 25 June 1942. In the foreground can be seen the damaged tail of a TBF-1 Avenger (Bureau # 00380), the only survivor of six Torpedo Squadron Eight (VT-8) TBFs that attacked Nagumo's carriers on 4 June 1942. No hits were scored in this, the Avenger's first combat mission of the war – not an auspicious start for an aircraft that was to end up with an outstanding record in action. The ship in the right distance is probably USS *Ballard* (AVD-10).

HMS *Mauritius* and RMS *Queen Mary*

A view taken on board HMS *Mauritius*, a 'Colony' class cruiser, at sea in August 1942 escorting the famous Cunard White Star liner RMS *Queen Mary*, by then being used as a troop ship. On 28 August the cruiser visited the island after which she was named.

In the left foreground is one of the cranes used for handling *Mauritius*'s seaplanes and ship's boats, with the barrels of one of the 4-inch twin mounts that comprised the cruiser's secondary armament projecting beyond this. The boats can be seen in between the funnel and mainmast, while in the bottom right-hand corner the tailplane and port wing tips of one of the ship's Supermarine Walrus seaplanes are visible. At the base of the funnel are two Carley floats, items that had been in use with the Royal Navy since 1915 and which, with the growth of wartime ships' complements became largely ubiquitous. As life-saving equipment the Carley float was useful in that many could be carried, stowed more or less anywhere on a ship, but beyond this it provided only the most basic means to effect its purpose: it kept men afloat, but not much more. Note how the ship's Admiralty Disruptive paint scheme is different each side – evident from the obvious 'break' on the centre line of the funnel.

The *Queen Mary* had been requisitioned from her owners in March 1940 and during the course of the war steamed some 650,000 miles, carrying close to one million soldiers. On one voyage in 1943 she carried, in addition to her 943 crew, some 15,740 troops, making a total of 16,683 souls on board, a record which seems unlikely to be broken.

Only two months after this photograph was taken a different escorting cruiser, HMS *Curacoa*, was accidentally rammed and sunk by *Queen Mary* off the west coast of Scotland. Loaded with troops, the liner could not afford to stop, and so three quarters of the cruiser's crew were drowned.

On board HM Submarine *Tribune*

These photographs are part of a series of some seventy which were all taken by Jack Bryson, an official photographer for the Ministry of Information, during the filming of *Close Quarters* in 1942. Their purpose was as publicity stills for the feature film, which detailed a routine British submarine patrol in the North Sea and off the coast of Norway, and was made using 'officers and men of His Majesty's submarines'. While many of the photographs are clearly posed, all give a good impression of the claustrophobic conditions on board all submarines, as well as the somewhat informal manner of dress adopted (even though all present were doubtless tidied up for filming).

(right) HMS *Tribune* at Holy Loch
Tribune lying alongside the submarine depot ship HMS *Forth* at Holy Loch, Scotland in the dawn light.

(below) Stowing a torpedo
A Chief Petty Officer and a Torpedo Instructor supervise the stowing of a torpedo. The 'T'-class submarines carried 16 Mk.VIII 21-inch torpedoes, and with these weighing about 1½ tons each, as well as having an 800-pound high explosive warhead, correct stowing was vital, especially since, when on patrol, up to a dozen members of the submarine's crew lived in the same compartment.

The engine room
General view of the interior of the engine room on board HMS *Tribune*.

(right) Checking the depth gauge
The Second Coxswain of HMS *Tribune*, Petty Officer Hedley Charles Woodley at his diving station on the forward hydroplanes. The depth gauge in the picture shows that the submarine is on the surface, a clear indication that this photograph was posed during shooting of the film.

(left) Forward periscope
Lieutenant R. Bulkeley at the forward periscope of *Tribune*, with a stoker working the periscope operating handle, and an Engine Room Artificer responsible for the diving operation.

HMS _Tribune_ running on the surface in Scottish waters
This is a wonderfully atmospheric view looking aft from the
conning tower of _Tribune_. The prominent triangular object is
the submarine's High Frequency Direction Finder (HF/DF,
nicknamed 'Huff-Duff') for intercepting radio signals.

'O' class submarine
The other photographs on these pages are part of the
same series by Jack Bryson showing other submarines in
Holy Loch. This is possibly HMS _Otway_, leaving the depot
ship HMS _Forth_.

Loading stores

Three submarines load stores alongside the depot ship HMS *Forth*. *Sibyl* is the inboard boat, with *P614* alongside. Kit-bags and hammocks on the casing indicate that *Sibyl* had probably come from another port in Britain since kit-bags were not carried on patrol.

Transferring a torpedo

Transferring a practice torpedo from HMS *Forth* to the submarine *P311*. HMS *Sibyl* (*P217*) is seen alongside and another submarine is seen in the background.

Operation Harpoon

As spring 1942 gave way to summer, and as shipping losses mounted simultaneously in the Atlantic, the British supply situation to Malta became critical. If Malta could not be sustained, with the Royal Navy chased away from the island, its garrison would be easy prey for a German invasion and North Africa would fall to the Axis. A series of crucial relief convoys was put in motion. In June, Operation Harpoon saw six merchant ships, escorted by five destroyers and covered by two carriers and a battleship, sail from Gibraltar to Malta. Four merchant ships and two destroyers were sunk by Italian cruisers and air attack. Simultaneously, a British eleven-ship convoy from the Middle East, escorted by light cruisers and codenamed Operation Vigorous, was beaten back by an Italian battle fleet and by intense Axis air attack, E-boats and a U-boat. Two merchantmen, a cruiser and three destroyers were lost and nothing at all reached Malta except more bad news.

A deceptively peaceful scene in Grand Harbour, Malta, early on the morning of 16 June 1942, the aftermath of Operation Harpoon. A motor launch heads down the harbour, while a damaged destroyer, down by the bows, is being helped into Dockyard Creek by a tug. This is almost certainly *Badsworth*, which had struck a mine off the island during the small hours as the convoy approached. In the foreground lies *Ithuriel*, with *Blankney* coming slowly up to port, while the destroyer in the distance is probably *Marne*.

These latter three, plus *Middleton*, were the only destroyers left seaworthy out of the convoy's escort. The crews of all were in the last stages of exhaustion. Of the six merchantmen that set out from Gibraltar, only two made it into Malta – a pitiful quantity of supplies compared to the losses suffered to deliver them. This was the time of the island's supreme trial. (In a graphic example of the unending, constantly changing demands placed on the ships of the Royal Navy and their crews, less than a month

earlier *Blankney* and *Middleton* had been in climes that could hardly be more different, ploughing through the mountainous North Atlantic.) The forlorn looking wreck lying off the bomb-damaged wharf in the foreground is all that remains of another destroyer, HMS *Gallant*, which had had her bows blown off by a mine off Pantelleria in January 1941, was towed stern first into Malta, but then further damaged in a bombing raid in April 1942. Beyond repair, she was later sunk as a blockship.

(right) Benito Mussolini on the cruiser *Montecuccoli*
Mussolini goes onboard the cruiser which docked at Naples following the action off Pantelleria in June 1942 that successfully attacked the ships of Operation Harpoon.

(left) Battle honours
Mussolini pins the *Medaglia d'Argento* to the uniform of Lt Cdr Fabio Tani in a ceremony ashore. Behind the *il Duce* is Admiral Riccardi.

(below) Naples
The destroyers (from left to right) *Malocello*, *Oriani*, *Ascari* and *Eugenio di Savoia*, which also took part in the action, at the quayside during the ceremony.

HMS *Phoebe*

HMS *Phoebe* was typical of the hard-worked cruisers of the Royal Navy, and saw extensive service in the Atlantic and Mediterranean. Completed in September 1940, she was twice torpedoed, in August 1941 and October 1942, both times going to the Brooklyn Navy Yard for repair. *Phoebe* was sold for scrapping in 1956.

(above) A mess deck on HMS *Phoebe*
Phoebe was typical of the hard-worked cruisers of the Royal Navy, and saw extensive service in the Mediterranean and Atlantic. Completed in September 1940, she was twice torpedoed, in August 1941 and October 1942, both times going to the Brooklyn Navy Yard for repair. She was sold for scrap in 1956.

(above left) Royal passage
Phoebe conveys HRH King George VI and Queen Elizabeth on a Royal visit to Northern Ireland in 1942. The King took a keen interest in naval matters on all levels.

Operation Pedestal

Two battleships, three carriers, seven cruisers, thirty-two destroyers and eight submarines were mustered to protect just fourteen merchantmen and their 85,000 tons of desperately crucial cargoes sailing from the Clyde to Malta. The convoy met with submarine, air and motor-torpedo-boat attacks along almost the entire length of its route. Of the carriers involved in Operation Pedestal, one, *Eagle*, was sunk by *U-73* on 11 August, along with nine of the mixed escort of cruisers and destroyers and nine of the convoy. Just five surviving merchantmen, including the urgently needed American-owned and British-crewed tanker *Ohio*, herself hit by an Italian torpedo and two German dive-bombers, limped into Grand Harbour, Valletta with 32,000 tons of supplies intact. This was a hugely risky and expensive re-supply operation which could easily have seen the convoy wiped out, and indicates how important a fighting presence in the Mediterranean was to the Royal Navy.

(right) HMS *Phoebe*
The forecastle of the cruiser *Phoebe* during Operation Pedestal.

(below) HMS *Eagle*
The aircraft carrier *Eagle* escorted by a destroyer during the preparatory stages of Operation Pedestal.

HMS *Indomitable*

Crewmen dispersing on the flight deck in relaxed mood early on in Operation Pedestal. Quite apart from the large numbers of sailors milling about, including members of a band, there are a number of other indicators that flying operations have not been taking place, nor are imminent. The radio masts along the sides of the deck are in the raised position – for flying operations they were lowered to the horizontal (as shown in later photographs). There are no arrester wires rigged, though the 'bowsprings' that held them clear of the flight deck for an aircraft's arrester hooks to engage can be seen just outboard of the hatched lines on the deck. Near the stern are half a dozen spare wing sections, presumably detached for maintenance, while in the foreground are two of the starboard crash barrier stanchions, lying on top of which are the heavy wire barriers, which could be rigged during landing to prevent aircraft from overshooting and running on into any parked on the forward part of the deck. This photograph was probably taken on 10 August 1942, the convoy having passed through the Straits of Gibraltar during the night, for by the next day it was being shadowed by Axis aircraft.

Sea Hurricanes on board HMS *Victorious* during Operation Pedestal

This photograph is dated 22 August 1942, which must be incorrect for the simple reason that HMS *Eagle* is in the background. It is more likely that it was taken at around the same time as the other photographs in this section, 10-11 August. The aircraft fitted to an outrigger in the foreground is Sea Hurricane 1B V7506 (7T) of 885 Squadron. (This squadron left *Victorious* on 21 August, confirming the mis-dating of the print.)

Early on the afternoon of 11 August, *U-73*, having slipped through the convoy's screen, put four torpedoes into *Eagle*'s port side, sinking the ship in just eight minutes. Fortunately, some four fifths of the crew were saved. Four of her Sea Hurricanes, in the air at the time, managed to land on other British carriers.

Preparations on HMS *Indomitable*

HMS *Eagle* seen from the flight deck of HMS *Indomitable*, sailing through a brilliant sun-lit western Mediterranean. The scene is still fairly relaxed, but signs of the battle to come are clear, with aircraft now on the deck of both carriers, arrestor wires rigged, and radio masts lowered. On board *Indomitable* is an intriguing mix of aircraft: there is a Sea Hurricane IB of 880 Squadron in the foreground, with Albacores belonging to 831 or 796 or possibly 827 Squadron, what appears to be a Martlet (possibly 806 Squadron) on the after lift, and a slightly out-of-place Swordfish at the starboard side of the flight deck. This photograph was taken on either 10 or 11 August. The Hawker Sea Hurricane IB was the Fleet Air Arm's first British single-seat fighter monoplane, and was basically a standard Hurricane but fitted with a V-frame arrester hook: unlike purpose-built carrier aircraft it did not have folding wings.

Fairey Albacores

Photographed through the struts of another aircraft, four Fairey Albacores are on anti-submarine patrol, protecting the convoy, 10–12 August 1942.

Indomitable is struck

On 12 August *Indomitable* was hit three times by dive-bombers, and although her armoured flight deck saved her from fatal damage, she was put out of action until March the following year.

(below) Ohio reaches Malta

One of the epic sea stories of the war reaches its conclusion as the last ship of Pedestal, the crippled tanker *Ohio*, slowly approaches Valletta, Malta, on 15 August 1942. The destroyer *Bramham* lies alongside to port, *Ohio*'s structure having been so weakened by repeated bomb and torpedo attacks that she is incapable of steaming on her own and needs a destroyer lashed on either side to support her – to starboard, mostly hidden by the tanker's superstructure, is *Penn*. Fenders hung between the ships prevented them from causing too much additional damage to one another as they moved slowly forward. Two more destroyers, other tugs and motor launches are in attendance. Only when *Ohio* was safely within Grand Harbour did the two destroyers hand her over to the tugs. This photograph was taken from another ship of the escort, possibly the destroyer *Ledbury*, which played a major part in *Ohio*'s survival. The exhaustion of the men in the foreground is evident (and understandable), most having been in action continuously for three days or more.

(opposite) Malta convoy
A peaceful view of a Malta-bound convoy and escort at sunset as seen from HMS *Euryalus*, one of the escorting warships, later in the year on 4 December.

Maltese watching *Ohio* and the destroyers arriving in the harbour
With the arrival of 10,000 tons of fuel oil to Malta, Operation Pedestal was a great strategic success. The British U-class submarines of the 10th Submarine Flotilla returned to Malta the following month, and more fighter aircraft arrived. Pressure on Axis supply lines, principally through Allied submarine and air attack on tankers and warships (all losses that Italy could hardly afford to replace), could be maintained through what was the decisive phase of the struggle for North Africa.

Survivors from Operation Pedestal
Survivors disembark from the destroyer *Ledbury* at Grand Harbour, Malta.

America goes on the offensive

Victory at Midway paved the way for the first American counter-attack against Japanese-occupied islands, meeting stiff ground and naval resistance. The Americans landed Marines at Guadalcanal in the Solomon Islands on 7 August. The next night, disaster struck as a joint American-Australian cruiser force was annihilated by Japanese cruisers near Savo Island, with four sunk and one damaged.

USS Quincy

Photographed from USS *Wasp* (CV-7) on the eve of the invasion of Guadalcanal at Noumea, New Caledonia, *Quincy* (CA-39) was one of the cruisers sunk during the Battle of Savo Island. Note *Quincy*'s signal flags and Measure 12, Modified, camouflage scheme.

(below) HMAS Canberra

The *Kent*-class Australian heavy cruiser is photographed on fire near Tulagi Island, in the southern Solomons during Operation Watchtower. An unidentified destroyer has pulled alongside to remove the crew. During the early hours of 9 August, while on patrol off Guadalcanal, she had been badly damaged in combat with a force of Japanese cruisers. *Canberra* was scuttled several hours later. Photograph taken from USS *Chicago* (CA-29).

(opposite) Ship's band

Members of a ship's band play on deck aboard a US Navy cruiser during 1942. Note the number of pegs deemed necessary to keep the sheet music in place.

(opposite) The Battle of the Eastern Solomons
Within two weeks of the US landings on Guadalcanal, American and Japanese carriers fought the Battle of the Eastern Solomons. This incredible photograph of an exploding Japanese bomb aboard USS *Enterprise* killed the photographer who took it, Robert Frederick Read, on 24 August 1942.

(left) Damage to USS *Enterprise*
This photograph shows the damage sustained to the starboard quarter gallery of USS *Enterprise*, received from a bomb hit during the Battle of the Eastern Solomons.

(below) Wreck of Japanese cargo ship
This photograph of the *Kinugawa Maru*, beached on the Guadalcanal shore, was taken in November 1943. She had been sunk by US aircraft on 15 November 1942, while attempting to deliver men and supplies to Japanese forces holding the northern part of the island. Savo Island is in the distance.

The Soviet Navy during 1942

Throughout 1942 the Soviet Navy continued to provide support for the army, and in particular for the defenders of Leningrad and Sevastopol. But with the German advance stalling against these stoutly defended cities, they were also able to go onto the offensive, in particular against coastal shipping, not only in the Baltic and Black Seas, but in the Arctic too.

The cruiser *Kirov* after a bomb hit at Leningrad
On 4 April 1942 *Kirov* was hit by a bomb and suffered no fewer than ten near misses, while twenty days later she was struck by two more bombs, necessitating repairs which kept the ship out of action until 1943. Intermittently, the *Luftwaffe* had a serious effect on Soviet surface operations.

The destroyer leader *Tashkent* enters Sevastopol
In June 1942 the final German-Romanian attack on Sevastopol was launched, and the Soviet Black Sea Fleet was kept busy carrying reinforcements into the fortress port and taking the wounded out, all the while providing fire support. It lost three destroyers and many smaller vessels to air attack. Axis midget submarines and MTBs compounded the difficulties facing the Soviets in Sevastopol harbour. On 27 June the last large Soviet warship to enter the beleaguered port, the destroyer leader *Tashkent*, brought 944 men into the fortress and evacuated 2,300 wounded and civilians, all the while under intense air attack. Shipping nearly 2,000 tons of water through bomb damage and near-misses, she had to be towed to Novorossiysk where she settled on the shallow bottom. She was destroyed by bombs five days later.

Submarine *D-4* alongside *Tashkent*
The old submarine *D-4* alongside *Tashkent* during resupply of Sevastopol in 1942. Built after World War One, *D-4* was the first Soviet submarine built specifically for the Black Sea, but the design suffered from many faults and was unsuccessful. She was sunk by German forces off Yevpatoria the following year.

Submarine *Shch-212* at Poti

The submarine is shown here heading out on a combat sortie. In the background is the battleship *Parizhskaya Kommuna*. By autumn 1942 the bulk of the Soviet Black Sea Fleet was forced to concentrate at Poti and Batumi as more and more of its bases were overrun by the German army. Poti became crucial in the resupply of another base, Tuapse; submarines harried German coastal shipping from the Bosporus up to the Crimea, and cruisers and destroyers carried 45,000 men to the defence of Tuapse by mid-October. Tuapse was saved.

(right) Submarine *Shch-421*

Sitting down on the far right is the commander of the submarine, *Kapitan-Leitenant* A. F. Vidyaev. When an Allied convoy passed the North Cape, four or five Soviet submarines would get into position between the inbound convoy and the Norwegian coast, waiting for the convoy to pass before turning into the coast to harry Axis shipping. After PQ 13 and QP 9 had run in the last week of March 1942, *Shch-421* was engaged in this way when she ran into a fresh German minefield laid in Tana Fjord. Severely damaged, her crew transferred to submarine *K-22* and she was scuttled.

(left) Soviet minesweeper

On board a Soviet minesweeper of the 'Tral' class, looking aft, in wet weather.

HMS *Formidable* during Operation Torch

Originally conceived as a joint Anglo-US operation of 90,000 troops from each army to go ahead in spring 1942, in fact the operation went ahead in November with mostly American forces, despite strong dissent in the US high command about the value of the 'soft underbelly' strategy. Joined by several British assault and supply convoys from British waters, an American army in over a hundred ships traversed the Atlantic from Norfolk, Virginia, heading for Casablanca in Morocco. The whole force arrived without loss – a sign of the growing efficacy of anti-submarine tactics, technology and intelligence. This was the most ambitious and largest amphibious landing of the war thus far. The Americans also brought with them a well-developed publicity machine. When the Americans landed in North Africa, there were twenty-two foreign correspondents and photographers in Algiers. Within nine months there were 150. A French squadron in Casablanca harbour, including the powerful but immobile battleship *Jean Bart*, and the cruiser *Primaguet*, and local shore batteries, put up resistance but were eventually silenced and a cease-fire was agreed. Algiers was captured, though Oran proved more stubborn. Throughout, Axis submarine attacks on supply convoys were sustained but avenged with a number of counter-sinkings informed by 'Ultra' intelligence.

Observing operations

In these photographs, Royal Naval officers, including Captain A. G. Talbot of *Formidable*, and men observe operations through binoculars.

Preparing for take-off

Grumman Martlet IIs or IVs of 888 Squadron and Supermarine Seafires (either Ibs or IIcs) of 885 Squadron ranged ready for take-off on the flight deck of HMS *Formidable* during operations in support of Operation Torch. The Martlet (the British name for the American Wildcat) had a habit of behaving rather unpredictably on take-off and landing, resulting in plenty of spectators, such as those in the foreground of the photograph, whenever there were flight deck-operations involving these aircraft. Note also the way that the carrier's camouflage paint scheme has been carried over the flight deck.

Bombing up a Fairey Albacore

Flight attendants secure the torpedoes on a Fairey Albacore I of 820 Squadron on the flight deck of *Formidable*, November 1942. Basically a torpedo aircraft, the Albacore was used to provide close support for the landings and to bomb airfields.

Severe bomb damage to the stern of HMS *Delhi*
The anti-aircraft cruiser suffered bomb damage in Algiers Bay during mopping-up operations in December 1942 during the aftermath of Operation Torch. Note the men standing on the lower deck of the cruiser.

The cruiser *Dupleix*
Although the Germans managed to get the sea cocks closed to prevent her sinking, the sabotage measures were so thorough that everything – magazines, torpedoes, etc. – went up, rendering the ship a complete wreck. The explosions were so violent there were a number of casualties on the quayside, and the ship burned for twenty days.

Toulon

In World War Two the greatest number of ships to be destroyed in one single action occurred in the early morning of 27 November 1942 at the French naval base and arsenal of Toulon, when the French Navy fulfilled the promise made two and a half years previously not to let its ships fall into German or Italian hands.

This dramatic event had been prompted by the Allied invasion of Algeria and Morocco earlier in the month. The German high command, fearful that this could lead in turn to a landing in the Vichy-controlled southern half of France, resolved to occupy the area. While this was taking place, unopposed by the Vichy regime, which recognized that to do so would have been futile, there was much deliberation as to whether or not to attempt to seize the powerful French fleet (which included most of the ships which escaped from Mers el-Kebir) at Toulon. By the time the decision had been made to carry this out the French had taken matters into their own hands, and prepared all the ships for scuttling.

As soon as the German forces began to advance on the port the order was given to scuttle, and in the space of just a few hours over eighty ships were sunk at their moorings or blown up by their crews. The German operation was an almost complete failure, with just a handful of vessels left afloat and operational. Five submarines managed to escape from the harbour: of these one was then scuttled by its crew just outside; one was interned in Spain; and three, *Casabianca*, *Glorieux*, and *Marsouin*, eventually made it to North Africa to be greeted by a rapturous reception and to join the Allies. In all, three battleships, seven cruisers, a seaplane carrier, thirty-four destroyers and escorts, twelve submarines and fifty-seven other vessels were destroyed or put out of action.

In Britain initial reports stated that the French commanding officers and sabotage parties had gone down with their ships. In fact, despite the colossal destruction, a fair amount of fighting in and around the dockyard, and many men – both French crews and German would-be captors – only leaving ships as they were sinking, fatal casualties amounted to just twelve French, and one unfortunate German. Some 27,888 French seamen were temporarily made PoWs. A number of the ships were raised over the following eighteen months, often to be sunk again in Allied air raids, but very few were ever put back into service.

The cruiser *Marseillaise*
The commanding officer of the *Marseillaise* deliberately scuttled the ship in such a manner to make salvage more difficult.

The day after the scuttling

An RAF reconnaissance photograph shows the ships at the main jetties at Quai Milhoud. With smoke obscuring much of the scene it was impossible to tell precisely what damage had been done, in particular internally and below the waterline, but it was clear that a lot of the ships were either bottomed or capsized. As usual the RAF's photo interpreters were able to work out a lot from small details; for example they deduced that the apparently intact *Strasbourg* (right) was in fact low in the water, and therefore quite badly damaged. Next to her at jetty No. 5, the cruiser *Colbert* was burning furiously, the smoke almost entirely hiding the equally aflame *Algérie* at jetty No. 4 and *Marseillaise* at No. 3.

(above) The burnt-out remains of the cruiser *Colbert*
Note how thoroughly the scuttling was carried out, with the ship not only sunk but the main gun turrets blown apart with 70 kg demolition charges. The four small rectangular antennae on the yards are for her French-designed *Détecteur Electro-Magnétique* (DEM): radar developed and manufactured by the Sadir Company, which could detect aircraft at a range of 50 km. There were similar installations fitted on board *Strasbourg* and *Algérie*.

The seaplane carrier *Commandant Teste* and the battleship *Provence*
Both ships had been at Mers el-Kebir where the latter was severely damaged, and now both were scuttled at Toulon, next to the Ilôt Vauban. The two ships had been part of the *Division des Ecoles*, and both went down with the Germans actually on board. Just visible next to *Commandant Teste* are the masts of a small supply ship, the *Hamelin*, also scuttled. In front of the ships can be seen the floats supporting anti-torpedo netting, which had, ironically, served to impede the five submarines which attempted to escape.

Another view of *Dupleix*
A hauting view seen between the funnels of a *contre-torpilleur*, almost certainly *Gerfaut*, scuttled on the opposite side of the Darse de Missiessy.

The Climax of the U-Boat War

'The sea war is the U-boat war' said Admiral Dönitz to his staff in February 1943. By then, the *Führer der Kriegsmarine* had nearly 350 submarines at his disposal. Almost a third of these were at sea at any one time, the remainder completing their lengthy training, trials and work-up periods, or under repairs and refits. The war against the U-boat might have been entering its fourth new year, but the elite arm of the *Kriegsmarine* still had a lot of fight left within.

The Allies were obliged to adopt a two-pronged approach to finishing off the U-boat threat. Reliant at the outbreak of war on evasive convoying and whatever defence a few hard-pressed escorts could muster, superior Allied technology and training, invested in 1942, achieved a critical mass which allowed the initiative to be wrested away from the U-boats.

In early 1943, Britain suffered from acute shortages. Imports had dropped to just a third of their pre-war level, and crucial supplies of oil dried up so that by the end of 1942 her reserves held enough for only three months at most. The success of the Allied policy of routing convoys away from gathering packs of U-boats had decreased to the point of near impossibility. There were too many slow convoys and stragglers and too many U-boats, and the German *B-Dienst* could still read British convoy signals. In the face of aggressive wolf-packs, two convoys, SC 118 and SC 121, lost thirteen ships each. Twenty-two ships of 141,000 tons were sunk out of convoys HX 229 and SC 122 in March 1943, constituting the worst Allied convoy battle of the whole war. Within the month of March nearly a hundred Allied merchantmen had been sunk, for only fifteen U-boats out of action – just half the number of new submarines entering service in the same period. And by mid-May it was estimated that there were 120 U-boats operating in the North Atlantic and that about 90 per cent of these were lurking in the area north of 40° North. Heavy losses continued to reflect the fact that the mid-Atlantic gap was swamped with over a hundred U-boats every day. At one point the Admiralty considered abandoning convoying altogether. But however daunting, the menace simply could not be evaded: it had to be tackled and destroyed.

From early 1943 the Allies kept abreast of German attempts at increasing the security of their Triton-coded radio traffic. This gave them detailed information on impending German operations. It allowed the Allies to dispatch supplementary escort support forces ('hunter-killer' groups, often including an escort carrier and powerful new destroyer escorts) to aid targeted convoys, while analysis of cumulative attack data facilitated the development of better anti-submarine tactics. And as U-boats were increasingly sent to sea with less and less experienced commanders and crew, the level of expertise within Allied anti-submarine personnel – from the 'back room boys' ashore to the escort captains at sea – grew.

At the same time, Ultra intercepts revealed to the Allies that the British losses of March were directly attributable to the German reading of British warning and re-routing signals. This discovery led to changes in British coding, removing this advantage from U-boat operations.

An Obstacle to Victory?

Taking advantage of renewed Triton decryptions and HF/DF, aircraft became one of the most decisive weapons of anti-submarine warfare, whether flown from escort carriers or operated from land. Halifaxes, Sunderlands and Flying Fortresses were hastily converted, but by far the most effective were American B-24Ds – known as Liberators. These giant aircraft, carrying a crew of eight or ten and with enough fuel to stay on patrol for upwards of sixteen hours or 2,000 miles at a stretch, were able to provide almost constant cover for convoys ranging across the Atlantic.

Admiral King, Commander-in-Chief US Navy, always regarded the Pacific as the natural focus of his attentions and yet simultaneously retained personal control over US Navy anti-submarine operations worldwide. The US Navy operated over a hundred Liberators, all in the Pacific. The western half of the Atlantic did not have a single VLR aircraft until May 1943 when a US Army Air Force Liberator squadron arrived in Newfoundland. There was not a single American Liberator allocated to Canada or Iceland before then. In fact, the US Navy did not assume sole control of anti-submarine aircraft until September. The other issue was that RAF Bomber Command refused to release long-range aircraft from their strategic bombing role, and RAF Coastal Command had to make do with being the third priority of American production. Sir Arthur 'Bomber' Harris argued that instead of giving more resources to this 'obstacle to victory', a more efficient use of such aircraft was in the bombing of U-boat bases among myriad other industrial, infrastructure and civilian targets. But to the sailor ploughing slowly across the Atlantic – perhaps conveying aviation fuel to keep Bomber Command's fleet in the air, among other supplies – the presence of a Liberator above him was infinitely more comforting and effective.

Finally entering the battle in limited numbers in April and May 1943, and flying from the British Isles, Iceland and Newfoundland, Liberators helped to close the dreaded 'air gap' and patrolled the Western Approaches and the Bay of Biscay for U-boats exiting and entering French bases. The U-boats, accustomed to an area of the Atlantic where they were at least able to sit on the surface, ventilate the crew spaces and recharge their batteries, were now in danger at all times.

So important was this long-range air cover deemed to be to victory over the U-boat in 1943 that the official historian of the Royal Navy later concluded that 'if the Allies had lost the battle of the Atlantic in the spring of 1943 history would have judged the cause to be the lack of two more squadrons of VLR aircraft'. While admittedly uninformed of Allied code breaking, such was its continued general secrecy until 1974, his judgement is stark. The withholding of VLR aircraft from naval control by the RAF arguably stands as perhaps the greatest error of misjudgement of the British war.

As the spring of 1943 wore on and the Battle of the Atlantic hung in its final balance, advances produced a new-wavelength centimetric radar, ASV III, which was undetectable by the Metox RWR. This improved kit was rushed out to Allied aircraft and warships. At the same time a new British depth-finding sonar began to prove effective in concert with American-improved 'Hedgehog'.

The battle of Convoy ONS 5 in April 1943 showed the complexity of the anti-submarine campaign. Forty-eight escorted merchant ships were attacked by no fewer than forty U-boats, and twelve Allied ships were sunk; but the combination of growing tactical skill and exploitation of new technology on and above the sea accounted for the sinking of eight U-boats – a new and unsustainable rate of loss for the U-boat arm. The inability of the U-boats to act on the surface, even at night, led to anti-aircraft guns being fitted but while they brought a temporary surprise to Allied aircraft, they could not stem the new tide. It was their turn to experience decimation. The turning point of the Battle of the Atlantic had been reached.

The Hunter Becomes the Hunted

Convoys were now used as bait to draw out the U-boats. Convoy escorts, well-practised, held their own or called in 'hunter-killer' support groups, which had been hastily assembled after the disasters of March. These ranged across the convoy routes, foraging for prey with HF/DF and reacting to warnings from the Submarine Tracking Rooms. Armed with improved depth charges, reliable electronics, high-definition radar and HF/DF and in co-operation with air support, they began to take a serious toll on U-boats. The 'Happy Time' was well and truly over, as morale in the U-boat service plummeted. More and more U-boat berths remained empty as boats failed to return from missions.

Convoy SC 130, departing Halifax bound for Britain, saw the culmination of all that Allied anti-submarine science had brought forth; thirty-seven vessels transited the Atlantic unmolested – not one was sunk – while a support group and Liberators, sticking with the convoy all the way across the ocean, accounted for six U-boats sunk. As one U-boat officer ruefully admitted: 'The idea of a convoy with its own air defences smashed our basic concept of U-boat warfare.'

Six more U-boats were lost attempting to tackle other convoys during May. By early June 1943, despite a construction rate of around forty boats per month and a total fleet of four hundred, an unprecedented forty-one U-boats had been lost, forcing Dönitz to admit privately that Germany would lose the Battle of the Atlantic if the situation persisted. Within two months, over fifty more U-boats had been lost while Allied merchant ship production overtook losses and never dipped below again. In the face of mounting emergency, Dönitz ordered the U-boats out of the North Atlantic to rest and re-equip.

They re-entered the Atlantic armed with the FaT (*Flächenabsuchender Torpedo*, which ran an irregular course incorporating 180-degree turns) and the T-5 '*Zaunkönig*' or 'Gnat' electric acoustic homing torpedo, designed to target convoy escorts running at high speed. The British, anticipating such a weapon, had developed a countermeasure to the T-5 in the shape of the 'Foxer' towed noisemaking decoy, as well as devising an air-dropped acoustic torpedo of their own, codenamed 'Fido'. 'Fido' made life very uncomfortable for surfaced U-boats, as any attempt to crash dive while under attack would produce a particularly attractive noise target.

During August, forty-one U-boats were lost to this deadly combination of accurate Allied aerial reconnaissance, timely signals intelligence and effective sub-killing technologies and tactics. The Bay of Biscay, home of many of the U-boat bases, became a no-go area for surfaced U-boats; pinned down by constant Allied air patrols, their only tactic was to crawl underwater all the way into their bases from many miles away.

Half-hearted U-boat re-entry to the Atlantic in the autumn resulted in losses as appalling as in the late spring. It is perhaps not too much to say that the U-boat threat had, after months and years of painful work, been neutered in a matter of weeks, by a small number of well-employed aircraft and escort vessels employing the fruitful bough of Allied technological resources. By the end of the year, 237 U-boats had been lost. And as American industrial capacity delivered sufficient weaponry to take the offensive simultaneously in the Atlantic and the Pacific, the *Kriegsmarine* would be forced to turn towards its own industrial reinvigoration to try and redress the imbalance. During 1943 German industry under the guidance of Albert Speer adopted American-style mass-production for the first time to deliver the number of tanks and U-boats required. Simultaneously, increasingly radical technological solutions were sought in its struggle to overcome Allied tactical and material dominance. But control of the Atlantic had been lost to the Allies and would not be regained.

The Italian Navy Runs Out of Steam

Likewise, by 1943 the offensive capabilities of Italian submarines had largely been neutralized by the advancing state of Allied anti-submarine warfare. Simultaneously, the process of interdicting Italian trade tonnage, already seriously damaged, was speeded up. British coastal forces, including the new Fairmile D MTB/MGB type, grew in strength. Equipped with hydrophones, mines and shallow-running torpedoes to counter flat-bottomed Axis transports, eighty such craft operated in the sometimes-stormy Mediterranean in January 1943, increasing to 171 a year later. As the Allied ground forces moved west across North Africa towards Tunis, so the MTB forces moved with it. The convoy routes between Sicily and Tunisia – nicknamed the 'Death Route' by demoralized Italian sailors – became dominated by the Royal Navy and Allied air forces acting out of Malta and from bases along the captured North African coast. Axis troops more frequently arrived in North Africa by transport aeroplane than by sea, flying into a desperate situation. Attrition of the Italian merchant navy far outstripped the launching of new tonnage. American bombing attacks further reduced the Italian warship fleet and many harbour facilities were razed. The last Italian air raid on Malta occurred in February 1943.

By the spring, the Axis position along the southern Mediterranean littoral was hopeless, and in May the Germans and Italian army corps, numbering close to a quarter of a million men, surrendered at Tunis. Italy's capability and will to wage war was crumbling to pieces. And in June the Germans lost the momentous tank battle of Kursk, effectively Nazism's last major offensive on the Eastern Front. From then until the end of the war their land forces were in general retreat.

Codenamed Operation Husky, and supported by a powerful escort and bombardment force of a monitor, six battleships, two carriers, seventeen cruisers and nearly fifty destroyers, the Allies made crossings from Bizerte in Tunisia and Malta to put eight divisions – 180,000 men – ashore in large amphibious landings in Sicily in July. German beach-head counterattacks were beaten off by inshore gunfire support from cruisers and destroyers, though German dive-bombers succeeded in sinking some American ships. Smaller-scale amphibious hops, guarded by British MTBs from Malta, attempted to outflank Axis positions around the north east of the island, but could not prevent almost 110,000 German and Italian troops and 10,000 vehicles escaping across the Straits of Messina to the mainland (in some cases, using craft built for the abandoned invasion of Britain in 1940). Meanwhile, with the exception of the *X MAS* force which switched to the German side, the attitude of the Italian Navy to Allied incursion into Italy was ambivalent. At the insistence of Dönitz, forces were sent south but they were light and offered only token resistance. The still-potent Italian battleships remained in port. Half of the

dozen Italian submarines sent to interfere with the Husky landings were lost within ten days.

On 25 September, Mussolini was dismissed in Rome by Italian king Victor Emmanuel, and Marshal Badoglio appointed in his stead. With Sicily in Allied hands, increased secret negotiations hastened the Italian armistice of 8 September, which resulted in an immediate German offensive occupation of chaotic Italy and action against her navy. The new battleship *Roma* was sunk with FX-1400 (Fritz-X) radio-controlled bombs on 9 September as the bulk of the Italian fleet made its way to Bone and Malta to surrender to the British Mediterranean fleet.

Backed up by five carriers, Allied amphibious landings went in against light German defences at Taranto and stiff resistance at Salerno between 8–12 September. A second FX-1400 severely damaged the American light cruiser *Savannah* off Salerno harbour, and the British cruiser *Uganda* and battleship *Warspite* would soon receive similar punishment while contributing to the massive shore bombardment. Despite the ports of Bari and Brindisi falling (and to the west, Corsica and Sardinia being captured), the Allied advance became heavily bogged down by November and was locked in terrible stalemate at Monte Cassino by the end of the year.

At the Allied tripartite conference in Teheran in November, it was agreed to give part of the surrendered Italian fleet to the Soviet Navy (principally the battleship *Giulio Cesare*, to be renamed the *Novorossiysk*), and that the USSR would receive Königsberg, a permanent warm-water port in the Baltic, later to be renamed Kaliningrad.

Meanwhile, stubborn German resistance further to the east meant that the Ukrainian Black Sea port of Odessa remained in German hands, supplied by convoys from Romania (whose oil the German war effort now largely depended upon). Squadrons of swift Soviet motor boats harried them. Among a range of ex-US warships to be donated, many patrol torpedo boats of different types were handed over to the USSR in 1943, in whose service they would prove of great worth.

The Japanese Retreat from the Southern Frontier

From the end of 1942 and into 1943, Japanese forces began to be dislodged from a number of their most far-flung locations. Split into three groups under General Douglas MacArthur (South-West Pacific Area), Admiral William Halsey (South Pacific Area) and Admiral Chester Nimitz (Central and North Pacific Areas), vast American forces of men, ships and aircraft fought their way from atoll to atoll, defeating or leap-frogging the Japanese forces around the perimeter of conquered territories. Capture of enemy-held airfields was a top priority.

In February 1943 the Japanese force of 12,000 remaining men were withdrawn from Guadalcanal by destroyer, ceding a vital victory to the US Marines. For the first time, the Japanese had been handed a decisive defeat in the air, at sea and on the ground. And in the first week of March, the Japanese were taught that they could not run slow convoys of transports during the day with inadequate air cover without great risk. Eight transports en route between Rabaul and New Guinea, escorted by eight destroyers, were attacked by American bombers using new skip-bombing tactics. Over the course of two days, the battle of the Bismarck Sea saw all eight transports and half the destroyers sunk by bombing and strafing.

On 18 April, US P-38 fighters, acting on intelligence intercepts, shot down Admiral Yamamoto's aeroplane as he flew from Rabaul to Bougainville, killing him. Meanwhile, Japanese reinforcements were being sent using fast destroyer forces down 'The Slot' in an effort to relieve the beleaguered land garrisons. Over the next few months, the central Solomons became the scene of several hard-fought surface actions. For the Americans, on balance the victors of these battles, the purely offensive phase of the Pacific war had begun and they pressed to the north west towards Bougainville and Rabaul. Fear of American carrier aircraft and a lack of friendly land-based air cover kept the Japanese from approaching American fleets without their own carrier battle fleet in attendance.

By this time, mass-produced Liberty ships were pouring out of American shipyards at a rate of about 140 per month. By the middle of 1943, American shipyards were churning out *Essex* class fleet carriers every eight weeks, as well as light carriers every six weeks. Furthermore, superior new aircraft types – in particular the Grumman F6F Hellcat fighter – and improved radar and fighter control were introduced to the fleet

With a growing fleet of large and light fast carriers backed up by an efficient fleet train – conferring the ability to conduct sustained and wide-ranging operations at an unprecedented pace and intensity – Nimitz in the central Pacific pushed south west from Midway. The Japanese Navy, increasingly composed of forces thrown together as best as losses and its far-flung commitments could provide, was still attempting to contest the Solomons well into November 1943. Having failed to prevent an American invasion fleet from landing on Bougainville on 1 November – threatening their hitherto-unmolested major fleet base at Rabaul – the Japanese lost a light cruiser and a destroyer and two other warships damaged at the Battle of Empress Augusta Bay. Three days later they suffered a further serious setback when a fleet of nine powerful 8-inch gunned cruisers under Vice Admiral Kurita, despatched from Truk to stop the consolidation of the American landings on Bougainville, was caught and badly battered in crowded Rabaul harbour by a surprise air raid by a hundred US carrier aircraft. Japanese air groups sent to interfere were largely wiped out, and the Japanese lost all hope of contesting the Bougainville landings.

As a result, it was only a matter of time before Rabaul became isolated and neutralized as a forward naval base for the Japanese. With most of the Solomons now in American hands, US land-based airpower would now keep Rabaul under constant air attack, wearing away local Japanese air groups struggling to defend the base. As the Americans pressed on, the lid was kept on Rabaul and it became increasingly suffocated as the frontline moved north and west.

Supported by heavy battleships, a US fleet invaded the Gilbert Islands, which were captured in November after a suicidal last stand by the Japanese garrison on the island of Tarawa. Only one hundred prisoners were taken out of the garrison strength of 4,700 defenders. The overwhelming strength of American carrier power was clearly demonstrated during this campaign. Eighteen carriers were almost unopposed by the Japanese who had lost most of their own carrier groups in the Solomons.

The irreversible attrition of Japanese aviation, cruiser and destroyer forces in terms of numbers and of fighting efficiency, and the loss of the Solomons bases, together served to weaken the logistical and combat foundations upon which Japan's south-eastern expansion had been built. The Japanese Navy could not field enough light forces to act both with the fleet and in defence of Japanese shipping, let alone use them to reinforce precarious outposts in the ground war. It was losing aircraft and pilots and less and less did it enjoy friendly local air superiority.

Thereafter, without the means to end the war it had begun, strategic mobility was worn away as Japan found itself fighting defensively on hugely separated fronts against a range of enemies: Chinese, American, British and Commonwealth. Of these, the US Navy was alone able to sustain five major efforts against the Japanese: a long-range submarine *guerre de course* against Japanese mercantile shipping; fleet actions against concentrations of naval shipping; an island-hopping strategy using enormous amphibious forces to leapfrog major pockets of Japanese resistance; a devastating carrier air offensive that was eventually able to carry the war to the Japanese homeland; and the facilitation of a strategic bombing campaign launched from islands that the navy and marines had captured.

The Ongoing Menace of German Capital Ships

Increasingly isolated and contributing less and less to the Axis war effort, nonetheless the remaining *Kriegsmarine* capital ships could not be ignored by the Royal Navy. Sister-ship to the *Bismarck* and likewise one of the most powerful weapons afloat, the *Tirpitz* had a chequered operational history. Hitler was nervous of her loss to British aircraft carriers potentially operating with the Arctic convoys and would not authorize her use until the whereabouts of the British carriers could be established. But even in harbour she posed a threat that the British paid a disproportionate amount of attention to countering.

A number of daring torpedo-bombing raids by Fleet Air Arm Barracudas damaged her, making her a static target. But despite repeated attempts, including abortive tries with British human torpedoes codenamed 'Chariots', she could not be knocked out. Mirroring tactics pioneered by the Italians and Japanese, an audacious plan had been hatched by the British to attack the German battleship and her 11-inch gunned consort *Scharnhorst* at anchor in Altenfjord in Norway using midget submarines called X-craft, each carrying two 2-ton explosive saddle charges. In September, six such craft, towed by submarines, set out for the fjord. Two were lost on the passage to Norway; another sank during the approach to the *Tirpitz* and one failed at the last minute to attack the *Scharnhorst*. This left two to get through to the *Tirpitz*. Placing their charges underneath the huge battleship's hull, the midget sub crews bailed out and watched as the Germans tried in vain to shift the ship out of the way; the charges went up, putting the battleship out of commission for a further six months – a valuable strategic result and another blow to German naval pride.

A year after their failure at the Battle of the Barents Sea against convoy JW 51B, German surface units again felt pressure to demonstrate their strategic worth in the Arctic. In December 1943 Allied convoy JW 55B, eastbound to Russia, was targeted by the German battlecruiser *Scharnhorst* sortieing from Norway, but an intercepting force of British cruisers supported by the battleship *Duke of York* brought her to action at long range, where the 14-inch guns of the British battleship battered the German ship into a hulk. The Battle of the North Cape demonstrated British expertise in fleet handling, use of radar and low-light fighting skills. Now just the damaged *Tirpitz* remained alone as the last vestige of German capital ship power.

Meanwhile, the neutering of the threat of massed U-boat attacks in the Atlantic had removed the final major obstacle to a massive transferral to Britain of American and Canadian men, tanks, weapons, supplies, transports, landing ships, hospital ships and a million and one other things needed for the commencement of the invasion of Nazi-occupied Europe. And simultaneously, the situation in the Pacific showed that an American victory was, for all practical purposes, inevitable – but at what cost?

Navies in exile: Greece

Some of a series of photographs of the Greek cruiser, HHMS *Giorgios Averoff,* Flagship of Rear-Admiral A. Sakellariou, Commander-in-Chief of the Royal Hellenic Navy. The 10,200-ton cruiser had been bought by Greece while under construction at Livorno in Italy in 1909. Despite a major refit in France during 1925–7, by 1941 the ship's speed had dropped to 16 knots and so, rather than stay in Greek waters to be sunk by the *Luftwaffe,* on 22 April she left for Alexandria where two days later she was placed under the orders of Admiral Cunningham.

During 1941–4 *Averoff* operated with the Allied navies in the Middle East and Indian Ocean theatres where her lack of speed was of little importance and her powerful main battery would be more than adequate to deal with any German raiders. In April 1944 the ship was one of a number of Greek warships which were briefly the scene of mutinies, but on 17 October of that year the old warrior led the Greek fleet that dropped anchor in Faliron Bay, Athens, at the end of the Nazi occupation. On 15 May 1945 she arrived at Rhodes to mark the accession of the Dodecanese from Italy.

After the end of the World War Two the old warrior became first a naval headquarters ship, and then from 1957 a training ship at the Greek naval academy at Poros, before finally returning to Faliron in 1985 to become a museum ship, where she remains to this day.

(right) HHMS *Giorgios Averoff*
Seen from the quarterdeck, anti-aircraft gunnery exercises are taking place after the conclusion of Divisions. Two of *Averoff*'s 3-inch anti-aircraft guns can be seen, prominent on either side of the after superstructure with anti-splinter protection around them, while the machine guns on the roof of the after main turret and on the platform between the legs of the tripod mainmast are also in use. In the foreground is a large-base (possibly 9-foot) portable rangefinder.

(left) Independence Day
Morning divisions on board *Averoff,* and preparations for celebrating Greek Independence Day (25 March), a major occasion for the sailors of the Greek ships in the Allied navies. Admiral Sakellariou is in the centre of the quarter deck, facing forward. Note the naval band playing beneath the main guns, and the AA machine guns on the turret roof. The pale object in the foreground is the aft rangefinder, covered by a tarpaulin.

Navies in exile: Netherlands

The majority of the Netherlands' warships based in European waters escaped when the country was invaded by Germany in 1940, and at once began to serve alongside the Royal Navy. An outstanding combat record ensued. Ships sunk were replaced by new ones built in British shipyards. However, when Japan invaded the Netherlands East Indies two years later there were far heavier losses before the surviving vessels escaped to Australia and Ceylon.

HNIMS *Tromp* in Australia
The cruiser *Tromp* at Sydney for visit and repairs, 1942–4. Before the war the ship had been designated as a flotilla leader; during the war she took part in the defence of the Netherlands East Indies until damage by Japanese destroyers during Allied attempts to thwart the invasion of Bali forced her to retire to Australia for repairs. This probably saved her from sharing the fate of most of the rest of the Allied ships, sunk during the following weeks. Later she served with the British East Indies Fleet and with the US 7th Fleet.

Submarine-killers
Two famous Netherlands 'submarine-killers': on the left is *Zwaardvisch* ('T'-class) which sank *U-168* in the Java Sea in October 1944, and on the right is *O-21* which sank *U-95* in the Tyrrhenian Sea in November 1941. Of *U-168*'s crew, twenty-three lost their lives and twenty-two were rescued. *U-95* had only just entered the Mediterranean and was sunk with thirty-five of her crew, twelve surviving and being taken prisoner. These were not the only instances of a Netherlands submarine sinking another submarine: *Dolfijn* ('S'-class) sank the Italian *Malachite* near Sardinia on 9 February 1943. This photograph was taken at Amsterdam on 2 September 1948.

The 'terrible twins'
The big gunboats HNIMS *Soemba* (above), in the Netherlands East Indies, pre-war but post-1932, dressed overall, with masthead ensign and 'Double Prince Jack', and *Flores* (right), in a North African harbour, probably Algiers (she was deployed to the Mediterranean in 1943, her commanding officer losing his life off Italy), were known as the 'terrible twins'. Heavily armed for their size, with three 150mm guns plus proper fire control, as well as possessing an armoured deck, they turned out to be ideal vessels for shore bombardment, and both were extensively engaged in operations off Italy and during the invasion of Normandy.

The balance of power changes in the Atlantic

At the start of 1943, the U-boat had succeeded in denying Britain so many essential cargoes that British national reserves held only three months' worth of oil. Over 300 U-boats were at the command of Admiral Dönitz, and Allied convoys in the early months of the year suffered great losses. Yet during the course of the year, the Battle of the Atlantic turned in favour of the Allies, as a combined anti-submarine offensive by skilled escorts and patrol aircraft increasingly took effect. By the middle of the year, as fewer and fewer of his boats returned from their missions, Dönitz ordered the temporary withdrawal of his force from the Atlantic.

The laughing swordfish

This boat is believed to be *U-744*, commissioned in June 1943. The photograph epitomizes the much happier times of the U-Boat with the 'Laughing Swordfish' emblem that adorned boats of the Ninth U-Boat Flotilla based at Brest. By 1944, U-boat operations in the Atlantic had dwindled almost to inactivity as integrated Allied anti-submarine measures dominated the sea space.

Under siege from the air

Aircraft became the U-boats' worst enemy. Armed with search radar, HF/DF, effective depth charges, 'Fido' acoustic homing torpedoes, machine guns and Leigh lights for night attacks, carrier-borne and land-based patrol aircraft could keep watch for U-boats around convoys, and shorter-ranged medium bombers and fighters flying from land bases could also surprise a submarine on the surface. In 1943, U-boats received air warning radar and heavier anti-aircraft armament in an attempt to beat off the attentions of Allied anti-submarine aircraft but to little avail.

Liberator factory

The importance of the maritime VLR aircraft to the closure of the mid-Atlantic 'air gap', leading to the defeat of the U-boats, is difficult to exaggerate. One of the most effective VLR types was the B-24 Liberator, flown by RAF Coastal Command, the Royal Canadian Air Force and the US Navy. Introduced in 1941, the Liberator holds the record as the most numerously built Allied aircraft of the war, with over 18,000 examples produced. The Ford Motor Company boasted of turning one out per day at the peak of their productivity. But the main claimant to the ranks of new aircraft coming off American production lines was the US Army Air Force, who used the Liberator as a strategic bomber over Germany and in the Pacific. As a result of their stranglehold on production, it was not until the spring of 1943 that even one maritime Liberator squadron began to operate over the western half of the Atlantic. In concert with squadrons flying earlier models from Iceland and the British Isles, its effect was immediate and lasting.

The Arctic, 1943

Arctic convoys continued throughout 1943, the most dramatic occurring in appalling conditions at the very end of December when JW 55A and JW 55B were set to converge on opposite tracks between Loch Ewe in Scotland, and Russia. The British expected an attack by the *Scharnhorst* and destroyers sailing north out of Altenfjord. To cover the incoming and outgoing convoys and bring the battlecruiser to battle, the British deployed their 8-inch cruisers *Belfast*, *Sheffield* and *Norfolk* with the eastbound JW 55B while Admiral Bruce Fraser in the *King George V*-class battleship *Duke of York*, accompanied by *Jamaica*, steamed eastwards from Iceland to provide support. Thirty miles east of the convoy, detecting the *Scharnhorst* using the *Belfast*'s radar set, Vice-Admiral Burnett attacked using *Norfolk*, hitting and forcing the German battlecruiser to turn away and work round to attempt an attack on the convoy. Anticipating this move, Burnett headed for the convoy and regained contact with the *Scharnhorst*. Re-opening fire, the British cruisers scored hits but *Norfolk* was badly damaged by the 11-inch shells of the *Scharnhorst*. Admiral Bey in the German battlecruiser turned south away from the engagement; meanwhile Fraser's force was closing from the south west, guided by radar reports from Burnett's cruisers. By 4 p.m. the *Duke of York* made radar contact at 22 miles and moved in for the kill. The whole scene illuminated by star shell, and battered on one side by Burnett's cruisers and the 14-inch shells of the British battleship on the other, the *Scharnhorst* was overwhelmed, and sunk by torpedo with large loss of life. Meanwhile the convoy reached safety in Murmansk.

The icy North
Looking forward on the port side of the bridge superstructure of HMS *Narcissus*, 23 January 1943, position approximate 50°N, 51°W. The build-up of ice on board ships serving in the Arctic may have looked spectacular but was potentially very dangerous. Despite the cheerful expression on the face of this sailor, living and working conditions were appalling.

Soviet destroyers in echelon
Soviet Type VIIU destroyers in 1943. The design of these ships was a modification of the initial series to enable them to operate in the harsh conditions of the Arctic. They could also transit between the Arctic and Baltic seas via the White Sea Canal.

Pushing through the ice

Seen from the *Dido* class cruiser HMS *Scylla*, merchant ships and an escort destroyer of convoy JW 53 pass through pack ice during their voyage on 15–27 February 1943. There is a seal on the ice in the foreground. JW 53 left Liverpool on 15 February 1943 and arrived at Kola Inlet, Russia, on 27 February 1943. Of the twenty-nine merchant vessels which left British waters, twenty eight arrived safely; one was sunk in port by aircraft attack. One escort vessel was also lost. The escorting aircraft carrier, HMS *Dasher*, had to divert to Iceland following ice damage during a storm.

HMS *Duke of York*

The battleship, *Duke of York*, Admiral Bruce Fraser's flagship at the Battle of the North Cape, opens fire with her guns.

A British 4-inch gun and crew

An obviously posed photograph, dated November 1943, of a naval gunnery team loading a 4-inch anti-aircraft gun. Several thousand 4-inch guns of various Marks were made, and were fitted in every type of British warship from aircraft carriers to trawlers, as well as to Defensively Equipped Merchant Ships (DEMS). In the anti-aircraft role they had a reach of 39,000 feet at 80 degrees elevation, though were not particularly accurate at long range. These dual-purpose HA (High Angle) guns could also be used against surface targets if needed.

Amphibious exercises in the English Channel

The success of Operation Torch – the landings in North Africa in November 1942 – encouraged the Allies to step up their preparations for an amphibious re-entry into France. New craft were constructed and training exercises mounted throughout 1943. Here, lines of LCI(S)s emerge from a smoke screen while on exercise in the English Channel in 1943. LCI(S) or Landing Craft, Infantry (Small) were designed by the British company Fairmile and built of wood. One hundred of these craft were constructed using prefabrication techniques. In order to provide some protection for their seventeen-man crew and the 100-odd troops they could carry, half-inch armour plate was fitted. With a top speed of 14½ knots, they were faster than most landing craft, and proved a considerable success during the invasion of France, even though the troops were disembarked by the thoroughly precarious means of removable wooden brows balanced over the crafts' transom bows. Of note are the two distinct camouflage schemes in use.

The Tunisian port of Sousse after Allied bombing
Taken by a War Office photographer, this view shows an Axis ship and wrecked port installations in June 1943 after the port's capture. Sousse had been one of Rommel's main supply ports, and was quickly brought back into use as a base for British motor torpedo boats.

Algiers
Two Liberty ships are on fire behind light cruiser USS *Savannah* (CL-42) after air attack on Algiers, 16 June 1943. During the war 2,710 Liberty ships would be built in American shipyards, using increasingly streamlined pre-fabrication mass-production techniques. *Savannah* had returned to Algiers to replenish ammunition after bombardment duties off Sicily.

The Allies invade Italy

When it became clear that the proposed Allied invasion of western Europe could not be mounted before 1944, agreement was reached within the Allied command that subordinate plans to invade Italy could be put in motion. Using forces plucked from the successful campaign in North Africa, landings were made first at Sicily, then across the Straits of Messina and into mainland Italy at Salerno and Taranto.

British troops of Montgomery's Eighth Army emerge from the bow ramp of *LST-383*, a US Navy landing ship, on the beach at Salerno on the Italian mainland. This particular Landing Ship Tank was later used to attain a beach-head at Anzio and then in the Normandy landings.

Exhausted and poorly equipped, British troops from the 50th (Tyne Tees) and 51st (Highland) Divisions, having fought a long campaign against Rommel in the North African deserts, were needlessly added to fresh American troops of the US Fifth Army in the assault on Salerno. But, after having been deceived about their destination and purpose, nearly 200 men refused to join in the assault, and were arrested for disobeying orders. Within six weeks, after a trial for which their defence had no time to prepare evidence, all but one had been found guilty of mutiny, their sentences ranging from five years' penal servitude to death.

Pack animals ashore

While coming ashore from landing craft in Sicily in early August 1943, American soldiers lead rather reluctant mules through the surf towards the beach. Beasts of burden were used to help transport Allied supplies over Italy's rugged terrain.

Operation Avalanche

Touchdown in the surf, September 1943: US military vehicles of the 817th Engineer Aviation Battalion roll off an LST ramp during landing operations in Salerno on mainland Italy. Troops stand on the deck of the ship. A US-operated Supermarine Spitfire lies nose-down in the surf, mistakenly shot down by American anti-aircraft guns. According to the US Air Force, the pilot suffered only 'a scratch on the back of his hand'.

Surrender of the Italian fleet

After the Italian Government had agreed the Allied terms for an armistice the main body of the Italian fleet sailed for Malta to pass under British control. Air attacks by their former ally resulted in the destruction of the battleship *Roma* with heavy loss of life, but the remainder of the fleet made it to Malta. On 11 September Admiral Cunningham was able to signal to London: 'Be pleased to inform Their Lordships that the Italian battle fleet now lies under the guns of the fortress of Malta'.

These photographs are part of a series taken by Lieutenant Cotter at Kalafrana Bay on 14 September and St Paul's Bay on 22 September 1943 and show units of Admiral Da Zara's fleet at anchor with members of their crews on deck. All are taken from small boats, photographers not being allowed on board the ships.

(below) *Italia* at anchor
Battleship *Italia* (ex-*Littorio*) in Kalafrana Bay.

(above) Keeping watch
A Maltese sentry stands watch over Italian battleships, Kalafrana Bay.

Line-up in St Paul's Bay
From left to right: Italian submarines *Ciro Menotti*, *Jalea* and *Zoea*, then the escort-torpedo-boat *Orione*, the seaplane carrier *Giuseppe Miraglia*, the requisitioned liner *Luana* and the submarine on the other side of her is probably the *Axum* and then the *Galatea*.

The crew of the *Galatea*
Seen from a different angle, *Galatea* is in the foreground with *Axum* behind her and then the *Luana* and *Giuseppe Miraglia*.

Worse fates
Battleship *Vittorio Veneto* in Kalafrana Bay. In the foreground, with salvage work clearly still in progress, is the *Breconshire*, sunk in August 1942 after the Battle of Sirte.

The expansion of US output

President Roosevelt stops at Kaiser Shipyard in Richmond, California, during an 8,000-mile tour of the United States, visiting industries and the armed forces. In the car with him are Harry Hopkins (left) and Henry Kaiser, known to some as the 'father of modern American shipbuilding' – to others, simply as 'Sir Launchalot'. By 1943 the industrial output of the United States was far outstripping that of its allies and enemies combined, and Kaiser's became famous for producing a Liberty ship in four days, one of over 2,750 ships built to the same basic British design requirement. Hopkins was a pro-British diplomat and advisor to Roosevelt, popular with Churchill and instrumental in arranging Lend-Lease in 1941.

The Japanese Emperor aboard *Musashi*
Japanese Emperor Hirohito (front centre) with naval officers beneath the powerful anti-aircraft and secondary armament of the super-battleship *Musashi*, at Yokosuka naval base in June 1943. Loyalty to the Emperor was the central tenet of the Japanese armed forces in World War Two, and led to a psychology that demanded a willingness to pay the ultimate price in battle. On land, at sea and in the air, Japanese forces – led by fanatical officers – proved extremely tough for the Allies to beat, even resorting to suicide tactics when the increasingly dire operational situation demanded.

The Southern Pacific fight-back

Victory at Guadalcanal in February 1943 gave the US a base which enabled their forces to accelerate the process of counter-advance, pushing the Japanese frontier back through the Solomons. The Japanese Navy was forced to adopt a perpetually reactive stance as its carrier air power was ground away in support of beleaguered land garrisons.

HMNZS *Leander*
The light cruiser *Leander* at anchor in Solomon Islands waters, 25 July 1943, photographed from USS *Nicholas* (DD-449). *Leander* was on loan from the Royal Navy to the Royal New Zealand Navy.

Cruiser survivors
Throughout the summer and into the autumn, the Americans and Japanese fought hard for the central Solomons at the cruiser-destroyer battles of Kula Gulf, Vella Gulf, Horaniu and Vella Lavella, the Americans, despite losses emerging victorious in the first week of October. Oily survivors of USS *Helena* (CL-50) clamber aboard USS *Nicholas* (DD-449) after the battle of Kula Gulf, 5–6 July 1943.

Amphibious landing
American and Australian soldiers look at the camera as their landing craft heads into shore somewhere in New Guinea, possibly the Huon Peninsula near Lae, during Operation Postern in early September. During the operation, Japanese 'Betty', 'Val' and 'Zero' aircraft, based at Rabaul in New Britain, attacked the amphibious shipping off-shore, killing a hundred Allied personnel. This campaign, overseen by General Douglas MacArthur, was a success despite a distinct lack of naval support.

Replenishment at sea

The Americans, operating across vast distances for weeks at a time, pioneered the efficient use of replenishment at sea (RAS) using specially-equipped naval tankers, a massive force-multiplier. Also crucial was the vast support fleet of repair ships, tankers, freighters and floating docks, which were steadily moving closer to Japan using anchorages provided by suitable atolls such as Kwajalein in the Marshalls, Manus in the Admiralty Islands and Ulithi in the Western Carolines. The American fleet had to provide not only a striking force but its own base of operations – as well as carrying an air force and an army along with it. This photograph shows USS *Minneapolis* (CA-36) refuelling at sea from a navy oiler during the Marshall Islands operation in December. The oiler is one of the few that were fitted with a Mark 37 gun director, visible atop her bridge. Note the red navigation light on the oiler's port bridge wing.

Shooting practice

USS *Biloxi* firing her guns while steaming in a turn, during shakedown, October 1943.

Plotting the battle
A photograph by Edward Steichen shows busy crewmen working on charts and communications systems aboard the Essex class aircraft carrier *Lexington* (CV-16) – nicknamed 'The Blue Ghost' due to her all-over dark blue 'camouflage' – en route to striking against Japanese targets in the Gilberts and Marshall Islands in late November 1943.

Taking 'cover'
American crew flatten themselves on the deck of their aircraft carrier as Japanese aircraft attack during the battle for the Marshall Islands on 3 December 1943. The wide expanses of the flight deck gave little if any shelter for the exposed flight operations crew should they be caught in the open during action.

A courageous rescue
An F6F Hellcat of Air Group 6 crash lands after it fails to clear the flight deck of USS *Enterprise* after being waved off from landing, 1 November 1943. Its left wing is buried among the port side deck anti-aircraft guns, crewmen – probably lucky to be alive – looking on. The catapult officer, Lieutenant Walter Chewning, can be seen clambering up the side of the forward fuselage to rescue the pilot, Ensign Byron Johnson, from the blazing cockpit.

Soviet and Axis operations in 1943

During 1943 the Soviet advance began in earnest, with the large warships, such as battleships and cruisers, being used to bombard German and Romanian positions ashore, while smaller ones operated in coastal waters and rivers.

(right) *MAS* craft in the Black Sea
The Italian Navy contributed a squadron of these *MAS* craft, four midget submarines and some crashboats, all sent to the Black Sea by continental rail. Though small, this force enabled the Axis to use the sea for supply and transport, and offensive operations. This photograph shows elements of the *IV Flottiglia MAS-Marnero Sezione MAS* at Sevastopol, January 1943. They sank a Soviet cruiser.

Romanian escort
Units of the Romanian Navy escort a Romanian convoy on the way to its destination.

Loading a torpedo
Loading torpedoes onto a Soviet K-class submarine. Soviet torpedoes were not terribly effective – the depth-keeping and firing mechanisms were unreliable and many torpedoes passed under their targets; some detonated after missing, others just sank. Those that made a hit did not always detonate properly, although this was a problem not restricted to Soviet submarines. Soviet doctrine was to dive immediately after releasing torpedoes, and detonations were often freely translated as 'hits'.

Destroyer *Stalin*
On board the *Novik* class destroyer *Stalin*. These older ships formed the backbone of the Soviet destroyer strength at the start of the war, being distributed among all four fleets. *Stalin* was one of the few to survive the war.

The littoral
One of the most important functions of the Soviet Navy was moving troops in river and coastal environments. However, he Soviet Navy did not construct specialized landing ships or craft, and in delivering men amphibiously had to rely on warships, transport conversions, civilian ferry barges and other small craft.

Battleship fire support
The battleship *Parizhskaya Kommuna* bombarding enemy positions. During 1943 she reverted to her original name, *Sevastopol*.

The Royal Navy's intricate work
Although the German Navy did not have enough stocks of mines to cause decisive
damage to shipping in British coastal waters, minesweepers still had a vital role to play in
safeguarding sea lanes. This photograph shows officers aboard Motor Minesweeper 136
enjoying a cup of ship's cocoa, very welcome in cold weather.

'Chariots' of fire

Royal Navy officers conduct trials of the 'Chariot' human torpedo underwater craft, which was designed to carry explosives to attack enemy ships. Once in range, the two crew members would bail out and wait to be rescued. Seven were lost in attacks off Italian ports and two off Libya in January 1943; two were also lost in late December attempting to attack the battleship *Tirpitz* in Oftofjord, Norway. She had already been damaged by British X-craft midget submarines three months previously, although three X-craft were lost in the operation. For the crews it was a peculiarly dangerous way to go to war.

a mere feint – almost complete strategic and tactical surprise was achieved by the Allies. From headquarters in Portsmouth, Admiral Sir Bertram Ramsay as Allied Naval Commander-in-Chief of Operation Neptune, the maritime facet of Overlord, co-ordinated an enormous number and range of vessels in the assault phase and the build-up of supplies. The forces comprised 1,213 warships, 4,126 landing craft of all sizes and cargoes, 736 support ships and 864 merchant vessels – a total of almost seven thousand vessels, of which 79 per cent were British and Canadian, 16 per cent American and 4 per cent from other allies. The equipment transported across the Channel also included a range of ingenious vessels and Mulberry/Gooseberry artificial harbours created specifically for the establishment and subsequent maintenance of the Normandy beach-head.

Meanwhile a complex, deep-layered defence comprising British and American destroyers, frigates and MTBs patrolled apportioned sectors of the western and eastern Channel on the lookout for any German attempts to reach the invasion shipping lanes. *Schnorkel*-equipped U-boats, infiltrating narrow tidal coastal waters being plyed constantly by large volumes of shipping on predictable routes, would present a difficult challenge to Allied anti-submarine air and surface forces. But with Allied superiority assured and with Ultra intercepts continuing to inform the Allies of German counter-attack plans, no major German naval units could hope to make a decisive intervention. Through pre-emptive Allied saturation of the skies around the U-boat bases in the Bay of Biscay, and constant local patrolling, U-boat and E-boat interference was kept to a minimum as the crucial toehold was gained.

By the end of D-Day, over sixty thousand shells had been fired at German defences by naval craft, and over 175,000 troops of many nationalities had been put ashore on an established beach-head that stretched for 56 miles. Hitler's much-vaunted Atlantic Wall, which had taken the Germans four years to construct and absorbed a large percentage of materiel and labour, fell in just one day.

Still, Allied warships had to be alert to tip-and-run raids by powerful German torpedo-boat flotillas based to the east at Le Havre and to the west at Cherbourg. Once convinced that the Allied landings were the genuine article, seventeen U-boats were mustered by the *Kriegsmarine* for operations in the Channel; those without *Schnorkels* were destroyed first and all boats of the first wave were accounted for by 15 June. Seven had been sunk and three damaged by British escorts. By mid-June almost all the E-boats had been sunk by air attack in Le Havre.

In the days after 6 June, blockships, Gooseberry breakwaters and the Mulberry harbours were manoeuvred into position off Gold and Omaha beaches. By the end of Operation Overlord, on 5 July, one million Allied men and thousands of vehicles, weapons and tons of stores had been put ashore in Normandy. Over 80,000 vehicles were landed for the Americans alone in just eleven days.

In return for their heavy losses, the U-boats had managed to sink a meagre five transports and one landing craft; only one escort was sunk and three knocked out. Withdrawn from the Channel and forced to flee their French bases during August as the Allied ground offensive split and the Americans swung towards the western coast, the U-boats headed for Norway.

Further Allied Amphibious Landings

While Operation Cobra – the elimination of resistance in Brittany and the capture of its ports in particular – and the swing towards Paris took place to the north, Operation Anvil went in to the Mediterranean beaches between Cannes and Toulon on 15 August. An American and a French corps went ashore and were quickly successful in forcing the German occupiers to retreat to the north east. These were the last major amphibious actions in the European war. Marseilles was seized, and through this port Allied troops were also gathered for the final push on Germany. The British opposed Anvil, preferring to maintain the pressure that General Alexander was applying in Italy as a means of getting to Vienna before the Soviets. Here, Churchill's arguments failed to be heeded by his allies, as Britain rapidly became the junior partner in the Big Three. As a result, support for the Italian campaign was diverted to the American forces intended for Anvil. But control of the sea in the western Mediterranean, won by the Royal Navy, had created the conditions to complete the liberation of France from the south.

Meanwhile, in the Baltic, the long bitter fight for Leningrad continued, Soviet naval forces acting in support of their comrades under arms ashore. Moored with their guns covering the city, the battleships and cruisers of the Soviet Navy acted as static batteries. Their fire, however, while terrifying in volume, was not particularly accurate or decisive.

By April 1944 in the Black Sea the German garrison in Odessa was threatened with encirclement. Overwhelming Soviet power generated a breakthrough and despite furious orders from Hitler not to evacuate, the German and Romanian armies of the Crimea – some 150,000 men – were brought away by air and sea as Soviet naval brigades stormed through the ravaged city. Abandoned Axis casualties numbered more than half the quantity successfully evacuated.

The US Fast Carrier Task Forces in the Pacific

With the frontline fleet of brand new carriers, modern aircraft and powerful escorts expanding ever more, the relentless American march towards Japan went on. During February and March 1944 the Marshall Islands were captured, with no survivors from a garrison of 2,000 defenders on the final atoll to be taken, Eniwetok. With ten Japanese troops killed for every American casualty, the Admiralty Islands and New Britain also fell and the Japanese fleet base at Rabaul became increasingly untenable. Finally, Rabaul was snuffed out and the Japanese base at Truk was pummelled by US carrier air groups.

Nine days after Operation Overlord went ashore from the grey waters of the English Channel, nearly 130,000 troops were landed by over 500 ships against fierce resistance on the island of Saipan in the Marianas, in what was to be the largest amphibious operation of the Pacific war.

Having expected the Marianas to be attacked next, the Japanese attempted to deploy a force to prevent any landings. A very potent Japanese fleet – consisting of five battleships, five fleet carriers, four light carriers, thirteen cruisers and twenty-eight destroyers – was assembled. But even this was outweighed by the naval firepower and staying power assembled by the Americans in Task Force 58: seven fleet carriers, eight light carriers, seven battleships, twenty-one cruisers and sixty-nine destroyers. Naval history had never seen the like of it.

Instituted in August 1943 under Admiral Sherman, the Fast Carrier Task Forces were the main striking force of the US Navy in the latter stages of the war, operating under the guises of Task Force 38 and 58 depending on whether the same ships were operationally assigned to Admiral Halsey's Third or Admiral Spruance's Fifth Pacific Fleets. The core of the Fast Carrier Force consisted of the fleet carriers of the *Essex* class, supported by the *Enterprise* and *Saratoga* and the *Independence* class light carriers capable of 32 knots. Operationally divided into carrier task groups, each group included between three and five 30-knot carriers and a powerful escort of new fast battleships, cruisers and destroyers. Each *Essex* class carrier could carry thirty-six F6F Hellcat fighters, thirty-six SB2C-1 Helldiver dive bombers and eighteen Avenger torpedo aircraft. Of Admiral Mitscher's force assembled for the Marianas operation, six large carriers were of the *Essex* class – the seventh, the older *Enterprise*.

Able to make proper use of air warning radar, Admiral Mitscher's force was warned of an incoming Japanese carrier-launched attack and met it 50 miles out in the Philippine Sea; in aerial combat, more than two hundred Japanese aircraft out of just one raid were shot down for only twenty-three US fighters. Judging – unusually, for a carrier-based force – that the best form of offence was defence if the enemy was likely to attack from a large number of bases, Mitscher's tactics were essentially reactive and greatly successful. Meanwhile, American submarines, acting as pickets, sank the carriers *Taiho* and *Shokaku*. Next day, Mitscher launched an air strike and sank the *Hiyo* and some tankers, and the Japanese fleet, seriously knocked, withdrew to Okinawa.

At 'The Great Marianas Turkey Shoot', as the Battle of the Philippine Sea became known to the American fliers, a total of between 300 and 400 Japanese aircraft were destroyed by Hellcats from Task Force 58. Japanese carrier aviation was almost annihilated and the safety of the American landings on the Marianas was ensured.

Three weeks of nightmarish ground fighting followed, resulting in the slaughter of almost the entire Japanese garrison of 27,000 men. The Japanese cabinet resigned. At the end of July the Americans landed on Tinian and cleared it of resistance within a week. Meanwhile, 10,000 Japanese men were killed trying without success to dislodge an American invasion of Guam, ending on 10 August. The capture of the Marianas provided yet more bases from which naval and air forces could interdict Japan's lines of communication, cut her empire in half, isolate the Philippines, apply even more pressure to her suffering merchant marine and take the fight direct to the home islands through long-range bombing.

The Crucible of Leyte Gulf

On 25 October 1944, the US Navy returned to the Philippines, from whence they had been expelled in early 1942. Still able to field powerful battleship forces, the Imperial Japanese Navy attempted to interfere with the invasion by throwing Admiral Kurita's force including the 18-inch gunned *Yamato* and *Musashi* and other battleships round the north of Leyte while a slower group of battleships including the *Fuso* and *Yamashiro* under Admiral Nishimura passed to the south through the Surigao Strait. American submarines had already struck Kurita's force as it passed through the Palawan Passage, sinking or seriously damaging three cruisers, including his flagship *Atago*. Rounding the far side of Leyte, both Kurita and Nishimura's forces ran into the teeth of the escort carriers and older battleships providing cover for the landings. *Musashi* was sunk by carrier planes in the Sibuyan Sea. Nishimura's fleet was hammered by American surface forces. *Fuso* was sunk by a torpedo attack launched by destroyers in the Surigao Strait while US battleships and cruisers of Admiral Oldendorf's Task Group 77 stood off and with their main armament inflicted a defeat in detail upon the rest of Nishimura's fleet, the admiral going down with his blazing battleship *Yamashiro*. Three out of the four carriers in Admiral Ozawa's main body of the Japanese fleet were also sunk by Mitscher off Cape Engaño. In total, the Japanese lost three battleships, four carriers, ten cruisers and eleven destroyers. The largest battle (or, more correctly, series of battles) in modern naval history, and the last major naval engagement of the war, had ended in serious

defeat for the Japanese. By the end of November, when the US carrier force withdrew, it had been in continual action at sea for almost eighty-four days.

With the main strength of the Japanese fleet all but destroyed, 200,000 US troops were put ashore on Leyte and for the next eight weeks a series of difficult overland and amphibious operations followed until the island was carried on Christmas Day. The largest battle of the Pacific war was the new-year prospect welcoming the battle-weary US troops as they looked across the San Bernadino Strait towards Luzon, and the Filipino capital, Manila.

The Unsung Hero of the Pacific

By the end of 1944, in the hands of the largest and most powerful navy ever built, one weapon achieved all that the *Kriegsmarine* had failed to. Steadily accounting for an increasing quantity of Japanese merchant ships plying between the home islands and the newly-acquired, disparate empire, the US submarine force was perhaps the lynchpin of the American victory over the Japanese civilian population, and certainly the most unsung factor in a post-war US Navy keen to emphasize the role its expensive surface units had played.

At the outbreak of war only forty submarines had been available for operations in the Pacific, from Manila in the Philippines, and Pearl Harbor. The most modern fleet boats of 1,500 tons were of the *Porpoise*, *Salmon, Sargo/Seadragon* and *Tambor* classes, based at Pearl Harbor. US fleet submarines were nearly half as big again as German submarines such as the Type IX, reflecting the need to cover much larger distances. The shorter-ranged 'S' class medium boats of 800 tons were intended for coastal defence and many were consequently based at Manila. Also available were the nine older 'V' boats of varying classes and sizes, the largest of 2,800 tons.

By the first week of January 1942 the Philippines had fallen to Japan and the Asiatic submarine base there withdrew to Java, and after the battle of the Java Sea at the end of January, Fremantle in Australia became the third home for the Asiatic fleet in a month. A month later, the command structure became yet more complex when these two fleets were joined by a third operating out of Brisbane.

Cautious Early Days

Trained primarily in the role of long-range scouts for the battle fleet which was now dislocated, and hitherto less concerned with targeting the Japanese merchant fleet, the US submarine force was given free rein to engage in unrestricted submarine warfare against any ships sailing under the Japanese flag. A cautious start ensued. Combat readiness was uniformly poor; US submarines were accustomed to attacking from depth using sonar bearings and not on the surface; Japanese anti-submarine capabilities were little known; and doctrine dictated that much of the time spent on patrol would be submerged and out of the sight of land-based enemy aircraft. These factors accounted for few successes, and it was not until August 1942 that the first major Japanese warship, the heavy cruiser *Kako*, was sunk by a US submarine, the *S-44* (later to be lost to enemy action off the Kurile Islands in October 1943).

At first, American submariners were taught to prioritize attacks on warships over merchantmen, and centralized command and wolf-pack gatherings were disliked in the US Navy, which preferred its submarines to operate alone and in radio silence. SJ surface and SD air-search radar began to be fitted to US submarines, particularly in the new *Gato* class (1,525 tons and 20 knots on the surface) which entered service in the summer of 1941 and of which type seventy-seven would be built, making them one of the more numerous classes. American submarines, like their German counterparts, experienced difficulties with their torpedoes, particularly in the case of arming and detonating on impact. The quality of the Mark XIV steam torpedo's secret magnetic detonator and the weapon's variable depth of running remained serious issues. 'Duds' meant attacks frequently did not produce the results a skilful approach had merited. Refusing to countenance a possibility of technical failure, an investigation of the firing pin was not ordered by the Bureau of Ordnance high command until the summer of 1943, when tests revealed that it was not sturdy enough to withstand impact without a risk of distorting; the fitting of a new type of stronger pin eventually solved the issue. But the supply of torpedoes was severely limited after stockpiles in Manila had been bombed in December 1941, exacerbated by manufacturing difficulties. Submarine 'kills' remained very low. After just six weeks of operations, despite plentiful targets, only six Japanese transports had been sunk, for the loss of two US submarines.

In truth, the American submarine force and its British and Dutch allies had failed to prevent the Japanese expansion which had proceeded, after all, along reasonably predictable lines. With over seventy boats available in the western and mid-Pacific theatres – more than the *Kriegsmarine* operated in the entire Atlantic after two years of war – by April 1942 the Americans had sunk 300,000 tons, constituting less than 25 per cent of the German total in the same four-month period. But the *Kriegsmarine*'s submarines had been practising their art in war conditions rather longer.

As the US submarine service went over to the offensive as best it could given the strain upon men and materiel, patrol records of claimed sinkings were often wildly optimistic and led to confusion about the true damage being done to the Japanese merchant tonnage total which stood at around seven million tons in December 1941. For the whole of 1942, 275 ships of 1.6 million tons were claimed by American submarine commanders. In fact, post-war analysis shows that only 180 ships of 725,000 tons had been sunk, constituting 10.8 per cent of the available tonnage. After one year of war, nine US submarines had been lost.

Japan's Achilles Heel

During 1943 and early 1944 the American submarine fleet received upgraded weapons including the new wakeless Mark XVIII electric torpedo (based on the German G7e, several having been washed up on US beaches during Operation *Paukenschlag*), employed increasingly well-honed wolf-pack tactics (but rarely involving more than three boats), and had the advantage of a growing range of forward bases located around the edge of the shrinking Japanese frontier. From these bases, such as Milne Bay in New Guinea, supported by tenders and protected by local patrol boats and detached destroyers, US submarines had less distance to transit to their patrol areas. Advantageously placed, they could more efficiently venture into ever-concentric Japanese shipping lanes and pick off merchant ships, in particular the oil tankers with their cargoes vital to sustaining the Japanese war effort.

Powerful and large submarines such as the *Balao* (119 built) and the refined *Tench* (80 built) classes, in the hands of increasingly able and daring skippers such as O'Kane, Grider and 'Mush' Morton, took the best lessons of the German U-boat campaign, honed them and applied great pressure to the Japanese war machine already at a significant disadvantage vis-à-vis the US industrial base. As sinkings rose, the Japanese began to pay more attention to anti-submarine operations, introducing new destroyer escorts and patrol craft. By the end of 1943, American

submarine losses due to enemy action and unserviceability were being outstripped by new commissioning; over the same period the Japanese lost over one and a half million tons of trade vessels and the effects were staggering.

Japan was as reliant on a large and efficient merchant marine as Britain. But in contrast to her Axis partner Germany, Japan did not obtain a single useful and productive industrial centre in all its territorial conquests since December 1941. Large capacity shipyards did not exist outside Japan or America (Singapore was just a maintenance base) and no factory or armament complexes existed with which the Japanese could have augmented their native capacity. But Japan, planning for a short war with a negotiated end, was singularly ill-prepared for the long-haul defence of its existing trade tonnage. And unlike Britain, Japan could not turn to external sources of shipping production to shore up her haemorrhaging merchant marine.

Neither did Japan dedicate enough resources to signals intelligence and those advances it did make were hardly applied to the protection of trade nor the interdiction of US merchant vessel traffic. Japanese pre-war planning had set too much store on the international agreements in place which had declared unrestricted submarine war illegal. As a result, the Japanese discounted the idea that their merchant tonnage would be in such a vulnerable situation. Assuming that its warships and not its trade would be the preferred target, merchant convoying was not adopted from the outset and when it was – not until November 1943, when monthly losses ran at 100,000 tons – it was run in an unco-ordinated and unscientific manner. In an effort to reduce disruption and time wastage, only small groups were convoyed, which failed to appreciate the merits of a concentration of escorts shepherding one large convoy, and also served to spread the small number of dedicated anti-submarine warships too thinly. Meanwhile, American Ultra intelligence – aided by a Japanese propensity to 'radio chatter' – enabled precise information on enemy dispositions and intentions to be exploited.

A Faulty Doctrine

Japanese ships, designed for the offensive application of power and commanded by men who subscribed to that ethos, were much less effective in the escort role as Allied destroyers, frigates and corvettes had been. The most highly trained men were employed in ships engaged in the fleet and not on anti-submarine operations. Only the largest and most offensive fleet ships were equipped with radar and certainly not for the detection of American submarines. Meanwhile, maritime anti-submarine patrols and air cover, proven decisive against the U-boat in the Atlantic theatre, were not a priority for the Japanese air force. Despite developing some excellent flying boat designs, the Japanese air force had no centimetric radar, no Leigh light equivalent, and no effective anti-submarine doctrine.

Compounding this parlous state of officially sanctioned ignorance, new merchant tonnage launchings were pitifully insufficient to keep track of losses, which by Allied (principally British) standards were mild. In 1942 Japan constructed a quarter of a million tons of shipping, which was trebled the following year and doubled in 1944, but by then it made no difference. Naval demands for materials and access to shipyards always took absolute precedence over the construction of mercantile hulls. At all times Japanese shipyards were clogged with a growing pile of hulls awaiting repair.

Japanese anti-submarine measures were unsuccessful in the main even when ramped up in the face of mounting and irreplaceable shipping losses. American submarines were good-depth boats and, unaware of their quarry's attributes in the early months of the war, the Japanese often set their depth charges to explode at too shallow a depth. A controversial information slip-up in Congress in 1943 helped the Japanese to recognize their error and it was soon rectified, to the cost of a number of American submarines. Local fishing boats and tramp vessels, nicknamed 'sampans' by US submariners, gave radio reports to shore bases if they spotted American boats, and would be fired upon erratically using deck-mounted guns. American submarine losses rose in correlation to the growing size and boldness of the sub fleet and the marginal increase in effectiveness of Japanese defences. Seventeen boats were lost in 1943.

It was not until autumn 1944 that the first radar sets were fitted to Japanese escorts. Concurrently, in a desperate and unworkable edict, Japanese merchant ships were ordered to sail only by day to reduce losses. Already suffering acute shortages of oil, the Japanese Navy had re-based itself nearer its fuel supplies at Singapore in early 1944.

The Stranglehold Intensifies

By early 1944 all Japanese tanker and fleet train routes had been discovered and were being plundered by bold young American commanders using reliable torpedoes. Monthly losses tipped 200,000 tons. The growing weakness of the Japanese economy – by 1944 the blockade was really biting hard, with civilian consumption of oil at just 4 per cent of 1941 levels and the Japanese fleet's mobility severely hampered – and the continual interdiction of lines of supply by American naval and air forces made it impossible to stem the spiralling rate of attrition. All the while, American production in all areas – fuel oil, naval and merchant shipping, aircraft, men and munitions – was constantly expanding.

Major Japanese warships were also picked off. Big Japanese task forces, centred around fleet and escort carriers, were targeted by American submarine forces acting in small packs. On 19 June 1944 the *Shokaku* and the flagship *Taiho* were sunk during the Battle of the Philippine Sea. The *Taiyo* was dispatched by USS *Rasher* in August off the Philippines. The USS *Barb* sank the *Unyo* off Hong Kong in September. The *Shinano* was sent to the bottom on 29 November, torpedoed by USS *Archerfish* while on a working-up voyage. The *Junyo* and *Chuyo* were torpedoed off Japan in December, the latter by USS *Sailfish*. The *Unryu* was sunk by USS *Redfish* off Shanghai that same month. The rebuilt battlecruiser *Kongo* and nine cruisers also fell prey to the silent service.

Japanese submarines comprised a diverse force of technically advanced boats, including large cruiser types and one-off special designs including the *Sen-Toku* (I-400) seaplane-carrying behemoths of 1944, designed to bomb the Panama Canal. Operating a fleet of easily the largest and longest-ranged submarines in the world, and with the best submarine torpedoes of any navy, the Japanese submarine force was almost exclusively designed for offensive fleet or special missions, and operated under a 'warship first' policy. However, it made only a small contribution to the attack on Allied warships or merchantmen, and suffered severe losses in the process. Figures show that just over 180 American merchantmen were sunk by Japanese submarines, totalling 900,000 tons. This compares to 5,200 ships totalling over 22 million tons sunk by German submarines. In broad terms there was no Japanese 'Battle of the Pacific' equivalent of a war on American trade and ever-lengthening supply lines. Very quickly many Japanese submarines, whatever their original purpose, became burdened with the job of running supplies to island garrisons cut off and hard-pressed by swift American counter-advances.

American air groups flew anti-submarine patrols from a large force of dedicated escort carriers such as the *Casablanca* class carrying nearly thirty aircraft, backed up by land-based patrol aircraft operating from a growing array of island bases.

By the end of 1944 the Japanese, like the Allies, had made strides in the development of Magnetic Anomaly Detection (MAD) gear but it was too little and too late to influence the war. British long-range 'T' and 'S' class submarines joined the fight, equipped with air and surface-search radar.

By the end of the war, fifty-two US Navy submarines had been lost to enemy action, accident or malfunction. At least two US boats – the *Tullibee* and *Tang* (commanded by Richard O'Kane), and possibly the *Growler* – were sunk in 1944 by their own torpedoes returning on a circular run. Ninety per cent of the total Japanese merchant tonnage was lost. Men in submarines made up less than 2 per cent of the entire total of men mobilized within the US Navy in the Pacific, yet they accounted for approximately five million tons of total Japanese tonnage sunk during the war. US carrier-based air power, traditionally highlighted as the 'leitmotif' of the Pacific War, accounted for approximately 40 per cent of the Japanese merchant tonnage sunk. Submarines sank 55 per cent (though carrier aircraft sank slightly more Japanese warships than the US Navy's underwater arm).

US submarine aces would not sink as many ships or so much aggregate tonnage as leading German commanders because targets were generally smaller and fewer overall in the Pacific, and these were spread across a wider nexus of routes. But as a service, it wiped out the Japanese merchant marine, halted the Imperial Japanese Navy's remaining units for the want of fuel, and brought the Japanese economy to its knees. In short, it achieved in the Pacific what the U-Boat Arm had set out and failed to do to the British in the Atlantic. The writing was on the wall by the turn of 1945; Japanese defeat was certain if not yet accomplished.

The Normandy invasion

In the evening of 5 June, minesweepers set to work off the Normandy coast, while early in the morning of 6 June, British midget submarines laid markers off the intended landing beaches. As an enormous aerial armada consisting of transport planes, towed gliders, bombers and fighter escorts rumbled overhead, at 0530 hours the big guns of the Allied fleet opened up an accurate and paralyzing fire, several miles off shore, before being augmented by cruisers and eventually the rockets and shellfire from specially-equipped landing craft as the landings forces, escorted by MGB and destroyer flotillas, closed in to the beaches on a massive front. Naval clearance teams went ashore with the troops to clear beach obstacles.

(above) A busy Devon port
In preparation for the invasion, artillery equipment is loaded aboard LCTs at Brixham on the south coast of England on 1 June 1944.

(below) Piping the invasion
The paddle steamer HMS *Aristocrat* sails for Arromanches during the Normandy landings, 6 June 1944. Electrical Officer, Sub-Lieutenant A. Mitchell, of Glasgow, Scotland, plays HMS *Aristocrat* away on the bagpipes as she leaves her depot ship HMS *Despatch* to sail for Normandy. HMS *Adventure* and various transports lie beyond.

Landing craft and barrage balloons
Landing Ships and Tank Landing Craft seen from the cruiser HMS *Frobisher* off the south coast of England twelve hours before D-Day. The barrel of one of the cruiser's 7.5-inch guns can be seen in the foreground. Above the armada are barrage balloons, silhouetted against the grey sky.

British coastal forces on patrol
British 71½-foot motor gunboats return from a patrol off Cherbourg, on the lookout for any E-boats and R-boats attempting to interfere with the Allied invasion. Built at Hythe by the British Powerboat Company, these craft had a speed of up to 40 knots and were armed with a 2pdr, two Oerlikons and four machine guns.

Omaha Beach, D-Day
While Robert Capa's famous 'blurred' images are probably the best-known photographs of the D-Day landings, this picture, taken from on board an American landing craft off Omaha Beach, is surely just as powerful. It graphically conveys the reality of assaulting the exposed beach through the surf while under heavy fire from the entrenched defenders on the cliffs above.

Evacuation of casualties
Beach casualties being brought on board the cruiser HMS *Frobisher*, one of the cruisers which took part in the bombardment before and during the landings.

Landing ships beached

By the end of D-Day, over 175,000 troops had been put ashore. Meanwhile additional troops, equipment and supply convoys were formed up across the Channel in readiness for being landed on the days following 6 June. The success of the landings depended on the protection of the cross-Channel lines of communication, because as long as German forces could be brought to the battlefield by rail and road (under heavy Allied air pressure), all Allied resources had to be brought across by sea and safeguarded. In this photograph, USS *LST-325* (left) and USS *LST-388* unload while stranded at low tide during resupply operations on 12 June 1944.

'Mulberry' Harbours

The 'Mulberry' harbours were an ingenious solution to the lack of accessible harbour facilities on the French coast. An outer floating breakwater made up of 'bombardons' contained an inner fixed breakwater consisting of 'Phoenixes' and scuttled blockships; together these were known as 'Gooseberries'. After construction, the finished 'Phoenix' caissons were flooded and sunk to the sea floor to hide them from German reconnaissance flights. On D-1, they were refloated and towed across the Channel.

General aerial view of the 'Mulberry' off Arromanches. The outer ring of vessels is the breakwater formed from partially sunken blockships and concrete 'Phoenix' caissons. Closer to shore is the long jetty formed of Lobnitz pierhead units, connected to the shore by floating pontoons known as 'Whales'. Around and between these elements of the artificial harbour, ships and smaller craft come and go in large numbers in an area of approximately two square miles, equal to that of the harbour of Gibraltar.

'Phoenixes' off Arromanches

Blockships, 'Gooseberry' breakwaters and the 'Mulberry' harbours were manoeuvred into position off Gold and Omaha beaches. Here, concrete 'Phoenix' caissons are laid in line off Gold Beach at Arromanches, while a soldier makes a hazardous wire-rope crossing.

Torpedoed LCT

LCT 608 delivered her cargo and, after a terrifying fifteen-hour voyage, made it back to Portsmouth despite having being torpedoed on the way to France. However, she still had to be scrapped.

(overleaf) Low tide

The scene on one of the Normandy beaches after the landings, with supplies being brought ashore from ships out at sea, and the debris of war everywhere.

Toulon: the French fleet returns home

The ceremonial re-entry of the French fleet into Toulon took place on 13 November 1944. After the Anvil landings in the south of France it had been expected that Toulon would take about three weeks to capture; in fact such was the morale of the defending German forces that the city fell in less than a week.

(above) French cruisers return

Tricolores flying, the French cruisers *Georges Leygues* (right) and *Emile Bertin* enter the harbour. *Georges Leygues* had begun the war as part of France's élite *Force de Raid* but after the armistice spent most of the next two and a half years at Dakar. At the end of 1942 the ship rejoined the Allies, first heading to the USA for a major refit to sort out the defects resulting from her prolonged inactivity and generally to bring her up to date. *Emile Bertin* meanwhile spent the same period at Martinique in the French West Indies, before also going to America for refit in the summer of 1943.

On the original print the censor has asked for the US-model SA air search and SF surface search (both also used for gunnery fire control) on the cruisers' foremasts, and other electronics on the yards, to be touched out.

(above) Scrapping the *Strasbourg*

An altogether sorrier sight: the battleship *Strasbourg*, seaplane carrier *Commandant Teste*, and cruiser *La Galissonnière*, which had been scuttled twenty months previously. All three ships had subsequently been raised, and then towed to the Baie du Lazaret opposite the dockyard, where a basin was dredged to accommodate them. By the time this photograph was taken the cruiser had capsized, while the *Strasbourg* had clearly undergone a certain amount of scrapping – note how the top of her tower bridge and the barrels of her forward guns are missing. While some thought was given to returning the relatively undamaged *Commandant Teste* to service after the war, in the end all three ships were broken up.

On parade in Toulon

After the ceremonial re-entry of the ships, events moved ashore, where Admiral Cunningham of the Royal Navy (Commander-in-Chief, Mediterranean Fleet), Admiral Hewitt (US Navy), and Rear-Admiral Lemonnier, commander of the Free French ships, took the salute, inspected the guard, and laid wreaths at the Toulon war memorial. This view shows some of the French Navy units during the ceremonial parade.

Reinforcing the Soviet Navy

In lieu of Italian ships allocated to the Soviet Union following the Italian armistice, various Allied vessels were transferred instead.

(left) Submarine and submarine chasers
Soviet submarine *S.17* at a Northern Fleet base in 1944, and Lend-Lease Submarine Chasers (SCs) with *BO.216* in the foreground. Under Lend-Lease terms, the USA supplied ten minesweepers, fifty torpedo boats and seventy-eight 110-foot submarine chasers to the Soviet Navy between 1943 and 1945. Slowly these were returned to America after the war, or scrapped or scuttled. Built of wood, capable of 22 knots and armed with a 3-inch gun and 20mm (or later a 40mm Bofors gun) and small radar sets, these SCs were versatile coastal anti-submarine boats capable of a wide range of inshore patrol and escort work.

(right) D3 motor boat at speed
Motor boat D3 type TKA.116 in 1944. These were a more conventional type of motor torpedo boat than the G-5, with a less extreme performance but better crew accommodation and more able to cope with sea conditions. Some were adapted as patrol boats with depth charges and additional guns in place of torpedoes, as shown here.

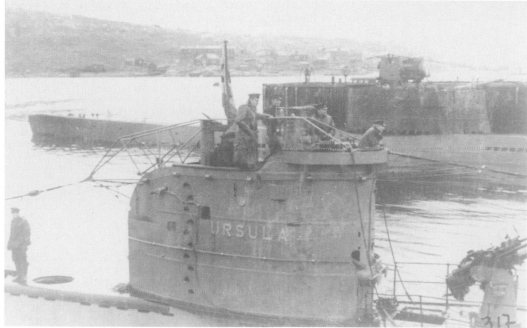

(left) *Ursula* changes ownership
During 1944 a number of British warships were transferred to the Soviet Union, amongst which were the submarines *Sunfish*, *Ursula*, *Unison*, and *Unbroken*. *Sunfish* was unfortunately the victim of 'friendly fire' before she arrived, being sunk by RAF aircraft off northern Norway on 27 July.

(opposite) A well-travelled 'flush-decker'
Another ship transferred was the destroyer *Brighton*. She had been USS *Cowell* (DD-167), one of the 'flush-deckers' transferred to the Royal Navy four years previously. In Soviet service she became *Zharki*, and was returned to Britain in 1949.

HMS *Howe* passing through the Suez Canal

The battleship *Howe*, flagship of Commander-in-Chief Pacific Fleet, Admiral Sir Bruce Fraser, is seen passing through the Suez Canal on her way to join the British Pacific Fleet on 14 July 1944.

The British Eastern Fleet

On board HMS *Queen Elizabeth*, flagship of Commander-in-Chief Eastern Fleet, Admiral Sir James Somerville, in the Bay of Bengal, during the action against the Japanese at Sabang in mid-April 1944. In this photograph, a line has been fired from the stern of *Queen Elizabeth* across the bows of HMAS *Nepal* (ex- HMS *Norseman*, renamed January 1942), which has come to receive a package.

On board HMS *Queen Elizabeth*

From under the 15-inch guns of *Queen Elizabeth*, HMS *Valiant* and FFS *Richelieu* can be seen in the light of a setting sun. By the end of 1943, the point had been reached in the war when the battleship lost its primacy to the aircraft carrier, led by the pre-eminence of the type in wide-ranging, pacy American operations. Carriers were capable of sinking each other and everything else at a range far outside that threatened by battleships. They could provide essential air cover over fleets and project an umbrella over land forces against attacking aircraft better than the AA guns of battleships. For the British it was certainly cheaper to build escort carriers than to continue to build expensive battleships which were of limited utility when the German Navy had increasingly few of their own. There was little that the battleship could do which the carrier could not now take over. That said, the inclusion of old 15-inch gunned British battleships of the *Queen Elizabeth* and 'R' classes with ocean-going convoys was important, as no raider of inferior gun power and armour could risk tackling them. Thus their value was in deterrence, as seen in early 1941 when the battlecruisers *Scharnhorst* and *Gneisenau* stayed away from three convoys escorted by British battleships. They also made good AA escorts for carriers, though expensive ones.

Carrier raids on Truk
Using the Marshalls as a springboard on his way to the Marianas, Admiral Nimitz pulverized
Truk, the main fleet base of the Japanese in the central Pacific, with relentless air attacks
launched from his carriers. Here, Grumman F6F-3 Hellcat fighters land on USS *Enterprise*
(CV-6) after covering strikes on Truk in February 1944. Flight deck crewmen are folding

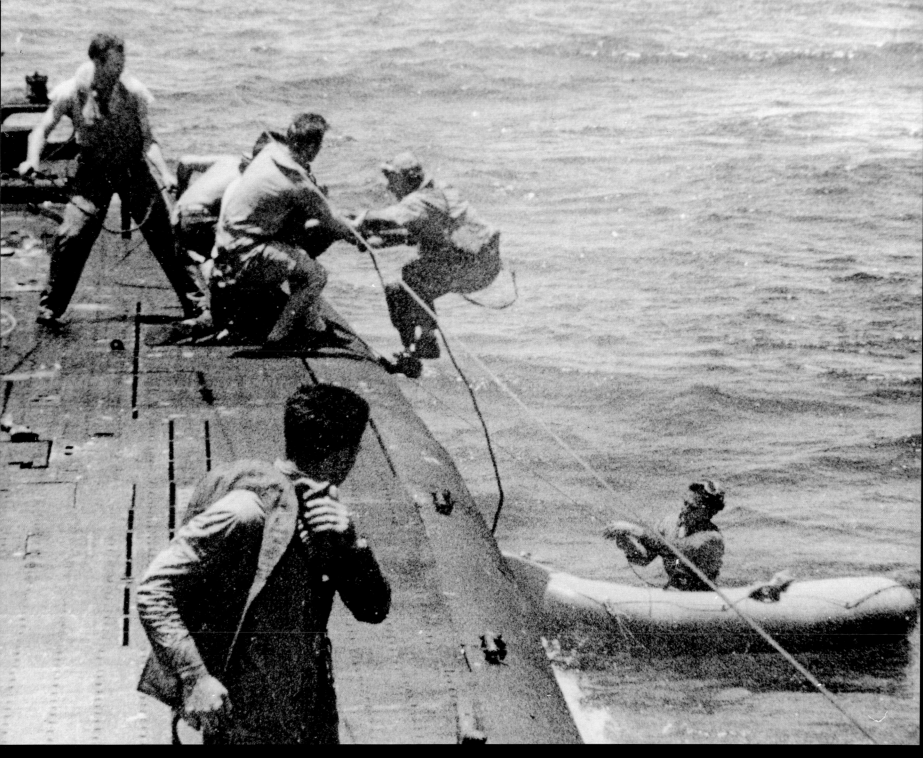

Rescuing downed aircrew by submarine
USS *Tang* rescues US Navy fliers, seen here climbing aboard, in Truk lagoon, April 1944. The Allies were far better equipped than the Japanese to recover their own aircrew. This helped preserve the aggregate experience levels and morale of naval aviation squadrons, while in contrast, Japanese losses ground away both these elements of their operational effectiveness.

The Marianas

The fight for the Marianas was a crucial step in the American advance on Japan's home islands. In June 1944, when the Americans invaded the Marianas, the Japanese main fleet met them in battle. The resulting engagement, known either as the Battle of the Philippine Sea or the Battle of the Marianas, ended in complete defeat for Japan. Carrier Task Force 58's Hellcat fighter squadrons destroyed large numbers of Japanese aircraft, ensuring the safety of the amphibious landings on the Marianas. Meanwhile, battleships performed fire support and AA escort for the carriers and US Marines. Japan lost three aircraft carriers sunk and hundreds of aircraft shot down.

(right) *Junyo* **damaged**
On board the Japanese aircraft carrier *Junyo* after the battle. Her funnel, usually so distinctive on account of its rakish angle, is missing, having been blasted by a bomb hit. Her sister ship, *Hiyo*, was sunk during the battle, as were two other carriers, the *Taiho* and *Shokaku*.

(left) Bomber shoot-down
A Japanese twin-engined bomber shot down in an attack on TF-52 escort carriers, 18 June 1944, during the Marianas operation, taken from on aboard USS *Kitkun Bay* (CVE-71). Sometimes this image is captioned as a suicide attack, but these were not introduced formally until the autumn.

The assault at Saipan
US Army reinforcements disembarking from LSTs form a graceful curve as they proceed across a coral reef towards the beach at Saipan, 17 June 1944.

Bombarding Japanese positions
The battleship USS *New Mexico* (BB-40) prepares to fire during the bombardment of Saipan, 15 June 1944. Note time-fuze setters on the left side of each gun mount, each holding three 'fixed' rounds of ammunition; barrels of 20mm machine guns at the extreme right; and triple 14-inch guns in the background.

Leyte Gulf and the Philippines

When Leyte in the Philippines was invaded in October 1944 the Japanese fleet, despite the mauling it had received three months earlier, came out to do battle with the Americans once again. Outnumbered and out-classed, it was unable to take advantage of some serious mistakes made by the American command, and by the end of a series of actions which together go to make up the greatest naval battle in history – Leyte Gulf – it had ceased to be a fighting force in any real sense.

(above) The Americans under attack at Leyte
Carrier Division 25 under attack by Japanese aircraft: two Destroyer Escorts and USS *Gambier Bay* (CVE-73) lay a smoke screen during the invasion of the Philippines, 25 October 1944. The escort carrier *Gambier Bay*, sunk off Samar later that day by Admiral Kurita's heavy cruisers, was one of only two carriers ever sunk entirely by gunfire from surface warships – the other being HMS *Glorious*, sunk by the *Scharnhorst* off Norway in 1940. Interestingly, *Gambier Bay*'s 5-inch gun is believed to have scored at least three hits on her attackers.

Japanese attempts to fight back
The Japanese fleet, heading for the American landing forces off Leyte, fell upon the escorting carriers. In the ensuing engagement, the Americans lost two carriers and three destroyers and escorts, but the Japanese were driven off with heavy losses. Here the carrier *Gambier Bay* (CVE-73) is seen on fire after being hit, viewed from on board her sister-ship *Kitkun Bay* (CVE-71).

Readying for a torpedo strike

US Navy armourers arming a TBM Avenger with a torpedo aboard USS *San Jacinto*, probably for a strike on Admiral Ozawa's Japanese carrier force off Cape Engaño on 25 October. *San Jacinto* was one of five light carriers in Admiral Halsey's enormously powerful Third Fleet, whose main striking edge was provided by no fewer than six fleet carriers.

The *Zuikaku* goes down

Crew members of the sinking Japanese aircraft carrier *Zuikaku* salute as the naval ensign is lowered during the engagement off Cape Engaño, 25 October 1944.

(opposite and above) The U-Boat bunker at Brest

Two views of one of the U-boat pens at Brest, on 18 September 1944, the image opposite showing a 40-foot hole in the roof which had received a direct hit during Allied bombing. In spite of RAF Bomber Command's claims, not one U-boat was proved to have been destroyed by strategic bombing of the hardened bomb-proof U-boat bunkers, such as those at Brest and La Rochelle, during the entire war. On the other hand, tactical bombing of roads, railways and canals and air-laid mines did indeed delay and disrupt U-boat manufacture, launchings and patrols; the introduction of the potent Type XXI boat was heavily affected in this way.

Destroyer action inshore

On the evening of 8 June the powerful, mixed British, Canadian and Polish ships of the 10th Destroyer Flotilla intercepted a force of three German destroyers and a torpedo boat off the Ile de Batz, sinking destroyer *ZH1*, driving *Z32* ashore and wrecking her, and damaging *Z24* and the torpedo boat *T24*. This engagement – one of the few actions between fleet destroyers of the war – left the Cherbourg E-boat flotillas as the only local surface forces capable of interfering with the Allied cross-Channel buildup. This photograph, from September 1944, shows *Z32* lying wrecked off the Brittany coast. She was damaged and driven ashore after a chase by HMCS *Haida*. Later, when reconnaissance aircraft reported that she had a maintenance crew working on her and that her guns were manned, she was attacked and torpedoed by British Motor Torpedo Boats of Light Coastal Forces, led by Lieutenant Tom Cartwright, who dashed in under the enemy's coastal guns to finish her off.

The demise of the *Tirpitz*

The battleship *Tirpitz* was attacked and damaged many times, by aeroplane and by mini-submarine, but was not destroyed until RAF Lancaster heavy bombers dropped 12,000-pound Tallboy bombs on her in November 1944.

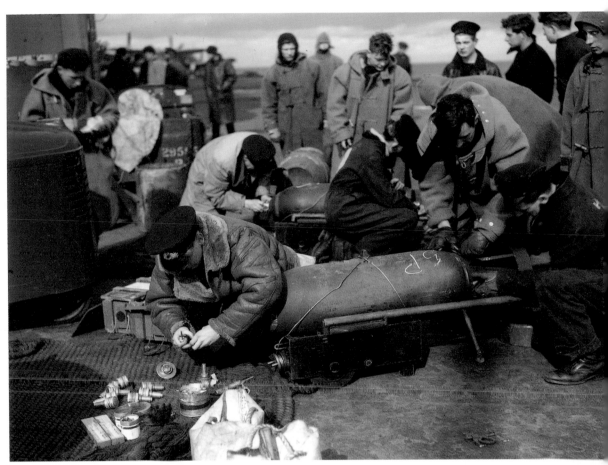

Bombing-up a Barracuda
Fleet Air Arm personnel preparing and fuzing bombs on the flight deck of an aircraft carrier. The bombs were then loaded onto Fairey Barracuda aircraft (visible in the background, probably from 827 or 830 Squadrons), which attacked the German battleship in Altenfjord, Norway in April 1944, but did not sink her.

(opposite) The *Tirpitz* capsized
Breaking up the German battleship *Tirpitz*. Pride of the German Navy, the 35,000-ton battleship *Tirpitz* was finally sunk in a Norwegian fjord off the little island of Hakoya by RAF Lancasters in November 1944 whereupon she capsized off Tromso, taking the German capital fleet strategy to its death. Here the Norwegians are busy breaking up the battleship.

The *Yamakaze* sinks below the waves
Dramatic periscope shot of the Japanese destroyer *Yamakaze* sinking in Japanese waters
after being torpedoed by USS *Nautilus* on 25 June 1942. By 1944, the American submarine
stranglehold over Japanese shipping lanes had intensified to the point where the Japanese
fleet's operational radius was severely curtailed for want of fuel oil. Merchant ships simply
could not get through to the home islands, and as the submarine blockade bit hard,
considerable privation was experienced in Japan.

Hauling survivors aboard a US submarine
British and Australian prisoner-of-war survivors being
rescued by men on the deck of USS *Sealion*, after the
Japanese ship *Rakuyo Maru* was sunk in the China Sea in
September 1944. She was carrying a cargo of rubber and,
unbeknownst to the crew of the attacking submarine,
1,300 Allied prisoners of war. Hit by two torpedoes, she
fortunately took twelve hours to sink, giving the PoWs
time to make rafts and organize themselves with food and
water. The Japanese crew had immediately abandoned ship
in the only available lifeboats.

(overleaf) A quiet moment
An American sailor relaxes in his bunk aboard a submarine.
In addition to his arresting collection of pin-ups, he is
reading *The Stray Lamb* by Thorne Smith, an American
writer of comically bawdy fantasy fiction. On a cramped
submarine with sixty-five other men, opportunities for
recreation were few and far between.

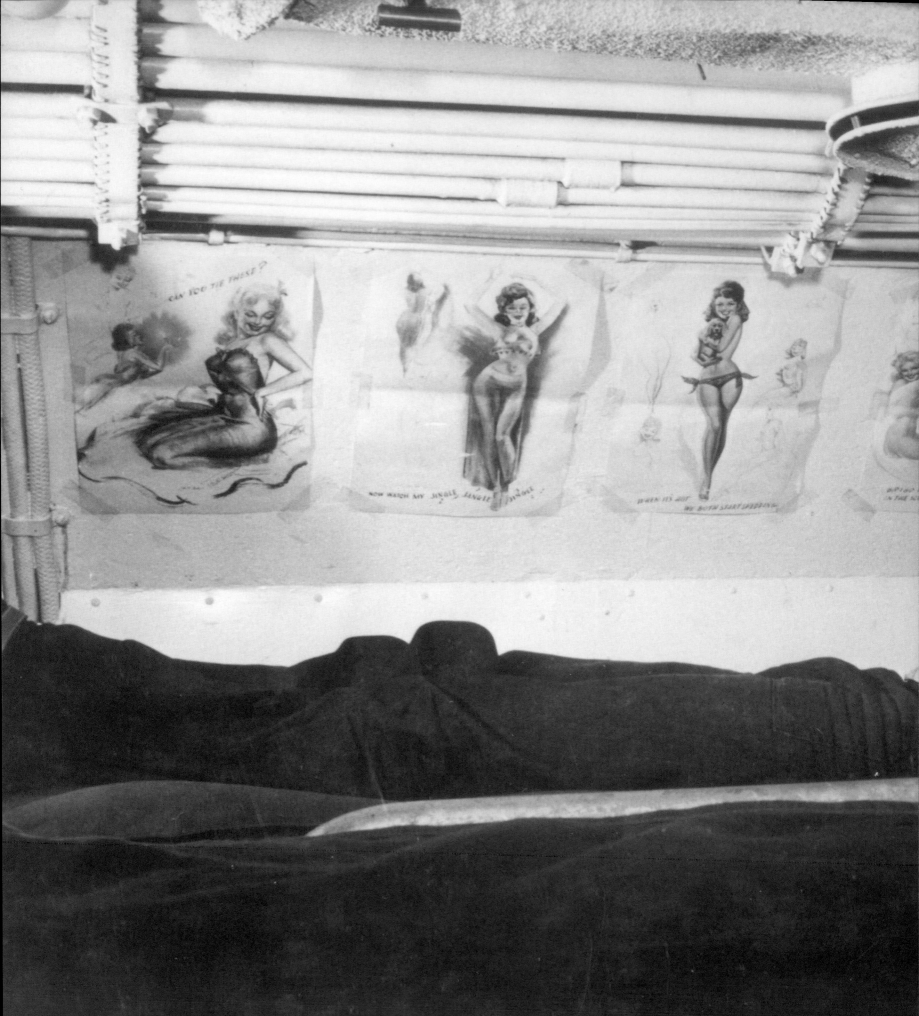

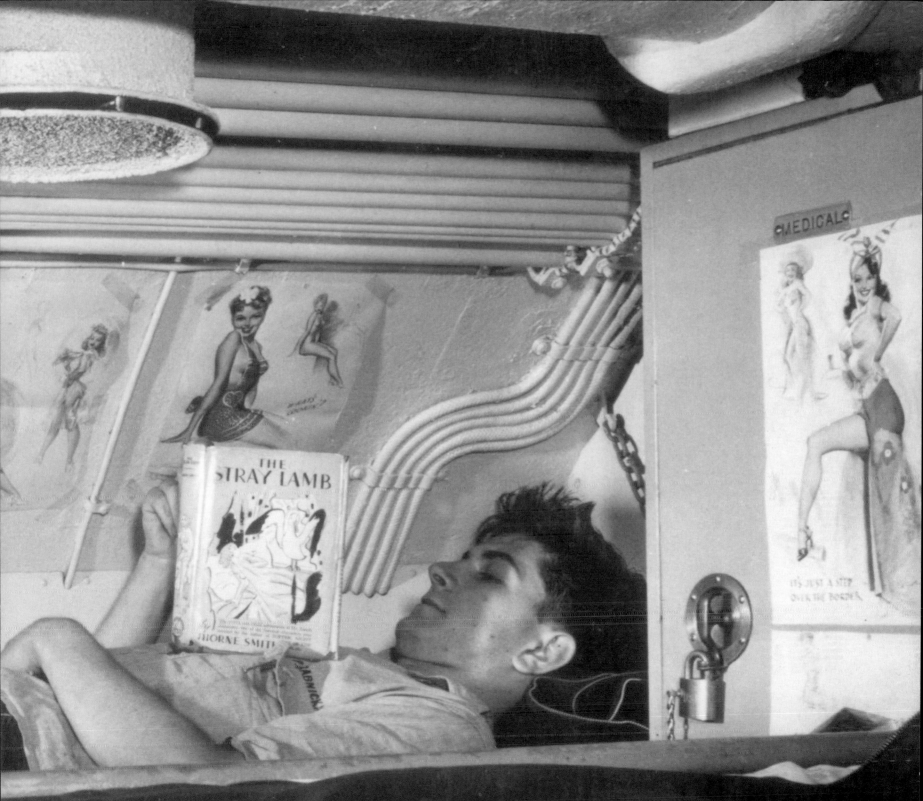

The German Search for Technological Salvation

Fascinated by technology, German policy was geared to producing qualitatively improved variants or new weapons as and when they could be developed and deployed, instead of concentrating on producing larger numbers of tried-and-tested kit. The ability to dedicate superior resources to research and development allowed the Allies, increasingly in a winning position, to identify and focus their energies upon real battle-winning applications. This technological race could not be won by the Germans and the Japanese.

However, Dönitz saw new weapons and technology as essential to his attempt to regain the initiative once held so near-decisively by the U-Boat Arm. With the Type VII and Type IX becoming obsolescent in the face of Allied strides in anti-submarine countermeasures, in late 1944 two new classes of submarines were introduced to the *Kriegsmarine*: the radical Type XXI oceanic and Type XXIII coastal boats.

Streamlined, equipped with a diesel-electric powerplant and high-performance battery giving 17 knots submerged and with outstanding underwater endurance, the Type XXI represented a quantum leap in capability for the U-Boat Arm. Equipped with the T3 pattern-runner (FaT) and T5 anti-escort torpedoes, the Type XXI and Type XXII could have posed a huge problem for the Allies had they been constructed in sufficient numbers to threaten the hard-won control of Atlantic and coastal waters. Some authorities claim that had it been available in 1941, the Allies would certainly have lost the Battle of the Atlantic. Contrary to earlier practice, sections of the Type XXI and Type XXIII U-boats were built at inland factories for assembly at the shipyards of Blohm & Voss and Deutsche Werft in Hamburg, and by Deschimag and AG Weser in Bremen. Bomber Command and US Eighth Air Force strategic bombing of the Baltic ports severely hindered the production of these types from the outset. A few well-placed bombs could wreak a huge amount of disruption to boats whether on the stocks, freshly launched, or awaiting completion. By the end of 1944, sixty Type XXIs had been completed, but it was found impossible to conduct meaningful training anywhere due to Allied dominance in the air, so that the first boat to become operational did so only in April 1945.

Europe First

That same month, the German army in Italy surrendered. Despite a build-up of troops, munitions and supplies delivered by sea, the Allies had not been able to dislodge the occupiers from Italian soil. Much-needed resources had – rightly, in light of events – been drawn away from the drive north through Italy by Operations Overlord in Normandy and Anvil in southern France.

Meanwhile, squeezed mercilessly against the sea by the Soviet armies pushing along the Baltic coast from the east and south, German garrisons fell back one by one towards the west until by the end of January East Prussia was cut off from German-held territory. Huge numbers of refugees fleeing from the Soviet Army compounded the difficulties of coastal defence, re-supply and organisation. By February a continuous maritime evacuation operation was in place, much larger than that achieved by the Allied armies in the summer of 1940. Nearly two and a half million people were transported west, the majority out of the ever-decreasing German pocket in the Bay of Gdańsk; of the thousand-odd ships which carried them away, a quarter were lost, mostly to Soviet bombers and torpedo boats.

Soviet submarines were not idle at this time; three large German transports, crammed to the rails with refugees hurrying back to German ports, were torpedoed, resulting in truly colossal casualties. Of a total of nearly 17,000 passengers, only a thousand were saved – small wonder that these tragic episodes constitute the largest maritime disaster in history. To add to the miseries of German shipping, more and more magnetic and acoustic mines were being sown along the southern Baltic coast by the RAF. Within the first three months of 1945, nearly seventy Axis ships would be lost to mines, despite the best efforts of the overwhelmed remaining German minesweepers. Allied strategic bombing of ports, shipyards and shipping proceeded, almost unchecked by the crippled *Luftwaffe*, preparing the path for the British 21st Army Group, which pushed east across the northern German plain.

With the failure of the German winter counter-offensive in the Ardennes, the western Allied armies fought to capture the Ruhr and major German cities; meanwhile the main Soviet armies approached from the east. After the crossing of the Rhine in March with the help of teams of naval landing craft, the western Allies halted at the Elbe in April while the Soviets crossed the Oder and pressed on to encircle the embattled German capital. By May the heart of German territory was pierced from east to west. Shattered, the Third Reich collapsed and Hitler committed suicide in his *Führerbunker* in Berlin. Admiral Dönitz – Hitler's choice over the *Luftwaffe*'s Göring – was nominated as *Reichspräsident* of a regime which existed only in the past tense, and it was in his name that the announcements of the unconditional surrender of Germany were broadcast on 8 May 1945.

The End of the *Kriegsmarine*

By the time Germany surrendered, her capital fleet had been destroyed, and the major surface fleet consisted of only three operational cruisers: the *Leipzig*, *Prinz Eugen* and *Nurnberg*. German ports and harbours had been devastated; wreckage and unexploded ordnance choked much of them. The task of clearing the coastal waters of both sides' mines fell to the British, augmenting their own ships with German minesweepers pressed into service. Allied naval chiefs were still wary of the German armed forces still at large. The main worry for the Allies was that the *Kriegsmarine* still possessed nearly 400 U-boats in commission. Losses to tenacious U-boats operating unsupported in the Arctic had continued right up until 7 May, where over two-dozen U-boats were still on war patrol. Ordered to surrender, fewer than half of all U-boat captains complied; many chose to scuttle their boats. Even after the German capitulation, a number of U-boats continued to operate out of Japanese-held Penang in Malaysia. But except for this small pocket, the U-boat threat – the instrument of war that had done so much damage to the British in particular – existed no longer.

Their war on Allied trade had been colossal. The total figures for the war are estimated at 5,200 Allied and neutral vessels of over 22 million tons sunk worldwide. Of this figure, just over half the tonnage was British-owned, and just under 11 million tons were sunk solely in the Atlantic. The casualties within the multi-national crews lost with these ships numbered over 60,000. Over 25,000 British and Commonwealth seamen were drowned.

The *Kriegsmarine* practically ceased to exist. Germany had lost a total of 785 U-boats, two battleships, two battlecruisers, three pocket battleships, two elderly battleships, two heavy and five light cruisers, forty-four destroyers, and eighty-six minor warships and armed merchant raiders. 138,000 men were killed out of a force of 1,200,000. And of 39,000 German submariners, 28,000 were killed, and 5,000 taken captive – at 85 per cent, this constituted one of the highest loss ratios of any of the fighting arms of World War Two.

The afternoon before VE Day, the last sinking by a U-boat of a merchant vessel in European waters had been achieved by a Type XXIII coastal boat. The end of the war and the discovery of the *Elektro-boote* programme enabled Allied scientists to conduct tests of the ground-breaking technology and also examine the radical Walter closed-cycle boats. These latter boats – the V80 prototype, and Types XVIIA and XVIIB – utilized high-performance engines running on very unstable hydrogen-peroxide fuel. The *Kriegsmarine* had decided that the Walter technology was not yet reliable enough when it opted for the technically sound – albeit still revolutionary – Type XXI and Type XXIII.

These modern wonders would be pored over by Allied engineers in the months after Germany's surrender, pointing the way towards a future where naval strike power would be most lethally – and survivably – concentrated in fast and stealthy submarines. A few perceptive naval officers could already see the potential to be had from marrying such true submersibles with the power created by nuclear fission. In the east, the offensive application of that nascent technology was about to be unleashed on Japan from the bomb-bay of an American B-29 Superfortress.

The Curtain Falls on the Pacific Theatre

The product of the 'Manhattan Project', the two atomic bombs dropped on Hiroshima and Nagasaki in August served to demonstrate to the Japanese that their final, irreversible defeat was now beyond all doubt. Surrender documents were signed aboard the battleship USS *Missouri* on 2 September. In at the death, the battleship had been accorded the honour of immortalizing the triumph of American naval dominance. Yet the campaigns that had brought the US Navy to the Japanese coast had not relied upon battleships. The final American drive on the Japanese home islands had come, inexorably, from the Philippines through Okinawa, from the Marianas through Iwo Jima and from the Aleutians through the Kurile Islands – all powered by the marine 'bootneck' on one hand and the fast carrier on the other.

The Japanese, ignoring the terms of the Allies' Potsdam Declaration of 26 July, which promised 'prompt and utter destruction', had clung on to a last-ditch defence of the home islands as the only remaining option. While infantry forces were gathered and prepared, Japanese shipyards made one last effort and built large numbers of *Koryu* Type D midget submarines to be sent against Allied landing forces. Entering service in small numbers in May, 115 were constructed by August with nearly 500 further hulls at various stages of completion at the war's end. Advanced electric submarines of the *I-201* and *Ha-201* types were built in much smaller numbers but failed to be ready in time for service.

Over the first half of 1945, the noose had been tightening around Japan. But despite the overwhelming signs of inevitable defeat, Japan could not be forced into an attitude of defeatism. And with unconditional surrender the stated goal of Allied policy, the stage had been set for a vicious denouement. American landings were made at Luzon in the Philippines in January 1945. A month later, Iwo Jima became the focus of the American push, witnessing one of the most legendary ground struggles of the war.

Iwo Jima lay within 650 miles of Tokyo; in American possession by the middle of March, the strategic bombing of the Japanese home nation was re-doubled as fighter cover could be more efficiently provided to long-range bombers. Meanwhile, the Royal Navy, unable to disguise its strain after more than five and a half years of unrelenting service, was able to send a Pacific Fleet – focused on aircraft carriers flying largely American aircraft types – to join Admiral Spruance's US Fifth Fleet only in March 1945. US commanders had mixed feelings about the participation of the British on what was, by any standards, an American stage in the final acts of the Pacific war.

On 1 April the island of Okinawa was invaded. US aerial qualitative superiority – backed up with over-lapping air-warning radar cover and huge numerical advantage in modern fighter types – was allied with a mature and experienced pilot force to shoot down whole squadrons of Japanese aircraft. In tremendous battles over the island and out to sea, Japanese aerial losses numbered over five hundred planes; American losses were only a fifth of that.

At sea, the giant Japanese super-battleship *Yamato*, without air cover on a futile one-way mission to relieve the battered Japanese garrison on Okinawa, was sunk by bomb- and torpedo-armed carrier aircraft on 7 April. She had never fired her main armament at an equivalent enemy vessel. The aircraft, and by extension the aircraft carrier, had finally and unequivocally supplanted the battleship when this 64,000-ton, 16-inch armoured, 18-inch gunned symbol of Japan's traditional battle fleet blew up spectacularly with the loss of some 4,000 of her crew.

Kamikaze attacks reached their climax off Okinawa. US carriers were the main target but vessels of all size and power were exposed to the 'divine wind'. In one span of eighty terrifying minutes, the American destroyer USS *Laffey* was subjected to one of the most intense suicidal aerial assaults ever recorded. Armed with six 5-inch, twelve 40 mm and eleven 20 mm guns, she put up an incredible amount of flak against a force of fifty suicide aircraft, shooting down eleven. But against such saturation, she could not avoid the impact of six aircraft and four bombs. Yet the *Laffey* survived to be towed to Okinawa. In the three weeks of bitter fighting over Okinawa, over 250 Allied ships were hit by *kamikaze* attacks, mostly from deliberate crashes. But after some of the fiercest ground, air and sea fighting of the entire war, the island was captured on 21 June.

American submarines, having taken the lion's share of Japan's trade over the past thirty-six months, continued to punish the dwindling Japanese mercantile and naval shipping until the end of the war. One boat – USS *Batfish* – sank three Japanese submarines in a remarkable four days in February 1945. In June, three US wolf-packs took up position in the Sea of Japan. The remaining warships of the Japanese fleet, paralyzed by a lack of fuel and totally dominated by Allied air power, were unable to counter this move, among many others designed to accelerate and exploit Japanese weakness.

By this point, the vestigial Japanese empire could in no way sustain the war effort that had conquered it. Of the oil extracted from the territories conquered in 1942, 42 per cent had reached the home islands that year; only 15 per cent had arrived in 1943, and 5 per cent by 1944. In 1945 no oil reached Japan itself at all, as oil-transporting ships were sunk in large numbers by well co-ordinated American submarines. Concurrently, tactical air strikes destroyed fuel dumps and oil bases wherever they were in range, and the US Navy's blockade took its toll. Where possible, marines seized any local oil supplies and turned them over to the Allied war effort.

In July, Admiral Halsey's Third Fleet, in concert with the British carrier force, took up position 170 miles off Tokyo and launched bombing raids on coastal facilities, damaging airfields and industrial installations and sinking shipping in Yokosuka naval base. Meanwhile, British and American battleships fired 2,000 tons of shells into the Tokyo industrial district. Allied air power ranged over southern Japan almost unopposed, such was the crippled state of Japanese defences.

All the while, American factories, shipyards, depots and training facilities remained untouched and invulnerable, and expanded their capacity and rate of production. As the strategic bombing of Japan continued apace, resulting in hundreds of thousands of civilian deaths and the shattering of the remaining Japanese war infrastructure, US and British submarines performed lifeguard duty on watch for downed B-29 bomber aircrews. Literally dwarfed by the scale of the combat in the Pacific, two British X-craft mini submarines still managed to contribute, sinking the Japanese heavy cruiser *Takao* at Singapore in July, the crews winning two Victoria Crosses in the process.

Just as the European naval war had been started by the actions of a World War One-era German battleship, the Pacific war at sea was brought almost to a close by the knocking out of two modernized World War One-era Japanese battleships, the *Hyuga* and *Ise*. Having escaped destruction at Leyte Gulf they were sunk in shallow water at Kure by carrier aircraft. The *Haruna*, a modified 1915-built *Kongo* class battlecruiser, also settled on the bottom after receiving bomb damage at Kure.

The Soviet Union declared war on Japan on 8 August and invaded Manchuria the next day, racing against time to gain new land in East Asia before the end of hostilities. The speed and scale of this new front destroyed any Japanese hope that their large army could hold back its enemies' conventional forces. And while Soviet marines made outflanking attacks south west from Vladivostock down into the Korean peninsula, American preparations began for the amphibious invasion of the south Japanese home island of Kyushu.

Codenamed Operation Olympic and scheduled for November, this was to be followed up by Operation Cornet – an air-sea assault on the largest island, Honshu, in March 1946. But in a controversial move calculated to shorten the war and avoid the grim prospect of a lengthy and costly invasion outlined in these operations, the US Air Force was authorized to use atomic weapons. The first bomb over Hiroshima on 6 August elicited no formal response from the Japanese high command. But when the second exploded over Nagasaki three days later, the Japanese surrendered unconditionally. Though a general cease-fire order was issued on 15 August, the Allied fighting forces were by no means certain that the Japanese would lay down their arms (or refrain from launching fresh *kamikaze* attacks) so abruptly after nearly four years of total war. Therefore, the large Allied fleet off Japan's southern coastline remained at a high degree of readiness. In the event, such was their shattered morale and evaporated warfighting capability, the Japanese put up no further mass resistance. Three and a half years of war in the Pacific were at an end.

The Final Reckoning

The US Navy had lost two battleships, five fleet carriers, six escort carriers, ten cruisers, seventy-one destroyers and fifty-two submarines. Against these losses, the prodigious output and efficient management of American industry had assembled, by the Japanese surrender, eight battleships, twenty-six fleet carriers, 110 escort carriers, fifty-two cruisers, 349 destroyers, 298 escort vessels, 181 submarines and thousands of landing craft, transports and small vessels. These were supported by an unprecedented array of mobile logistical forces including 152 floating dry-docks. Aware of the implications of fighting the Imperial Japanese Navy in its home waters, and at a great distance from its own bases, the US Navy had begun experimenting with underway refuelling in the mid-1930s. The perfection of these techniques had made a high tempo of sustained operations possible.

By the war's end, the US Navy had expanded to employ 3,408,347 people in all capacities, including ninety thousand women. Over the course of the next twelve months, 3 million of these would need to be demobilized. Fifty-six thousand had died in the service of the US Navy, and 80,000 had been wounded.

By VJ Day, the Royal Navy had expanded to around 900,000 men and women. Fifty thousand had been killed in service. British Commonwealth naval losses had been heavy, comprising four battleships, two battlecruisers, five fleet carriers, five escort carriers, thirty-three cruisers, 154 destroyers, ninety submarines, and 138 light warships and armed merchant cruisers, as well as 1,307 auxiliary and minor warships and 1,326 landing ships and craft of all types. The Royal Navy fought well in World War Two, but the price for its vindication was high.

Britain and America alone emerged from the war as the major naval powers. The US Navy ended the war with 1,672 major naval vessels, the Royal Navy with 1,065. At the end of World War One, the US Navy had supplied a battle squadron to supplement the British Grand Fleet; at the end of World War Two, in the Pacific, the positions had been reversed. The Royal Navy had been relegated to a supportive rather than pre-eminent position which, relative to the new superpower, continued to decline in the years after the war. Showing signs of exhaustion, the swollen wartime navy was swiftly demobilized. Within four years it was at but one sixth of its wartime peak.

The US Navy was meanwhile reduced from four million to a strength of 484,000, the Marine Corps to 92,000, as the fleet dropped from 1,200 to fewer than 250 major warships within four years. The US Navy had unquestionably become the greatest maritime force. After the war, despite the expansion of the Soviet Navy, it would continue as the premier navy in the world, a position it maintains today — its capital ships now solely large aircraft carriers.

The Japanese Navy had started the war at roughly 70 per cent size of the US Navy. But eleven out of twelve battleships, twenty out of twenty-six carriers, thirty-eight out of forty-three cruisers, 115 destroyers and 120 submarines had been sunk. The battleship *Nagato* was left as the sole surviving — though heavily battered — capital ship. Most of the remaining ships were similarly so heavily damaged as to be of no military value by August 1945. Japan's last few carriers, including some only recently completed, were of equally little use due to the almost total absence of aircraft or pilots to fly them. In the course of the war, the Japanese Navy had employed 2,100,000 people, of whom 415,000 were killed or wounded.

The Italian Navy suffered 22,000 casualties and lost eleven cruisers, forty-four destroyers, forty-one escorts, thirty-three torpedo-boats, eighty-six submarines and 178 minor vessels. A number of major units were passed to foreign countries, in particular the Soviet Union, as war reparations. The French Navy, torn asunder in the first half of the war, had by VJ Day been reborn as a modern fighting force. Nevertheless, its losses were still heavy, including five battleships, ten cruisers, forty-nine destroyers, fifty-five submarines and well over a hundred smaller vessels, sunk in the service of various regimes or causes. Soviet Navy losses were 155,000 men — still only a small proportion of the millions lost on land. Emerging as a superpower, the Soviet Union would subscribe to an uncharacteristic naval expansion which would eventually be a major contributory factor in the bankruptcy of Soviet communism by the late 1980s.

For the defeated Axis navies, their immediate problems were generally subsumed within the catastrophic internal collapse of their home nations. Later, the process of post-war reconstruction of the Japanese Maritime Self-Defence Force, the Italian Navy and the German *Bundesmarine* would occur within a new Cold War political framework dominated by the requirements of NATO, SEATO and the closure of painful war memories.

Today, those few warships of World War Two vintage still remaining intact are the focus of increasing efforts to preserve them as touchstones to the past. For those vessels no longer in existence — and for the scenes which confronted the participants aboard them — the photographic record is perhaps the most immediate medium through which the war at sea — and the parts played by men and machines in fighting it — can be remembered.

Survivor of Leningrad
The Soviet battleship *Marat* in 1945, showing how her destroyed fore part had been patched up so that she was able to continue in service as a powerful floating battery in the defence of Leningrad .

Romanian monitor
A Romanian monitor of the *Mariupol* class in 1945. In August 1944 Romania had switched sides, and the small Royal Romanian Navy found itself fighting alongside its former foe, the Soviets, against its former allies, the Germans.

Sevastopol
The battleship *Sevastopol* heading west, near the coast of the Crimea, as the war in Europe comes to a close.

The battered Italian fleet

As the Allies advanced up Italy, the remaining units of the Italian Navy which had not sailed for Malta in 1943 or been subsequently sunk, fell into Allied hands. These included (left) the minelayer *Buffoluto*, photographed scuttled in the Prima Daisena at La Spezia in the spring of 1945. The mushroom on the funnel was a cooling device fitted to eliminate sparks, as the ship was usually used at night. More fortunate was the aircraft carrier *Aquila* (below), saved from scuttling by partisans, photographed here in Genoa in 1945. The Germans had intended it for use as a blockship.

US Third Fleet warships
American landings were made at Luzon in the new year
1945. En route to the Philippines, USS *Stephen Potter*
(DD-538) is in the right centre, closest to the camera.
The aircraft carrier at left is USS *Enterprise* (CV-6).

Sea of Japan
Task Force 58 raid on Japan. USS *Hornet*'s (CV-12) 40mm guns are firing on 16 February 1945, as the carrier's planes raid Tokyo. Note the expended shells and ready service ammunition to the right.

Iwo Jima

The island of Iwo Jima – now a by-word for the stereotypically fanatical Japanese rearguard – was invaded on 19 February. By the middle of March, when the island surrendered, over 20,000 Japanese lay dead. American casualties, at 4,305, were light in comparison, though still horrifying.

Streaming into battle

One of a series of remarkable photographs taken during the Iwo Jima invasion by Lieutenant Howard W. Whalen, a Boat Group Commander on the attack transport *Sanborn* (APA-193), who used a Leica 35mm camera to take several rolls of Kodachrome colour transparencies showing various aspects of the operation. Most show the vicinity of the 'Blue' Beaches, northernmost of Iwo Jima's eastern landing beaches, where *Sanborn*'s boats and amphibious tractors (LVTs) put marines and supplies ashore during the 19 February amphibious assault. In this image LVTs head for landing beaches on Iwo Jima. Note the explosions, with much smoke and dust, ashore. Mount Suribachi is at left.

Destruction on Iwo Jima

A nightmarish vision. Smashed by Japanese mortar and shellfire, trapped by Iwo's treacherous black-ash sands, amtracs and other vehicles of war lie knocked out on the black sands of the volcanic fortress.

Burial at sea
An Honor Guard fires the salute during a burial at sea for a casualty of the battle for Iwo Jima, taken on board USS *Hansford* (APA-106) while she was evacuating wounded men to Saipan, 25–28 February 1945.

Kamikaze attack on USS *Saratoga*
Crewmen aboard USS *Saratoga* (CV-3) fight fires resulting from the attack by a Japanese suicide aircraft on 21 February 1945.

Okinawa

As a final preliminary to the complete isolation of the Japanese home islands, on April Fools' Day 1945 the island of Okinawa was invaded. The prime difficulties in taking Okinawa lay not only in the 120,000 men defending it to the last man and bullet, but also its relative proximity to the remnants of the Japanese air force and navy in Japan and Taiwan.

The invasion begins
The vessels of the invasion fleet head towards the shore.

Amtracs and big guns
American battleship USS *Tennessee* (BB-43), a victim of the Japanese attack on Pearl Harbor, takes her revenge at Okinawa, 1 April 1945.

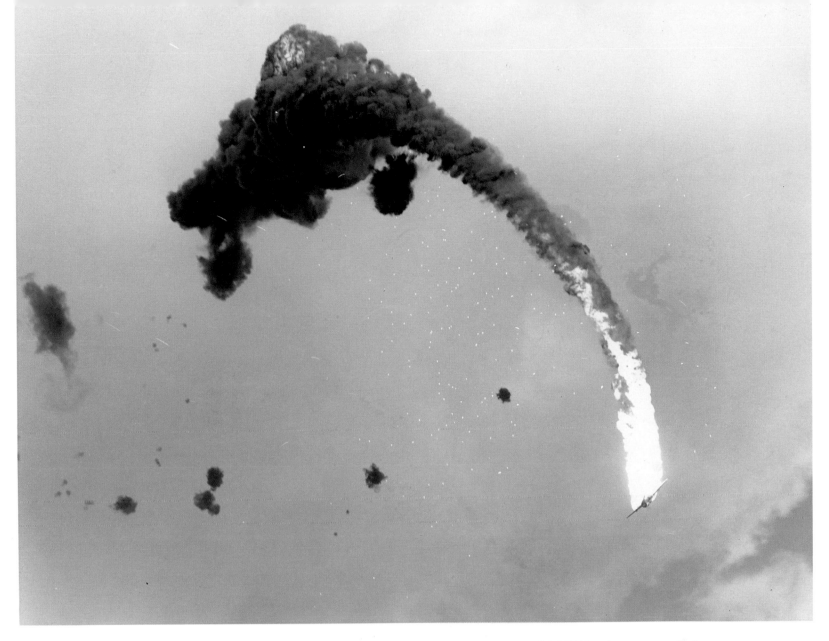

Japanese aircraft aflame
A Japanese Judy aircraft burns after being shot down by anti-aircraft fire from the aircraft carrier USS *Wasp* (CV-18) off the Ryukus, 18 March 1945.

Point blank
USS *Idaho* (BB-42) fires the guns of Turret Three at nearly point-blank range, during the bombardment of Okinawa. In these final stages of the Pacific war, American and British battleships were largely relegated to shore bombardment duties and to providing accurate radar-controlled AA cover for carrier battle groups, both roles of which the battleship could fulfil successfully but which were a far cry from being the traditional arbiter of sea power.

The split second before impact

A dramatic photograph of a Japanese *kamikaze* aircraft about to strike the starboard side of the battleship USS *Missouri* (BB-63), during battle off the coast of Okinawa, 3 May 1945. *Missouri* suffered hits from *kamikaze* aircraft twice. Suicidal attacks reached their peak during the unsuccessful Japanese defence of the island, the last stepping stone to the Japanese home islands.

Damage limitation

Firefighters aboard the *Ticonderoga* class aircraft carrier USS *Hancock* (CV-19) hose down damage caused by a Japanese *kamikaze* attack six days into the fight for Okinawa, 7 April 1945. The impact seriously damaged the *Hancock* and killed sixty-two of her crew. The casualties were buried at sea two days later. This was the third and last time the ship would be hit by *kamikaze* aircraft, and

The end of the *Kriegsmarine*

On 8 May, by signal from the *BdU*, all operational U-boats were ordered to surface, radio their position, jettison their ammunition and proceed to Allied ports, flying a black flag of surrender or a White Ensign. Aside from U-boats, the major units of the German surface fleet had ceased

Inspecting the *Lützow*
This is the wrecked pocket battleship *Lützow* (ex-*Deutschland*) in Soviet hands postwar.

The *Hipper* at Kiel
A striking view of the German cruiser *Admiral Hipper*, which was in dry dock at Kiel when the harbour was captured by the Allies. Both the German attempts to camouflage her and the damage caused by Allied bombers can be seen. *Hipper* had spent the last year and a half of the war used primarily for training new sailors, and supporting troops ashore on the Baltic front. Unlike some other German ships, she was too badly damaged to be returned to service, and was broken up for scrap the following year.

U-boat surrender

Two undamaged Type VIIC U-boats, *U-826* and *U-236* post-surrender. Only about 150 were ever delivered into Allied control; most made for British ports, although a few reached the USA. In Loch Eriboll and other northern and western British harbours, the U-boats were disarmed and their crews sent to prison camps in preparation for their repatriation. The rest of the U-boats were sunk by the Royal Navy off Lisahally in Northern Ireland over the remainder of the year in Operation Deadlight. But more than 220 U-boats were scuttled by their crews rather than suffer the indignity of a repeat of 1918.

Processing the U-boat crews

The Royal Navy are photographed taking over the German naval port and dockyard at Kiel. The assembled U-boat crews give their names and numbers to German personnel under the supervision of British naval officers.

The destroyer *Hatsuzakura*
Japanese officers leave the destroyer *Hatsuzakura* on 27 August 1945 to prepare for the entry of the Allied fleet into Tokyo Bay at the end of World War Two. Note the extremely neat and efficient appearance of the destroyer in marked contrast to the general condition of the Japanese fleet.

The formal ceremony of the Japanese surrender
The Japanese surrender took place on board USS *Missouri* in Tokyo Bay on 2 September 1945. The Japanese delegation was headed by Mamoru Shigemitsu of the Foreign Office and General Yoshijiro Umezu, Army Chief of Staff. The Allied delegation was made up of Admiral Nimitz of the USA; Chinese General Hsu Yung-chang; Admiral of the Fleet Sir Bruce Fraser; General Derevyanko of the USSR; Field Marshal Sir Thomas Blamey for Australia; Colonel Cosgrove for Canada; General Leclerc for France; Admiral Helfrich for the Netherlands and Air Commodore Sir Leonard Isitt for New Zealand.

Japan Surrenders

Japanese surrender followed soon after the second atomic bomb exploded above Nagasaki. The capitulation documents were signed aboard the new Iowa class battleship USS *Missouri* – the 'Mighty Mo' – on 2 September. While the surrender ceremony took place, another seven American, two British battleships and several cruisers stood on guard out in Tokyo Bay.

(above) The Allies in Tokyo Bay
Navy carrier aircraft pass over USS *Missouri* (BB-63), USS *Detroit* (CL-6) and other Allied warships in Tokyo Bay during the surrender ceremonies, 2 September 1945.

***Missouri* and Mount Fuji**
A close-up view of the bow of USS *Missouri* (BB-63) with Mount Fuji framed by her stem and anchor chain, in Sagami Wan or Tokyo Bay, Japan, circa 30 August 1945. British battleships and US cruisers are visible in the background.

The aftermath

The surviving ships of the Imperial Japanese Navy lying mostly heavily damaged, in their ports, were joined by those of the victorious Allies. Of the former, many of those which could be made seaworthy were converted for duties as repatriation transports, joining Allied vessels as the complex task of collecting, identifying, treating and transporting demobilized combatants, prisoners of war and indentured labour began in earnest.

(right) Cruiser *Aoba* in Kure

British Naval officers on board the Japanese cruiser *Aoba*, some time after the cessation of hostilities. Severly damaged by American bombing in July 1945, *Aoba* was resting on the floor of Kure harbour, where she had been serving as a floating anti-aircraft battery. Like all Japan's cruisers, *Aoba* had seen a very busy war, taking part in the capture of Guam and Wake, the Battles of the Coral Sea, Savo Island and Cape Esperance, during the latter of which she was seriously damaged by US gunfire, losing eighty of those on board, including Rear-Admiral Goto Aritomo. Repaired, she was damaged again by both air attack, and torpedoed by a US submarine before finishing up at Kure.

British shipping in Kure

Elements of the British Pacific Fleet in Kure harbour include the submarine depot ship *Adamant*, pictured here with submarines alongside. Among the ships in the background is the Japanese aircraft carrier *Katsuragi*, which was used for the repatriation of Japanese personnel. Between October 1945 and the following spring she brought home some 12,000 people. The Japanese naval academy at Eta Jima was used as the headquarters of the British Commonwealth occupation force.

(opposite) The *Junyo* and two *Ha-201* submarines

The impressive bulk of one of the few surviving Japanese aircraft carriers, the *Junyo* (launched 1942), at Sasebo, Japan after the armistice, on 26 September 1945. Two *Ha-201* class advanced electric submarines are alongside. Along with the larger *Sen Taka I 201*, these were the all-welded Japanese equivalent classes of the German Type XXI and XXIII class boats. They reached even faster speeds of 19 knots submerged, but Japan could not complete many or deploy them in time to have any effect.

Cricket on deck

The flight deck of British carrier *Formidable* in autumn 1945 while she transported 1,300 PoWs and internees from Japan to Sydney. The ship's hangars were rigged as dormitories. This is clearly a no-ball.

HMS Prince of Wales (William Blackwood & Sons Ltd, Edinburgh & London, 1944)

Friedman, Norman, *Naval Radar* (Conway Maritime Press, London, 1981)

Fukui, Shizuo, *Japanese Naval Vessels at the end of World War II* (Greenhill Books, London, 1992. Originally published in Japan by the Administrative Division, Second Demobilization Bureau, in 1947)

Goodenough, Simon, *War Maps* (St. Martin's Press, London, 1982)

Greene, Jack, & Massignani, Alessandro, *The Naval War in the Mediterranean 1940-1943* (Chatham Publishing, Rochester, 1998)

Green, William, *War Planes of the Second World War*, various volumes (Macdonald, London, 1961 etc.)

Grove, Eric, (ed.), *The Defeat of the Enemy Attack on Shipping, 1939-1945* (Navy Records Society, Ashgate, 1997)

Hadjiphoti, Litsa J., *Poros* (Editions Aeacus, Athens, 1981)

Hague, Arnold, *The Towns* (World Ship Society, Kendal, 1988)

Harman, Nicholas, *Dunkirk, the Necessary Myth* (Hodder & Stoughton, London, 1980)

Hattendorf, John B., *et al*, *British Naval Documents 1204-1960* (Navy Records Society, Ashgate, 1993)

Hawkins, Ian (ed.) *Destroyer* (Conway Maritime Press, London, 2003)

Hayward, Roger, *The Fleet Air Arm in Camera, 1912-1996* (Sutton Publishing, Stroud, Gloucestershire, in association with the Public Record Office, 1996)

Hodges, Peter, *Royal Navy Warship Camouflage, 1939-1945* (Altmark Publications, London, 1973)

Hood, Jean, *Come Hell and High Water* (Conway Maritime Press, London, 2006)

Humble, Richard, *Japanese High Seas Fleet* (Ballantine, London, 1974)

Hough, Richard, *The Hunting of Force Z* (Collins, London, 1963)

——, *Former Naval Person: Churchill and the Wars at Sea* (Weidenfeld and Nicolson, London, 1985)

Howarth, Stephen (ed.), *Men of War* (St. Martin's Press, New York, 1992)

Hughes, Quentin, *Fortress: Architecture and Military History in Malta* (Lund Humphries, London, 1969)

——, *Britain in the Mediterranean and the Defence of her Naval Stations* (Penpaled Books, Liverpool, 1981)

Humphries, Steve, *The Call of the Sea* (BBC Books, London, 1997)

Ireland, Bernard, *Naval History of World War II* (Collins, London, 1998)

Jenkins, Cdr C.A., *HMS Furious* (two volumes, Profile Publications, Windsor, Berkshire, 1972)

Jentschura, Hans Georg; Jung, Deiter; Mickel, Peter, (translated by Antony Preston and J. D. Brown), *Warships of the Imperial Japanese Navy 1869-1945* (Arms & Armour Press, London, 1977. Originally published in Germany in 1970 by J F Kehmanns Verlag as *Die Japanischen Kriegshiffe 1869-1945*)

Jordan, Gerald (ed.), *Naval Warfare in the Twentieth Century 1900-1945* (Croom Helm, London, 1977)

Keble Chatterton, Cdr E., *The Royal Navy: From April 1942 to June 1943* (Hutchinson & Co. Ltd, London, undated)

Kemp, Paul, *Liverpool and the Battle of the Atlantic* (Maritime Books, Liskeard, Cornwall, 1989)

Kemp, Peter, *A Pictorial History of the Sea War 1939-1945* (Arms & Armour Press, London, 1995)

Kennedy, Paul, *The Rise and Fall of British Naval Mastery* (Fontana, London, 3rd edn, 1991)

Lacroix, Eric, and Wells, Linton, II, *Japanese Cruisers of the Pacific War* (Chatham Publishing, London, 1997)

Lambert, John, & Ross, Al, *Allied Coastal Forces of World War II: Volume 1, Fairmile Designs and U.S. Submarine Chasers* (Conway Maritime Press, London, 1990)

Lavery, Brian, *Hostilities Only: Training the Wartime Royal Navy* (National Maritime Museum, Greenwich, 2004)

——, *Churchill's Navy: The Ships, Men and Organisation, 1939-1945* (Conway, London, 2006)

——, *River Class Frigates and the Battle of the Atlantic* (National Maritime Museum, Greenwich, 2006)

Leach, Derek, *Dover Harbour: Royal Gateway* (Riverdale Publications, Dover, for Dover Harbour Board, 2005)

Lengerer, Hans, & Trojka, Waldemar, *Japanese Warship at War* (Model Hobby, Katowice, Poland, 2006)

Lenton, H.T., & College, J.J., *Warships of World War II* (Ian Allan Ltd, Middlesex, 1962)

Lenton, H.T., *German Surface Warships* (Macdonald, London, 1966)

Lewinski, Jorge, *The Camera at War: War Photography from 1848 to the Present Day* (Simon & Schuster, London, 1986)

Lord, Walter, *The Miracle of Dunkirk* (Allan Lane, Middlesex, 1982)

Mallmann Showel, Jak, *The U-boat Century* (Chatham Publishing, London, 2006)

Matanle, Ivor, *World War II* (CLB Publishing, Godalming, Surrey, 1989)

McDougall, Philip, *Chatham Built Warships since 1860* (Maritime Books, Liskeard, Cornwall, 1982)

McLaren, Kevin, *Scotland from the Air 1939-49, Volume 1: Catalogue of the Luftwaffe Photographs in the National Monuments Record of Scotland* (Royal Commission on the Ancient and Historical Monuments of Scotland, 1999)

McLean, Ruari, *Half Seas Under* (Thomas Reed Publications, Bradford on Avon, Wiltshire, 2001)

Meister, Jürg, *Soviet Warships of the Second World War* (Macdonald & Janes, London, 1977)

Melson, Commodore P. J., CBE *White Ensign, Red Dragon* (Edinburgh Financial Publishing (Asia) Ltd, Hong Kong, 1997)

Mercer, Neil, *Camera at Sea: The History of the Royal Naval Photographic Branch 1919-1998* (Airlife, London, 1999)

Middlebrook, Martin, *Convoy* (Morrow, London, 1978)

Morison, Samuel Eliot, *History of United States Naval Operations in World War II* (fifteen volumes, Atlantic, Little Brown & Co., Boston, Mass, 1947-60)

Nesbit, Roy Conyers, *RAF, An Illustrated History* (Sutton Publishing, Stroud, Gloucestershire, in association with the RAF Museum, 1998)

Nicholson, Arthur, *Hostages to Fortune: Winston Churchill and the Loss of the Prince of Wales and Repulse* (Sutton Publishing Ltd, Stroud, Gloucestershire, 2005)

Overy, Richard, *Why the Allies Won* (W. W. Norton, London, 2nd edn, 2006)

Pack, S. W. C., *Invasion North Africa, 1942* (Ian Allan, Shepperton, Surrey, 1978)

Padfield, Peter, *The Battleship Era* (Pan Books Ltd, London, 1975)

Parkes, Oscar, OBE, *Ships of the Royal Navies and British Commonwealth of Nations* (Sampson Low, Marston & Co., Ltd, London, 1937)

Parshall, Jon & Tully, Anthony, *Shattered Sword: The Untold Story of the Battle of Midway* (Potomac Books, Washington DC, 2005)

Paterson, Lawrence, *U-boat War Patrol: the Hidden Photographic Diary of U-564* (Greenhill Books, London, 2004)

Pawle, Gerald, *The Secret War, 1939-45* (Harrap & Co., London, 1956)

Polmar, Norman, *Aircraft Carriers: A History of Carrier Aviation and its Influence on World Events, Vol. 1, 1909-1945* (Potomac Books, Dulles, Virginia, 2006)

Prange, Gordon W., with Goldstein, Donald M. & Dillon, Katherine V., *At Dawn We Slept: the Untold Story of Pearl Harbor* (Penguin Books, New York, 1982)

Preston, Antony; Gardiner, Robert; Hunt, Geoff (eds), *Camera at Sea, 1939-45* (Conway Maritime Press, Greenwich, 1978)

Preston, Antony, *The Royal Navy Submarine Service: A Centennial History* (Conway Maritime Press, London, 2001)

——, *The World's Worst Warships* (Conway Maritime Press, London, 2002)

Ramsey, Winston G. (ed.), *D-Day, Then and Now* (two volumes, After the Battle, London, 1995)

Ranft, Brian, *Technical Change and British Naval Policy 1860-1939* (London, 1977)

Raven, Alan, *King George V Class Battleships* (Bivouac Books Ltd, London, 1972)

——, *Town Class Cruisers* (Bivouac Books Ltd, London, 1975)

——, *War Built Destroyers, O to Z classes* (Bivouac Books Ltd, London, 1976)

——, *County Class Cruisers* (RSV Publishing, Brooklyn, New York, 1978)

—— & Lenton, H. Trevor, *Dido Class Cruisers* (Bivouac Books Ltd, London, 1973)

—— & Roberts, John, *Queen Elizabeth Class Battleships* (Bivouac Books Ltd, London, 1975)

Roskill, Stephen, *The War at Sea* (four volumes, HMSO, London, 1954-61)

——, *HMS Warspite* (Collins, London, 1957)

——, *The Navy at War, 1939-1945* (Collins, London, 1960, and subsequent editions)

Rohwer, Jürgen, *War at Sea, 1939-45* (Chatham, London, 1996. Originally published in Germany in 1992 by Urbes Verlag Hans Jürgen Hansen, München, as *Der Krieg zur See, 1939-45*)

—— & Hummelchen G., *Chronology of the War at Sea* (Ian Allan, London, 1972)

Rodger, N. A. M., (ed.), *Naval Power in the Twentieth Century* (Palgrave Macmillan, London, 1996)

Rousselot, Vice–Admiral d'Escadre Henri L. G., DSO DSC, *Rubis, Free French Submarine* (Profile Publications, Windsor, Berkshire, 1972)

Ruge, Friedrich, *Der Seekrieg: The German Navy's Story 1939-1945* (Naval Institute Press, Annapolis, MD, 1957)

——, *The Soviets as Naval Opponents 1941-1945* (Naval Institute Press, Annapolis, MD, 1979)

Shankland, Peter, & Hunter, Anthony, *Malta Convoy* (Collins, London, 1961)

Sharpe, Peter, *U-boat Fact File* (Midland Publishing Ltd, Leicester, 1998)

Silverstone, Paul H., *U.S. Warships of World War II* (Ian Allan Ltd, Shepperton, Surrey, 1965)

Smith, Gordon, *The War at Sea: Royal & Dominion Navy Actions in World War 2* (Ian Allan, London, 1989)

Spector, Ronald, *At War At Sea: Sailors and Naval Warfare in the Twentieth Century* (Penguin, New York, 2001)

Stern, Robert C., *Kriegsmarine* (Arms & Armour Press, London, 1979)

—, *US Navy 1942-1943* (Arms & Armour Press, London, 1990)

Syrett, David, *The Defeat of the German U-Boats: The Battle of the Atlantic* (University of South Carolina Press, Columbia, 1994)

—, (ed.), *The Battle of the Atlantic and Signals Intelligence: U-Boat Tracking Papers, 1941-1947* (Navy Records Society, Ashgate, 2002)

Talbot-Booth, Lt Cdr E. C., RNR, *All the World's Fighting Fleets*, 3rd edition (Sampson Low, Marston & Co., Ltd, London, n.d., but 1940)

Taylor, John R. W., *Fairey Aviation* (Chalford Publishing, Stroud, Gloucestershire, 1997)

Terzibaschitsch, Stefan, *Cruisers of the US Navy, 1922-1962* (Arms & Armour Press, London, 1988. Originally published in Germany in 1984 by Koehlers Verlagsgesellschaft mbH as *Kreuzer der U.S. Navy*)

Thomas, David A., *The Battle of the Java Sea* (André Deutsch Ltd, London, 1968)

—, *Crete 1941, the Battle at Sea* (André Deutsch Ltd, London, 1972)

Thompson, Julian, *The Imperial War Museum Book of the War at Sea* (Sidgwick & Jackson, London, in association with the Imperial War Museum, 1996)

Turner, Frank R., *The Maunsell Sea Forts* (three volumes, one co-written with William Stuart, plus booklet, published by the author, 1994-96)

Tute, Warren, *The Deadly Stroke* (Collins, London, 1973)

—, with John Costello & Terry Hughes, *D-Day* (Sidgwick & Jackson, London, 1974)

Various eds including Fred T. Jane, Oscar Parkes & Francis E. McMurtrie, *Jane's Fighting Ships*, (Sampson Low, Marston & Co., Ltd, London, annually from 1897, some reprinted by David & Charles, Newton Abbot, Devon)

Warlow, Lt Cdr B., *Shore Establishments of the Royal Navy* (Maritime Books, Liskeard, Cornwall, 2000)

Waterman, Lt Cdr J., *The Fleet Air Arm History* (Old Bond Street Publishing Co, London, n.d., but 1974)

Watton, Ross, *The Cruiser HMS Belfast* (Conway Maritime Press, London, 1985)

Watts, Anthony J., *Japanese Warships of World War II* (Ian Allan Ltd, Shepperton, Surrey, 1966)

Westwood, David, *The U-Boat Arm* (London, 2004)

Whitley, M. J., *Cruisers of World War Two: An International Encyclopedia* (Brockhampton Press, London, 1995)

Williams, David L., *Maritime Heritage, White's of Cowes* (Silver Link Publishing, Peterborough, 1993)

Willmott, H. P., *The Great Crusade: A New Complete History of the Second World War* (Free Press, New York, 1990)

Winklareth, Robert J., *Naval Shipbuilders of the World* (Chatham Publishing, London, 2000)

Woodman, Richard, *Arctic Convoys* (John Murray, London, 1994)

—, *Malta Convoys* (John Murray, London, 2000)

—, *The Real Cruel Sea* (John Murray, London, 2004)

Wootten, Eric, *Dusty Days in the Royal Navy* (Avon Books, London, 1996)

Young, Edward, *One of Our Submarines* (Penguin, London, 1954)

Articles

Barlow, Jeffrey G., 'World War II: Allied and German Naval Strategies', in Colin Gray & Roger Barnett (eds), *Seapower and Strategy* (London, 1989)

—'World War II: US and Japanese Naval Strategies', in Colin Gray & Roger Barnett (eds), *Seapower and Strategy* (London, 1989)

Bell, Christopher M., 'The "Singapore Strategy" and the Deterrence of Japan: Winston Churchill., the Admiralty and the Dispatch of Force Z', *The English Historical Review*, Vol. 116, 467 (June 2001)

Buckley, John, 'Air Power and the Battle of the Atlantic 1939-45', *Journal of Contemporary History*, Vol. 28, 1 (Jan 1993)

Courtney, Anthony, 'The Background of Russian Sea-Power', *International Affairs*, vol 30, 1 (Jan 1954)

Fuquea, David C., 'Task Force One: The Wasted Assets of the United States Battleship Fleet, 1942', *The Journal of Military History*, Vol. 61, 4 (Oct 1997)

Gardner, W. J. R., 'Prelude to Victory: The Battle of the Atlantic 1942-1943', *Mariner's Mirror*, Vol. 79, 3 (August 1993)

Gray, Colin, 'The Strategy of Blockade', in Lawrence Freedman (ed.), *War* (Oxford, 1994)

Hervieux, Pierre, 'Operation Seelöwe', *Warship 18* (1981)

—, 'The Royal Romanian Navy at War, 1941-1944', *Warship 2001-2002* (2001)

Herwig, Holger, 'Prelude to Weltblitzkrieg: Germany's Naval Policy toward the United States of America, 1939-41', *The Journal of Modern History*, Vol. 43, 4 (Dec 1971)

Howard Bailey, Christine, '"Operation Pedestal": The Role of Oral History in Uncovering the Past', *Mariner's Mirror*, Vol. 79, 4 (November 1993)

Jordan, John, 'French submarine development between the wars', *Warship 1991* (1991)

—, 'The 7,600-tonne Cruisers', *Warship 1995* (1995)

—, '*Emile Bertin*: fast minelaying cruiser', *Warship 1996* (1996)

Kennedy, Greg C., 'Great Britain's Maritime Strength and the British Merchant Marine, 1922-1935', *Mariner's Mirror*, vol 80, 1 (February 1994)

Lautenschlager, Karl, 'The Submarine in Naval Warfare, 1901-2001', *International Security*, Vol. 11, 3 (1986)

Maiolo, Joseph A., 'The Knockout Blow against the Import System: Admiralty Expectations of Nazi Germany's Naval Strategy, 1934-9', *Historical Research*, Vol. 72, 178 (June 1999)

McGoverm, Terrance, 'The Hawaiian Turrets: Naval Turrets in Oahu's Coast Defenses during World War II' *Fort*, Vol. 32 (2004)

McKernan, Luke, John Turner Obituary in *The Guardian*, 24 March 2007

Milner, Marc, 'Convoy Escorts: Tactics, Technology and Innovation in the Royal Canadian Navy, 1939-1943', *Military Affairs*, Vol. 48, 1 (Jan 1984)

O'Connor, Raymond G., 'The American Navy, 1939-41: The Enlisted Perspective', *Military Affairs*, Vol. 50, 4 (Oct 1986)

Pallud, Jean Paul, 'The French Navy at Toulon', *After the Battle*, No. 76 (1992)

—, 'The Norwegian Campaign', *After the Battle*, No. 126 (2004)

Rahn, Werner, 'German Naval Power in the First and Second World Wars', in N. A. M. Rodger (ed.), *Naval Power in the Twentieth Century* (London, 1996)

Ray, Thomas W., 'Naval Aviation Photographs in the National Archives', *Military Affairs*, Vol. 15, 4 (1951)

Reynolds, Clark G., 'The US Fleet-in-Being Strategy of 1942', *The Journal of Military History*, Vol. 58, 1 (Jan 1994)

Schenk, Dr Peter, 'Scapa Flow and the *U-47*', *After the Battle*, No. 72 (1991)

Simpson, Michael, 'Wings over the Sea: The Interaction of Air and Sea Power in the Mediterranean, 1940-42', in N. A. M. Rodger (ed.), *Naval Power in the Twentieth Century* (London, 1996)

Skinner, Ian, 'The Naval Threat on the Western Flank of Operation Neptune, June 1944', *Mariner's Mirror*, Vol. 80, 2 (May 1994)

Watkins, John, 'Action off the Ile de Batz, 9 June 1944: a view from HMS *Ashanti*', *Mariner's Mirror*, Vol. 78, 3 (August 1992)

Web sites

Battleships-Cruisers.co.uk: http://www.battleships-cruisers.co.uk/

CyberHeritage International: http://www.cyberheritage.co.uk/

Destroyer History [US]: www.destroyerhistory.org

Hypertext History of the Second World War: http://www.ibiblio.org/hyperwar/

Imperial War Museum: http://www.iwm.org.uk/

Italian Navy in World War II: www.regiamarina.net

Museum of the Battleship *Averoff*: http://users.hol.gr/~bsaverof/

Naval History.net: www.naval-history.net

Nihon Kaigun: http://www.combinedfleet.com/

U-boat net: www.uboat.net

US National Archives: http://www.nara.gov/

US Naval Historical Center: http://www.history.navy.mil/index.html

Index